THE GIRL ON THE BELVEDERE

THE GIRL ON THE BELVEDERE

FINDING MEANING THROUGH TRAVEL, FRIENDSHIP AND FRENCH: A MEMOIR

CHERYL Y. FORREST

PETRIFIED FOREST PRESS

Copyright © 2022 by Cheryl Y. Forrest

All rights reserved.

No part of this book may be reproduced in any form or by any electronic or mechanical means, including information storage and retrieval systems, without written permission from the author, except for the use of brief quotations in a book review.

Cover photo courtesy of Tulsa Historical Society & Museum

Cover design by Julia Wood of Resolute PR

For Anna, Ibrahim, Lucía, Celestina, and Susi

And especially for John, my husband

PROLOGUE

I knew they were going to bury the car. I was afraid they might bury it with me still sitting on top of it...

Yes, that's me on the cover, sitting on the Plymouth Belvedere, the time capsule buried in Tulsa, Oklahoma, in 1957 to celebrate the state's semi-centennial. I was four years old at the time. My father had been standing in the back of the crowd, holding me, when someone singled him out and asked him to bring me forward. I know this because I've seen the video clip online. My now-deceased father, looking so young, so surprised, and so happy, carried me to the front of the crowd as the sea of people parted around him to let us through. My mother followed him, smiling. My brother was not present in the segment. Most likely, he was already at the front of the crowd, being eight years old and feeling independent.

I don't remember whether my father placed me on the car himself or if he handed me to an official who performed the honors. I do remember that the hole in the earth, intended to be the Belvedere's resting place for the next fifty years, seemed immense, and frightened me. The car seemed to be suspended very high in the air, and I felt that I needed to sit very, very still.

A man in a hat took some photos, and then two other little girls joined me on the hood.

After the ceremony, my father said to me, "I won't be here in fifty years, but you will be, and you'll need to be here when they bring the Belvedere back up." My father was always taking us places where the past and future met. We went to see a lake filling slowly behind a new dam. We toured the inside of another dam and marveled at its immense turbine engines. We went downtown at dawn on more than one occasion to see the implosion of various outdated buildings. I think my father wanted us to see progress and to understand that nothing is permanent.

Over the years, I did occasionally think about that buried car —usually while on dates in high school. "I know where a car is buried downtown," I would say.

"No, you don't. There's no such thing. There's no buried car!" the boys invariably said.

"I'll show you," I countered and would point out the small plaque on the lawn outside the county courthouse.

In 2006, I was at a meeting at the Tulsa Historical Society when the president mentioned the buried Belvedere and announced that the society was taking the lead on the events surrounding its excavation in 2007. My first thought was, *Wow, someone else knows about that car!* As the president laid out her plans, I was amazed at their scope: dignitaries, national and international press, a car show, souvenirs, and live television coverage. I had just expected that there would be a small crowd of old-timers to witness the event, nothing more.

At the end of the meeting, I mentioned to the president that I had been placed on top that car before it was buried. I told her that someone had taken a number of photographs and that my father had tried, unsuccessfully, to find the photographer. "I'm interested in seeing those photos," I said.

The Girl on the Belvedere

"I think I've seen some photos of children sitting on the car," she said. "I'll let you know if we find them."

As the year advanced, it became obvious that the Belvedere-raising was indeed going to be a major media event. Car enthusiasts were coming from around the globe, and most hotel rooms in the city were full.

Two weeks before the event, I irrationally worried about my mortality. What if I only lived forty-nine years and eleven and one-half months after the burial? I needed to survive at least another two weeks; nearly fifty years before, I had promised my father that I would be there to see the car resurrected.

The anticipation was apparent throughout the community. Numerous local publications interviewed both my brother and me ahead of the event. "News today can be so depressing," I said in one interview, "but this is truly a joyous occasion. It just touches all types of heartstrings. It brings back 'the good old days.'" When asked about my thoughts on the car's condition, I said, "It has been fifty years, and none of us who were there fifty years ago look like we did then. We will see how well it has withstood time. I would expect there to be rust and some other ravages of time, just like for the rest of us."

At last, the day came. I was interviewed for *The Today Show*, and at that interview, I met Debbie, another little girl who had been placed on the car beside me. She was now a fifty-something like me. At the dig site, I was ushered into the VIP section, along with my husband and son.

When the moment arrived, the Belvedere was raised from the ground. Unfortunately, water poured out of it as it was hoisted up. A large water main nearby had broken at some point in the past fifty years and had flooded the vault.

No one really cared, though; this was a *party*. There were hundreds of members of the press there, scores of cameras, and thousands of fans. One man tapped me on the shoulder and asked, "Are you Cheryl Forrest?"

Surprised, I said, "Yes, that's me."

"I've been waiting to meet you for fifteen years," he said.

I panicked for a moment, but relaxed when I glanced behind him and saw his smiling wife and two young children. He probably wasn't a stalker if he had his family in tow; he was likely just a car enthusiast. "Where are you from?" I asked.

"Germany," he said. "I saw your photo in a car magazine fifteen years ago, and my wife and I decided that we would like to visit Tulsa, see the car, and meet you."

Stunned, I chatted with them for a few moments before they excused themselves to meet some of the other "celebrities," many of whom were actual, bona fide celebrities from car magazines and television shows.

One magazine reporter from France interviewed me, and as we chatted, I realized that I had been to his hometown, Hyères, on the French Riviera. Several months later, he was kind enough to send me a copy of his article, *"La Plymouth de Tulsa: 50 ans sous terre"* ["Tulsa's Plymouth: 50 years underground"].

My brother, Larry, and I chatted about our deceased parents, whom we had recently seen online in the video of the car's burial. We agreed that they would have enjoyed the hoopla surrounding the ceremony.

That evening, there was an event at the Civic Center. Larry told me later that when he arrived, he joined his daughter in the seats she had saved. Unbeknownst to her, she had selected the exact seats that our parents had occupied across many basketball seasons. How had she managed to pick the same two seats out of almost nine thousand? Was it merely a coincidence? Perhaps. I prefer to think that they were there in spirit.

The event that night drew car enthusiasts from England, Germany, the Netherlands, Austria, Finland, Canada, Denmark, and Australia. Two hundred journalists were credentialed, seven thousand tickets were sold, and one-tenth of all attendees were from foreign countries. It was televised, and after the introductions, a celebrity attempted—and failed—to start the rusted-out, push-button, fin-tailed Belvedere. No one really cared about the failure; the crowd was still jubilant.

I went onstage to see the car, touch it, and look at the spot where my four-year-old self had sat fifty years earlier. Debbie also joined me onstage, and we marveled at being reunited after so many years. At that moment, the car seemed very small to me and very low to the ground. In my memory, it had been so large, so high, so shiny, so important. No matter. I was still alive and very much present, there to fulfill my long-ago promise to my father. I thought that this was an ending of sorts, and it was. Little did I know that my true life, my authentic life, was just beginning, rather than cruising to a quiet conclusion.

TRAVELS, TRAVAILS, TUTUS, AND EPIPHANIES

1

TRAVELS

I was born into a middle-class family and grew up in a middle-class neighborhood. In many ways, we were unremarkable and no different from the families of thousands of other World War II veterans who were living the American dream: a nice home, a loving family, and a peaceful future after the turmoil and fear that accompanied the worldwide conflict.

It was a time of optimism, a time when a newly employed father could provide everything that his young children needed: a home, a small backyard, and some toys—roller skates, bicycles, dollhouses, and a basketball hoop on the driveway. The most important item was an education, and now that the war was over, a stay-at-home mother was an added bonus.

I have many wonderful memories of my family during that post-war era: a home-cooked meal on the table every night, playing with neighborhood friends after school each day, and reading library books while perched in my favorite mimosa tree on long, hot summer days. My family watched television together in those innocent days of early TV. We sometimes went for a drive on the weekends and brought along a picnic lunch. We had cookouts on nice summer Saturdays. My father read to me and played "The Globe Game," in which he gave me a country to find on the globe. He always rewarded my efforts with a wide smile. I was given piano lessons, swimming lessons, ice-skating lessons, and most importantly, ballet lessons. I never heard a word of complaint from either parent about the cost, the incessant driving, or the loss of their own leisure time after work.

When I close my eyes, I can still see my parents as they were in my early life: my mother dressed in a clean shirtwaist dress at four in the afternoon; my father, a mechanic for American Airlines at the new maintenance base in Tulsa, arriving home by five o'clock in his grey jumpsuit and then changing for dinner. In later years, his career advanced, and he went "upstairs" to management, and wore a dress shirt and tie instead of a jumpsuit. Management was literally located in the upper level of one of the Tulsa hangars.

I AM an airline brat and have been traveling since I was a small child. My father had served in the ground crew for the Flying Tigers during World War II, was stationed in China and India, and later helped build the Burma Road. My mother's family were railroad people, and my father briefly considered that career after the war, but he ultimately decided to follow his passion for all things aeronautical. In many ways, it was he who fostered my love of visiting new places.

I flew for the first time at the age of four; it was during the summer of the Belvedere time capsule burial. Before boarding, I asked my mother if it was going to hurt when we took off. "No," she said, "it's just like sitting in a car, but it's in the air."

I remember that first flight so clearly. I was awed as we walked into the magnificent Art Deco airport, which had hosted

The Girl on the Belvedere

Amelia Earhart, Will Rogers, and Wiley Post in its early days. I watched my father saunter up to the little American Airlines counter for our tickets, and then, together, we walked out through the gate in the chain-link fence that separated spectators from travelers and ascended the metal stairway onto the DC-6. Its silver aluminum skin was highlighted by the company's orange lightning-bolt logo.

Once we were strapped in and airborne, the stewardess came down the aisle and set up our dining trays, which featured pressed linens, sterling flatware, and crystal glasses. "Would you care for some strawberries?" she asked as she ladled some into my china bowl. "Cream with those?" she added.

Thus began our yearly vacations, which we highly anticipated and much enjoyed. They were our family's happiest times.

On that first trip, we flew to Los Angeles. When we arrived, we drove toward Disneyland in a rental car and were soon surrounded by orange groves; the trees grew right up to the edge of the road to Anaheim. We rolled into town and turned right at a T-shaped intersection. The lone stoplight swung overhead. After that, it was back into the orange groves.

We soon turned into the parking lot beneath the giant Disneyland sign, which had been visible above the trees from far away. Disneyland, with its nearly empty parking lot, was so new that Tomorrowland was not yet fully open. When we rode the Peter Pan ride, I really believed that I was seeing London below me. I knew Dumbo the Flying Elephant from my favorite Sunday night television show, *Walt Disney's Disneyland*, and seeing Cinderella's castle solidified my belief in fairy tales. The Teacups were my favorite: turning, turning, turning, foretelling my fondness for all kinds of turns in later ballet classes.

We visited Marineland, host to all manner of sea creatures. This beautiful marine park was located right on the majestic Pacific Ocean, and one attraction featured my favorite non-marine animal: a dog. Much to my delight, this little well-trained mutt "drove" a small motorboat around and around his large circular pool. The boat undoubtedly was on a track hidden under the surface, but again, I was a believer. *That dog is driving a boat,* I thought. *He's even wearing sunglasses!* Oh, the joy of being four years old.

My last memory of Marineland is preserved forever in my family's Kodak films. In it, we are standing along the railing above the cliffs, with nothing but empty air behind us. While my blond brother and glamorous mother smile at the camera, I duck under the railing, grab hold of it, lean out, and look down at the rocks along the shore far below. I was not reprimanded, which surprised me at the time. Weeks later, when we sat down to watch our home movies, my mother started in surprise at this episode. She looked at me in shock and said, "I didn't know you did that." Now, as an adult, I shudder to think of what might have happened.

The evening of our visit to Marineland, we had a fried chicken dinner at Knott's Berry Farm. We sat at a circular wooden table with a Lazy Susan turntable in the center that held every flavor of their famous jam. After dinner, we went outside to visit the Ghost Town, which was peopled by actors in mining costumes.

That night, we stayed at a motel in Santa Monica, right on the beach. My father held my hand the next morning as we prepared to cross the coastal highway. "Look both ways," he cautioned me, though I do not remember a single car on the highway, nor any buildings to block the view of the ocean. I crossed that two-lane divide with my father and soon stepped down onto the soft sand and into the surf. It was my first experience of California's glorious coast. Our home movies show me in my little yellow gingham swimsuit with a ruffle. My mother

The Girl on the Belvedere

looks like a movie star in her white one-piece, sporting white sunglasses, smiling at the camera.

Thirty-five years later, I went back to Disneyland. The approach was unrecognizable. There were no orange groves, no charming little street "nearby" in Anaheim, just concrete, concrete, concrete. I have never returned to Knott's Berry Farm, which is now a major amusement park. I prefer the memories of that four-year-old child, as hazy and indistinct as they are.

I did return to Marineland, although at first I didn't realize it. I was in California with my husband for a conference held at a resort on the coast. At one point, I walked along the cliffs above the ocean and thought that the view looked familiar, though I knew I had never visited this particular hotel. I later discovered that the resort was built upon the former site of the famous Marineland, which Sea World had acquired and torn down in the interim.

We visited Boston the summer before third grade, when I began learning about American history. We had already seen the historical sites in Washington, D.C. and New York City on a previous trip, and my father's choice of Boston was fortuitous for me. When my class read about Paul Revere's famous ride, I was excited to realize that I had already visited his house, and knew about "One if by land, and two if by sea." During that vacation, we also went to Salem, the site of the famous witch trials, and toured the House of the Seven Gables. My mother bought the Hawthorne novel for me, and I was so determined to read it that I memorized the first paragraph because I had to start over so many times.

I remember my first trip on a "real" jet—the kind without propellers. It was a Boeing 707 Astrojet, and it was brand new, with silvery-grey starburst wallpaper on the interior. The flying public was still dressing up at that point, and my mother and I wore our

Easter dresses, while my father and brother donned coats and ties. My father taught me how to read an airline timetable—there were no hubs at the time, and one planned one's own route—and asked me to sit in the front seat of our rental cars, where he taught me how to read a map and how to navigate roads large and small. I felt special, important, and grown up, especially since my older brother always sat in the back seat with my mother.

We only had one "driving" vacation. It was in 1966, the summer of the "Great Airline Strike." Five airlines were not flying, which left thousands of daily air passengers scrambling for transportation. The few airlines not on strike did not have any seats available for "non-revs," or non-revenue people like us, so we drove to Colorado. Our car did not have air conditioning, and it was so hot that my brother and I stuck our bare feet out of the windows. We daydreamed while gazing upon tall green stalks of corn set against bright blue skies—the colors of Oz.

After my seventh-grade year, we flew to Mexico City for two weeks. We stayed at the old Hotel Del Prado, undoubtedly upon the recommendation of my father's coworkers, all of whom were part of the travel-obsessed culture of American Airlines. We explored the city for days, eating the local food and wandering the streets and markets. I particularly remember Chapultepec Park on a Sunday, with entire families strolling hand in hand, all dressed in their church finery. People bought balloons from a vendor with an enormous colorful bouquet flying overhead or purchased huge tortillas from a man with a two-wheeled cart.

We attended a bullfight, which I hated. I had expected to enjoy the pageantry, which I did, but I was totally unprepared for the brutality. During the last event, the bull gored the matador and threw him high into the air. When the matador landed on his back, it gored him again. It was like a horrific ballet: the matador swirling, the bull tossing, the body flying, the bull stabbing. The bull was quickly dispatched, and the seemingly lifeless matador was carried out of the ring. I have no idea whether he lived or died, but one thing was certain: I had seen my first, and my last, bullfight.

We hired a guide named Rubio to drive us to the pyramids on one day and to Taxco on another. We stopped at every country club along the way to have drinks on manicured terraces. In retrospect, I realize that Rubio was probably an alcoholic, but my parents did not seem to care. He was also the "mayor" of many small towns. At one point, he startled my brother and me by putting a siren on the roof of his car and fooling us into turning around to see whether a police car was actually following us. While sitting in a restaurant at the base of the pyramids, Rubio taught us how to roll corn tortillas in the palms of our hands.

We stayed in Mexico City longer than expected; summer school at the *Ciudad Universitaria* had ended, and the returning American students—like all paying customers—had priority over us. We spent the first night sitting in chairs in the employee lounge at the airport and went to a hotel at midnight the next, returning by six a.m. so as to not lose our spot on the flight list. I read several James Bond novels in the Mexico City airport during those long hours of waiting. In my memory, that airport is just one big room, with a small wire stand of paperback books in English. Admittedly, James Bond was a little racy for me at age thirteen, but I read every one of them available. My brother and I sustained our teenage selves at the restaurant, which was a circular soda counter in the center of the room. We ordered bottles of Coca-Cola and what I still consider to be the best refried beans I've ever eaten. Our mother joined us for one lunch, but left after seeing a large rat scurry along the floor.

We finally flew out of Mexico City on the evening of the third day. We sat up front in the "lounge" of that Boeing 707, a semi-circle of seats around a coffee table complete with magazines. The stewardesses—not yet called flight attendants—sat in jump seats.

On another trip, this one to Montreal, we stayed on the second floor of temporary housing in the form of a two-story trailer because all regular hotel rooms in the city were sold out. This arrangement frightened my mother; she was concerned that we couldn't get out in case of fire. Every day, we took the train, the Expo Express, to the Montreal World's Fair, known as "Expo 67."

We again stayed in temporary housing in San Antonio when we visited "HemisFair '68," another world's fair. This time, though, it was a Quonset hut. We visited the as-yet-undiscovered Riverwalk and the famous Alamo, which my memory tells me was fronted with a simple gravel parking lot. We rented a Volkswagen Beetle on this trip, which was memorable because it was a standard shift, and I was learning to drive at the time. My father allowed me to drive in circles around that Quonset hut compound, which was instructive for me but undoubtedly bone-jarring for him.

In Acapulco, I met a boy, Tom, and we danced cheek-to-cheek on our hotel's rooftop before a sudden lightning storm sent us back to our waiting and worried families. The next day, while swimming in the Pacific, Tom and I lost track of the waves while talking and looked up just in time to see a giant wave curling over us before crashing down. I thought that my arms and legs were going to be torn from my body and that I was going to drown. In that moment, I truly understood the power of the sea.

Tom and I struggled back to the hotel pool, but before I could rinse off the head-to-toe sand, my father was standing in front of me, saying, "There is a young man who would like to meet you. He's sitting with his family at the pool." I followed my father and solemnly shook hands with the boy's father, then his mother, and then with the young man himself. I sat at one end of the group, while the young man sat at the other; our parents sat in between. This young man was from a very traditional Mexican family and was dressed for the occasion, wearing all white. I was wearing a sand-caked bikini. We did not speak; our parents carried the entire conversation. I don't remember who left first, his family or mine, but I do remember thinking, *What beautiful manners they have. What a genteel society they must live in.*

When I was a little older and flying solo on airline passes provided by my father, the stewardesses usually mistook me for a colleague and invariably asked, "Where are you based?" In truth, I did think about becoming a flight attendant at one point. My love of travel always beckoned. But then came the deregulation of the airlines and the advent of the T-shirts-and-flip-flops-are-fine-for-flying era. And with it came the destruction of the historical Art Deco masterpiece that was the magnificent early Tulsa airport. What a high price to pay for "progress."

2

TRAVAILS

Given all these wonderful experiences, one might think that I had a blissfully happy childhood, but I did not.

Yes, I traveled extensively. I was given birthday parties, gifts from Santa Claus, and baskets from the Easter Bunny. I roller-skated, watched the summer clouds drift by, and played kickball in the street. And yet, despite the fact that I could see that my parents enjoyed their young family, I could tell that something was wrong.

My parents displayed affection toward each other less and less as I grew up. I'm not sure what happened; I'm not sure what changed. By middle childhood though, something was different in our family, and I began to withdraw into myself.

No one prepared me for the situations I was about to encounter; no one clarified expectations of my behavior. When the maternal floodgates opened, my mother's angry words overpowered me, and left me ashamed and depressed. Her Dr. Jekyll and Mr. Hyde behavior made me feel untethered, adrift, and unable to anticipate when the other shoe was going to drop. As the years went by, I started to notice my shoulders actually slumping when I was in the same room as my mother, as if defending myself from a possible attack, or perhaps trying to disappear.

My parents never threatened me, never promised punishment by removing me from my excellent private schools or from my ballet classes. There were no horror stories like those featured on the news nowadays; there were just frequent explosions when I transgressed in some unanticipated way. I kept my head down, and had few real friends. I never spoke to anyone about the situation at home. To be fair, I don't think I even realized what was happening.

I treasured my time at the ballet studio where I could be myself. In fact, some of my best friends to this day are from that era—fellow refugees from the world of ballet. While becoming a dancer was my mother's ambition for me—an outgrowth of her college class, "Orchesis," the study of Greek chorus movement—it ultimately saved me from my father's silence toward me and my mother's inability to see me as a separate person.

My mother treated me as an extension of herself and expected me to achieve her own unfulfilled dreams. I would be in the ballet company, I would go to a certain high school, I would dress in a certain way, even staying in my church clothes on Sunday afternoons, while my neighborhood friends were allowed to change clothes and play outside. I had an image to maintain, and that image hinged on my mother's idea of "the good life," the life that she evidently desired.

So much of it depended on how I *looked*. My mother scrutinized my dress, my hair, even the width of my hips. "So-and-so's hips are only this big," she once said during my dancing days, demonstrating a tiny width with her hands that my five-foot-eight, 115-pound frame would never achieve, even though I was extremely thin. This was very hurtful. Ballet is a visual art, after all, so size and shape and proportion matter, but this was beyond my control. I would never have the slender hips that so I desired to see in the mirror.

I suppose that my mother did not see herself accurately. After all, I had inherited those hips directly from her. Or perhaps she was just frustrated that I was not a perfect replica of what she imagined herself to have been or that I had not attained teenaged perfection.

When I obtained my driver's license, which correctly stated that my green-and-gold eyes were hazel, my mother objected, "But your eyes are brown like mine!" Her eyes were indeed brown; in fact, they were so brown as to appear almost black. But mine were not. I was surprised into silence when confronted with the fact that my own mother didn't know my eye color. Had she never really looked at me? Did she not even *see* me?

Not being viewed as a distinct individual means that everything you strive for, everything you achieve, is not really *yours*; it belongs to someone else and is a reflection of her or him. Except for your mistakes, of course. Those belong totally and unconditionally to you. When this happens to you as a child, the message is that this is who you really are. You are the sum of your mistakes.

I do not remember my parents ever saying, "I love you," either to me or to each other. When tensions were high in the home, I would do anything to avoid their gaze. When they argued, I would retreat to my room and bury my nose in a book as soon as the angry words began. I was extremely careful whenever I made my small childhood requests. I saw enough anger in that house to want to avoid bringing it upon myself. I could never depend on emotional stability from them; I was always watching and waiting for the next explosion. It is amazing to me today that I found this atmosphere perfectly normal.

Somehow, I learned that I did not deserve attention, even though I craved it. At one point as a child, I took part in a hula-hoop competition in which I was the youngest contestant and clearly the best hula-hooper. Eventually, I looked around and realized that the two remaining contestants were losing the battle, so I simply stopped and walked away.

Why on earth did I do that? I was very disappointed that I didn't win, even though it clearly had been within my power to do so. Perhaps I did not wish to attract attention to myself, or was unsure of what type of attention I would receive if I won. Perhaps I thought it would be "nice" of me if I allowed one of the others to win. I'll never know the real reason I gave up that day, but it exemplified the constant theme of sacrifice in my life.

Of course, allowing others to go first or even to win on occasion is a form of being "nice" for children. But how is a child to know the difference between being genuinely "nice" and being bullied into giving way? The difference between being considerate and allowing oneself to be hurt? On the rare occasions when I was bullied at school and complained about it to my mother, the response was always "Just be nice to everyone." When a neighbor child or the children of visiting adults broke my toys—sometimes intentionally—the response was the same, often with the addition of the words, "Oh, well," as in, "Oh, well, just be nice to everyone." The toys were never replaced, the offending children were never reprimanded, and the neighboring or visiting parents were, to my knowledge, never told of their children's transgressions. Other children could treat me however they wished. Like all children, I had no power, but unlike most children, no one had my back. And I was never taught to stand up for myself.

At church, I lip-synced all the hymns. I mouthed the words, yet no sound came out, in spite of quizzical looks from those around me. Why? Was I ashamed of my voice and didn't want it to be heard? Years later, in an arts program, I was told by the chorus master of the Tulsa Opera that I had vocal talent that I should develop. I kept his comment to myself.

My parents often called me names, sometimes in anger and sometimes in jest, but those words always stung. I was "Pigpen," in honor of the character from *Charlie Brown*. I was "Ignats," a colloquialism for "ignoramus." I was tall and thin, so "Olive Oil" from *Popeye* was a favorite. My mother frequently said, "You look like *this*," or, "You look like *that*," commenting on the shortcomings of my looks at that particular moment. Appearances were extremely important to my mother. I was expected to be "cute," "well-dressed," "smart," and to get good grades. I perceived my mother's love as conditional; being loved just because I existed was not on offer.

I know now that I displayed signs of anxiety. I bit my nails. I hid inconsequential things. I lied to avoid punishment. I rocked myself to sleep every night, long after it was considered "normal" to do so. In first grade, I always wore a headband to corral my unruly locks. I pushed it back on my forehead over and over again until the teacher called my parents about it. That night, I found my father in the garage, sawing the tiny teeth off of the headband. I was humiliated, and couldn't understand why my teacher had called my parents. After all, I was a *good girl*. I did not understand the restlessness that accompanied my anxiety.

At the beginning of high school, we were instructed to ask one parent to write a "Character Study" of us. My mother volunteered, and I braced for the worst. Now everyone would know who I really was. Much to my surprise, my mother wrote a glowing account of my appearance, my behavior, my accomplishments. Who was this person she was writing about? And who had written that paragraph? My life was filled with many such confusing episodes.

The Girl on the Belvedere

I was never allowed to consider anything that deviated from what my parents had experienced, those refugees from the Great Depression whose survival depended upon thrift. My mother saved tin foil if there was even the slightest chance it could be reused. She recycled every bit of leftovers into other dishes. She balanced her checkbook to the penny, even once making a trip to the bank because her balance and the bank's balance differed by ten cents. When I asked if I could go to summer camp like other neighborhood children, I already knew the answer.

My brother tells me now that we were poor, though I never perceived that. I had new clothes every year, even if my mother made them or bought them from a discount store. I had plenty to eat. I had my own room, eventually with my own pink Princess telephone. I had a large-enough front yard and a backyard in which to play with neighborhood friends. However, even if there had been enough money for summer camp, the answer would have been the same: "No." By the time I was an accomplished ballet dancer, I knew better than to ask whether I could study in New York for the summer like so many of my friends. There had simply been too many years of "No," and too much of that oft-repeated phrase, "Money doesn't grow on trees."

Once, in grade school, I asked my mother, "Could we please get me a new dress from Utica Square?" It was then and still is a beautiful leafy shopping center in midtown Tulsa.

"No," was her immediate answer. "Money doesn't grow on trees."

I did not tell my mother that some "friends" at school had made fun of the stores where we bought my clothes. I had been too naive to lie or to refuse to tell them where we shopped when they asked, and I was shamed by their horrified looks and comments. I always learned the hard way that not everyone is "nice."

I honestly do not know what my parents' true financial situation was. I do know that they traveled a great deal in their later years, that they gifted my children money for their savings accounts, and that I received a moderately large inheritance. They were, I believe, typical children of the Depression and of the privation of World War II. They had survived—even flourished—with very little, and therefore, so should I. This is not necessarily a bad trait; money, unless it lifts one from true poverty, does not bring happiness.

Still, my mother persisted in claiming that our house was bigger (it was not), nicer (it was not), and in a better neighborhood (nope) than others' houses. My parents had endless arguments about their house in comparison to others'. My father always pointed out what I perceived as the rational truth, while my mother vehemently disagreed.

I do not pretend to understand what truly went on in that home, nor does it matter. A child believes whatever she is told. My mother was a damaged soul, and I suffered as a result. In a way, I continue to suffer.

I sometimes worry about being harmed, which in this day and age, is certainly realistic in some situations. What is disturbing, though, is my fear of being harmed in some way and being unable to respond. I fear being paralyzed by fear. I can only assume that the origin of these disturbing thoughts lies in the helplessness that every child feels when placed in difficult situations over which they have no control.

If I fell down and scraped my knee, my mother dried my tears. But if I were to cry over some childhood emotional trauma —what someone said or did—she did not. Sometimes, she even made fun of these tears. As soon as I was old enough to voice an opinion, I was put down, criticized, and made fun of.

Did my mother know the damage she caused in this way? Did she understand the anxiety, the depression, the constant starvation for positive attention, and eventually, the desire to leave one's childhood behind? I doubt it, because I knew her mother, my grandmother.

My grandmother usually ignored me, but that was better than the harsh words I received when I made myself visible and audible to her. My earliest memory of her came after a four-hour car trip to Missouri, where the entire extended family lived. I asked, "Grandma, may I please have a drink of water?"

"Yes, if you'll shut up."

Why did my mother not defend me, her very young child? Surely, this type of treatment of her children must have made her angry. But in reality, I never observed my mother react in any way to my grandmother's constant gossip or her criticism of family members beyond a tense smile and raised eyebrows.

My grandmother told me stories of my mother's youth, of her transgressions, and of the harsh punishments she received for not being perfect, for just being a child. Even as a young child myself, I knew that this behavior was wrong and that my mother had suffered greatly because of it. Yet I was unable to connect the dots and see that familial behaviors are inherited and passed along until one family member decides that it will stop at that moment, forever. Years later, as an adult, I could see that my mom had managed to improve upon the role of "mother," considering how she had been raised.

On the other hand, perhaps I am too hard on my maternal grandmother. She was born around the turn of the last century, and had endured the trauma of World War One, the Spanish Flu Pandemic of 1918, the Great Depression, and World War Two. My mother had tuberculosis as a child; my aunt nearly died of diphtheria. I'm certain that in those pre-vaccination, pre-antibiotic days, they suffered from many other dangerous childhood diseases as well. The stress of motherhood one hundred years ago was real, and it must have taken its toll on my grandmother's personality.

I do know that my grandmother was inordinately proud of my mother's looks. She would show me photos from my mother's youth and compare her to Elizabeth Taylor. My mother had indeed been a beauty queen throughout high school and college, but those types of accolades—focusing on one's inherited looks—do not necessarily bring happiness.

In spite of her natural beauty, I do not think my mother lived the life that she had wanted. Did any woman of that era? She was a talented artist and had been an art major in college, yet she had neither the time nor the means for self-expression once "life" occurred. She dressed beautifully, though her clothes always came from the discount stores. She had wonderful taste in furniture and home design, but little pocket money with which to indulge those tastes. She had not been able to attend the expensive private college that was her first choice; it was during the Depression, and while her father held a steady job during those uncertain times, his salary from the Frisco Railroad would not have stretched far enough to allow anything more than the local state university. What had she envisioned for herself? Perhaps a marriage to someone who earned more and could provide more material rewards? I will never know, but looking back, I can see her frustration and perhaps some depression. She made those hidden feelings known through her demands of perfection from me.

My maternal grandfather was a dear, dear man. He was quiet, affectionate, and, I think now, eager to keep the peace in a fault-finding household. He once presented me with a dimestore diamond ring, telling me that I was "his girl." I adored him. And he adored his wife, my querulous grandmother.

My other grandmother—my father's mother—I loved. She was poor, often moving from one garage apartment to another, but she was fascinating. She had been born in a dugout in New Mexico Territory to parents escaping the devastating aftermath of the Civil War. Their homestead was near the Santa Fe Trail, where her parents barely eked out a living by running a few head of cattle and helping wagons traverse a ravine. My great-grandparents eventually moved back to Missouri to raise their family, where my grandmother matured, married, and had three children of her own, including my father. She always had cold Coca-Colas, a bowl of buttered popcorn, and tales from her past awaiting us when we went to visit her. We didn't see her often, though; we always stayed with my mother's parents when we went to Missouri where both families lived.

I don't know why my father was so reluctant to spend more than an occasional afternoon with his mother when we visited Springfield, but I do know that in his generation, no one spoke of deep wounds. I think that his father—my grandfather, who died when I was a baby—drank heavily; it was whispered about by the females in my mother's family, who considered themselves superior, even though only a few generations back, my father's family had been very wealthy, socially prominent, and extremely well-educated. Perhaps his family's reversal of fortune combined with my maternal grandmother's disdain explains my father's silence and occasional explosive anger.

ONE TIME, I overheard one of my parents' many arguments, this one about drinking.

My mother said, "You would be a 'social drinker' if you could," a veiled reference to the taboo word "alcoholic."

"No, I wouldn't. I only have a drink once in a while, usually on Friday night if you make us whiskey sours."

"You drink too much."

"One beer on Saturday is not drinking too much."
"Yes, it is."
"No, it's not."

And on it went, undoubtedly a throwback to the open secret in my family that his father had been a "drinker."

In reality, my father drank rarely. He always said to me, even as a young child, "If you want a drink, you may have a sip of mine." I usually did take a small sip of his occasional single Saturday beer, and as a young adult, I did not feel the need to rebel by drinking underage. After all, alcohol was always available to me in moderation, if I so desired.

I will say this about my father: he was one of the most stoic people I have ever known. I never heard a word of complaint from him, and in all the years I lived at home he called in sick from work exactly once. On that day, he was so ill that he could barely lift his head from the pillow, but he simply said to me with a smile, "I'm not feeling well today." Years later, on the night he died, as my children were leaving with my husband, my father raised his head and said, "G'night, kids!" in a cheery voice, as though he were going to see them the next day.

His nickname was "Greek," given to him in high school, supposedly due to his fascination with Greek history. My brother thinks that our father's secret desire was to teach history, and this may be true—we grew up in a household with a bookshelf in the living room filled with my father's preferences and trips to the library for other genres. While I was home for several weeks with strep throat, he brought Victor Hugo's *Les Misérables* into my room and told me that I would enjoy reading it. I was in the fourth grade.

I do not think, however, that he was attuned to my mother's need for creative outlets. The term "Women's Liberation" was not coined until a quarter-century after their marriage, and I think he felt that he was fulfilling the obligations of a post-war

The Girl on the Belvedere

father: providing a decent home and a second car, and spending some time with the children in the evening. That's it. The rest of daily life was up to my mother. There were certainly no date nights, no restaurant meals to relieve my mother's fatigue and boredom, and certainly not a new house when my mother longed for one.

When I was fourteen, my mother found a beautiful home for sale in Maple Ridge, an affluent neighborhood in Tulsa. The house was easily affordable, and I saw her eyes sparkle with the elegance and graciousness she could bring to it, but my father said no—it would be "too much work," as it was an older mansion built during Tulsa's first oil boom. It would be another decade before they moved to a distant suburb and into a smaller, more modern home that was move-in ready. Even then, he refused to relocate the bronze-and-crystal chandelier that she had hand-carried home from Mexico City years before, and she resentfully "made do" with the ugly modern light fixture in the new dining room. Hiring an electrician to make the required transfer was evidently out of the question.

My mother also mentioned several times over the years that she would like to own a houseboat. Perhaps houseboats were very much in style in the fifties and represented the epitome of luxury. At least, that's what I thought she meant when I was a child. Looking back, however, I think she may have been searching for more—perhaps more peace, more tranquility, more beauty, and the absence of everyday stress. Maybe she wanted to take up painting again.

I realize now that over the years she had to give up many of her dreams. She frequently said to me, "When you make your bed, you have to lie in it." I was never entirely sure what she was referring to in her case. Did she mean her marriage? Her children? Her house? Her circumstances? My parents' financial situation was more affluent than that of her childhood. However, it still must not have matched her expectations.

My father always remained silent while observing the constant criticism I received from my mother. Did he know how injurious his silence could be? Or was it simply the non-reaction of a man who had come from an historically prominent family, only to grow up in grinding poverty and fight in a world war? Had his parents ignored him? Spoken harshly to him without loving concern? Were they so focused on economic survival that they paid him no mind? His temper was explosive, and while his anger toward me was not displayed often, it was a cause of fear and anxiety.

My father was a very quiet man, and I was never quite sure where I stood with him. He rarely expressed his emotions. He told me on his forty-third birthday, when I was eight, that if the house ever caught on fire, I was to get myself out and not to worry about him—he had lived his life. I understood that he was placing the value of my life above his, and that this was a declaration of his love for me. I understood, but now I wonder why he just couldn't tell me outright that he loved me.

Years later, when I was in college, my father said to me, "The best years of your life are still ahead of you." What did he mean? My future working life? Marriage? Children? At the time, sensing a sadness in his voice, I thought he meant having small children with all the innocence, joy, and laughter that they can bring. I didn't ask what he meant, and he did not elaborate. How sad, that on these rare occasions, he could not verbally express his emotions.

When I started piano lessons, he requested lessons from me when I returned from each session with my instructor. We sat down together at the green-speckled upright piano in the den that my father had added to our small house, and I showed him what I had learned that week. He did not acquire much proficiency—how could he, with a second-grader as a teacher? But he really seemed to enjoy practicing my simple assignments in his free time after work.

And here's a curious thing—I don't remember being asked whether I would like to take piano. One day, I came home from school and found that a piano had appeared. Had my father wanted music lessons when he was a child and wished to give me the opportunity he was denied? I'm certain that it had not been a possibility during his impoverished childhood. Yet he loved music of any kind. On weekends, the record player was usually belting out Tommy Dorsey, Glenn Miller, or other popular artists from the Big Band era. Evidently, he also loved the song "Stranger in Paradise." I didn't know this, though, until he saw me dance as one of the Slave Girls in the "Polovtsian Dances" from the opera *Prince Igor*. My father said to me after the performance, "I love the music that you danced. It was used for the Broadway show *Kismet* and is called "Stranger in Paradise." I had never heard of *Kismet* before this.

He had a lovely singing voice, and if I have any vocal talent, I inherited it from him. It makes me wonder why I was so afraid to be heard singing when I was young. Every child should sing, and sing loudly.

I know that education was important to my father; both Larry and I were sent to private schools. He had learned the value of education the hard way. My mother told me that before my father entered high school, he left the family farm and moved to Springfield to live with extended family in order to attend a better school.

In spite of his emphasis on education, my father made it clear to me early on that if they had only enough money for one child to attend college, it would be my brother, not me. After all, Larry would one day be supporting a family, while I would not. Perhaps my father's attitude on this subject came from his having had to work his way through college, while his parents paid for his sisters' tuition in full. He left college after two years and enlisted in the Army Air Corps because he could no longer afford the tuition. Still, even armed with this knowledge, I was dismayed to hear that my education might be complete after high school. I was too young to realize that while my parents saved nearly every penny they earned, they must have worried about the prospect of paying for college tuition at all. At the time, it just felt like another "No," another hint that perhaps I was of little worth. It added to my feeling of inadequacy.

CHILDHOOD IS CONFUSING ENOUGH without being emotionally abandoned by your parents and told in so many words that you are the least valuable member of the family. Now, I grieve for that unhappy child, that lost child, that child whose mind still goes blank when someone else speaks of their "happy childhood." However, I also try to see things from my parents' perspective and feel gratitude for the opportunities they gave me. In their experience, finances could suddenly become unstable through no fault of one's own. They had both grown up *without*. They were determined to give us a good education at the very least, plus some frivolities along the way.

Like everyone, I carry the inevitable wounds of childhood, though perhaps just a few more than most considering the barrage of constant criticism and the dismantling of dreams. Happily, I had ballet, which became the center of my world.

The strange thing, the thing that I now puzzle over the most, is my conviction that my parents did indeed love me. While neither ever said, "I love you," to me—I witnessed the surprise on my father's face when I said those three little words to him during his final illness—I have never doubted that they loved me. I was certainly not spoiled, but I wanted for nothing. I was never asked to take care of them; I was not saddled with household chores too advanced for my tender age. I was encouraged to go out and play with my friends or ride my bike. I worshipped my parents with the unconditional love of a child. I appreciated the fact that my mother wanted me to succeed in life, and I loved that my father enjoyed discussing faraway places with me.

Is happiness taught? Is it instinctual in some, absent in others? Are some children indeed "blissfully happy" in their childhood? Are others just "happy enough"? I do not know, but the phrases "I loved my parents" and "they loved me" call to mind their constancy and their concern.

Has the definition of a happy childhood changed? In that post-Depression, post-war era, perhaps providing a roof over one's head, three meals a day, and a good education was considered the epitome of successful parenting. It is probably unwise to view the past by current standards.

Of course, while I did not have an emotionally secure childhood, I had many moments of joy, of freedom, and certainly many unique opportunities. I have no regrets save for wishing that my parents had had a better relationship, one filled with quiet contentment and happiness. And, selfishly, I would have preferred a relationship between them that would have better supported a shy, creative child, a relationship that would have encouraged her to dream about the future rather than teach her to drift along, always wary of the next obstacle, the next collision. I would have preferred that they instill hope, confidence, and honesty rather than fear, hopelessness, and dependence. I'm certain that my parents did the best they could with what they had been given. What parent can say any different? I cannot. I myself was given much, was lacking much, and parented accordingly. Every parent has limitations, and most of us pray that those limitations will not injure our children.

My mother and father were wonderful grandparents to my children—trustworthy, careful, kind, and gentle. And my parents did become closer to one another when my father was diagnosed with a terminal illness. I was very happy to see it, but I was also sad that it had taken so long for them to regain the affection that they surely had enjoyed at the start of their marriage.

WHAT FOLLOWED MY CHILDHOOD? I went to college after all; my mother went back to work so that I could attend. If that's not love, what is? My father, however, accused me of wanting to get away from them when I expressed my desire to live on campus. I stood my ground for once and went so far as to apply to lesser schools where tuition, room, and board, combined, would cost no more than living at home and commuting to my first choice, the University of Tulsa. I won that battle. Happily, my mother wanted me to attend my first choice, and she announced that if I made that decision, she would pay for me to live on campus. I was thrilled. Once planted there—away from the very people making it possible—I began to bloom.

I was successful at TU and was accepted by my peers. The university was a refuge, a place of safety, hard work, and happiness. Each semester, I returned at the earliest possible moment and stayed until school closed at the end of the term. I wasn't afraid to be at home; I just did not want to face the constant criticism or be endlessly judged. Case in point: late in my college career, when I was taking eighteen credit hours one semester, my father claimed that my entire course load was not nearly as difficult as the three-credit-hour course my mother was taking to renew her teaching certification. I was dumbfounded.

I had goofed off a lot in high school, being happier and

much more engaged in the ballet studio. I just didn't care—until, that is, my senior year, when I began to pay attention, work hard, and straighten up, so that I could succeed at whatever university I attended. Once in college, I studied very hard. I spent hours in my dorm room, studying with a single goose-necked lamp shining down on my textbook, highlighters in my hand, or clacking away at my typewriter on a term paper.

And now, my parents were telling me that it was of no value, that college was easy for me, and that my mother's three hours were more difficult than my eighteen. Why did they do that? Were they trying to retain control of a child who was perhaps brighter and—through their own good offices—better educated than they? Was their self-esteem that low? Even now, all these years later, just thinking about such comments makes me tired. I will never know why they behaved that way, but that doesn't change the fact that I had found a home at the University of Tulsa, was academically successful, and had developed many solid friendships away from my parents' disapproving gaze. And I flourished.

While there, I performed with the college dance team, danced in a faculty music recital, and once choreographed the annual musical revue—in addition to all my studying. I graduated with honors, went on to attain a master's degree, married for love, taught school, danced in a small contemporary company, had children, and hoped that I was more successful at parenting than what I had observed in my own childhood. I achieved plenty—old habits die hard—and I kept right on achieving, unable to slow down, look around, take a deep breath and just *be*.

I can honestly say that I loved my parents. We eventually got along very well after my own marriage when I lived a thousand miles away. My mother telephoned me every Saturday, and we spoke for an hour or so. My parents visited us on the East Coast many times, and I always looked forward to their visits. We continued to get along after my husband and I moved back to Tulsa.

Lives are complicated, families are complicated, and mine was no exception. I think now that we were a loving but imperfect family, that my parents loved to the best of their limited abilities, and that I grew up in a home where deep thoughts were rarely expressed except in anger. Unhappily, this taught me fear, but it also taught me the difference between right and wrong. There are many types of love, many manifestations of it, and I choose to look at the positive aspects rather than singing "They Done Me Wrong." After all, they done me right in so many ways. And I miss them.

3

TUTUS

My young life—and most of my young adult life—was spent in and around the world of classical ballet. It was the kindness of Czeslaw Roman Jasinski that influenced me, guided me, and ultimately saved me. Mr. Jasinski, my teacher, and, eventually my artistic director, was joyous in his everyday dealings with us. His love of ballet was infectious, and we stretched, strived, and smiled through his classes and corrections.

He was a native of Warsaw, born in 1907 while Poland was under Russian occupation. That occupation gave way to that of the Germans during the horror of World War I. Jasinski described to me the effects of starvation upon him and his family as well as his gratitude for becoming an American citizen during the many hours of interviews I conducted with him. Those interviews formed the nucleus of his biography, *A Gypsy Prince from the Ballet Russe.* Jasinski always looked forward, never back, and those of us who danced under his direction in the company now known as Tulsa Ballet adored him.

Moscelyne Larkin, his ballerina wife, was half Native American and half Russian, and we frequently gauged her mood by what she wore. "Is she Indian or Russian today?" we would ask each other ahead of class. Her "Indian" colors were red or orange, and these were always accompanied by the most beautiful pieces of large turquoise jewelry. Her "Russian" colors were softer, often pale pink or lavender. Her Russian side was gregarious and larger than life, while her Indian side was quieter, more reserved, more solemn. She was a true Ballet Russe ballerina who did not step out of the house without "making an effort," as she liked to say. She was always in full makeup, a matching leotard and chiffon skirt, and something pretty around her low chignon.

When the company went on tour, we were expected to look as glamorous as she. When we left the theatre after a performance, we were required to wear street clothes with normal makeup, always removing the dramatic stage makeup necessary for performance. Upon joining the company, I learned how to arrange my hair in a "classical." Everyone hated the classical. It looked like something borrowed from the nineteenth century—which it was—with the hair swooped low over the ears into a roll at the nape of the neck. I was somewhat adept at applying the standard dancer's stage makeup—with eyes winged by eyeliner above and below—having already danced in local summer musicals.

The dance world at that time had countless unwritten rules beyond hair and makeup: one must never put one's feet on the seat in front of one when sitting out in the house, one must never have food or drink around the costumes in the dressing room, one must sew one's pointe shoe ribbons together after tucking them in so that they did not come loose on stage, and one ought to make the sign of the cross before leaving the safety of the wings for the bright lights of the stage. *"Merde!"* we called to each other before going onstage. Never, ever, "Break a leg!"

Finally, one always hung up one's costume; a costume was never to touch the floor.

I made the sign of the cross and said "*Merde!*" to my fellow dancers. I wore the hated hairdo and the makeup with thick false lashes. I sewed my ribbons after tying them. I hung up my costumes, but I balked at not having sodas in the dressing room. I simply hid the cans under my sweatpants or street clothes, or whatever was available in a heap on the floor. And, sometimes, I left the theatre without taking off my stage makeup.

AT SEVENTEEN, I danced in the first performance of *Roman Jasinski's The Nutcracker*, a production that would run annually for thirty-plus years. A lot was riding on that first performance. The company was almost fifteen years old at the time, and had developed from a group of students into a well-rehearsed, well-oiled machine that turned out several major performances a year, as well as short tours and school performances. The company's technique and repertoire were based on that of the legendary Ballet Russe, the former company of the artistic directors, Mr. Jasinski and Miss Larkin.

We dancers were not paid, except in pointe shoes. The company bought our shoes for us prior to each performance. It was the first step toward becoming a paid professional company.

We understood that the Tulsa premiere of *The Nutcracker* was important, and while we did not know that this production would run for over thirty years, we did know that the company was making its mark through its various performances. By this time, it had been written up in Dance Magazine and we dancers took for granted that the Southwestern Ballet Festival would feature us in the annual gala performance, rather than in the workshop performance. In a few short years the company would achieve "major company" status in the National Association of Regional Ballet and would change its name from Tulsa Civic Ballet to Tulsa Ballet Theatre as it became fully professional. It is now Tulsa Ballet, heralded as "a tier-one North American company" by the European press.

We could not see the future, though; all our thoughts were on the present and the success of the show. I was nervous the morning of that *Nutcracker* premiere, and took company class along with my equally nervous fellow dancers. That evening—at five o'clock, as I always wanted to be in the theatre early—I walked down the musty old hallway from the stage door to the soloists' dressing room, flipped on the light, pulled my old grey sweatpants over my leotard and tights, and donned my worn-out pointe shoes for warmup. I wrapped the ribbons around my ankles, and tucked the loose ends behind the knots.

I had performed these rituals many times, but this time was different. We were presenting a well-known, much-beloved, full-length classical ballet for the first time in Tulsa. We had presented full-length ballets before, but none so well known or as appealing as *The Nutcracker*. The press had been carrying stories for weeks, and I had butterflies in my stomach, and was hypersensitive to everything around me.

I loved that old theatre. The stage floor creaked, the lighting in the dressing rooms was poor, it had dangerously slick concrete steps leading down to the stage level, and there was a circular wrought iron staircase leading up to the corps de ballet dressing room on the second floor.

That night, I carefully made my way down those concrete steps; there was no handrail. Once out on the empty stage, I glanced into the darkened house as I found an abandoned ladder and grabbed ahold of it to begin my warmup. Mr. Jasinski was already there, grinding the crunchy rosin with his foot onto the old wooden stage so that his dancers would not slip. He was wearing his familiar overcoat and hat with a feather, and when he saw me on this particular evening, he smiled and said in his thick Polish accent, "*Ched-al* [Cheryl] ready to do da dance?"

Every few seconds, I heard the stage door slam shut as the other dancers began to arrive. A stagehand closed the red velvet house curtain, the audience gathered, the orchestra filed into the pit, and the show opened at eight o'clock.

In the dressing room, my partner in the "Arabian" wrapped her bleeding feet with care. Her feet were badly injured, but she had refused to seek treatment, fearing that she might be required to miss the premiere. We donned our first costumes and performance shoes, and continued to warm up in the wings until our entrance in "Land of the Snow." We continually rose up on pointe, checking our shoes, and watched the children in the party scene. "Snow" went well except for the fact that a stagehand had accidentally ripped one bag of "snow" during the battle scene between the mice and the soldiers, and we Snowflakes entered a stage already slick with confetti.

During the second act, my partner and I took our places and watched the conductor from the wings. We were waiting for his baton to drop, the signal for our immediate entrance in the "Arabian." We had learned from our rehearsals with the orchestra that we were unable to hear the first soft strains of the Tchaikovsky music. After our variation, we doubled over in the wings, gasping for air, while we watched the next group on stage.

Near the end of "Waltz of the Flowers," a panicked dancer exited with a loose hair ornament bobbing up and down on her forehead. There was little time before her next entrance, so I ran alongside her, securing the hairpiece with bobby pins as we flew from the front wing to the back. My handiwork lasted through most of her variation, but the ornament came loose again during her final pirouettes. She finished and took her final pose

—and took her bow—with a large bunch of plastic grapes hanging down her forehead, obscuring her nose.

The principal dancers, who were from New York City Ballet, asked me to show them to their last wing and then requested that I count down their last entrance for them. Our principals were always from the New York City Ballet. Mr. Jasinski enjoyed a very real connection to the legendary George Balanchine, the artistic director of that company. Jasinski had been the principal dancer in Balanchine's first solo company, and their friendship lasted their lifetimes. Year after year, Mr. Jasinski simply telephoned his friend in New York and said, "Giorgi Melitonovitch, who can you send me?" We Tulsa dancers were accustomed to performing behind the most famous ballet stars of the day.

I fell onstage during the coda of that first *Nutcracker* performance when one foot became entangled in my Arabian costume. Down I went, and up I popped, not missing a single step. A large bruise on my hip served as a daily reminder of the incident for weeks.

After the premiere, well-wishers crowded the stage: young ballet students around the dancers, and board members around the principals. There were also society mavens in formal gowns and furs mobbing the handsome NYCB principal dancer, Jacques d'Amboise. Mr. d'Amboise somehow managed to disentangle himself and exit the stage to deliver cold sodas to those of us already in our dressing rooms.

I left the theatre soon after. As I departed, I turned to watch the door shut, for while I would tour with the company in the spring, this one performance of *The Nutcracker* was my last performance in Tulsa, in this venerable old theatre that had hosted Pavlova, Caruso, Buddy Holly, and so many others.

∼

The Girl on the Belvedere

WE TOURED several cities that spring, and I continued to train through daily classes, but there was no pressure on me. I was leaving. I jumped, I turned, I stretched, and I simply enjoyed whatever skill I had developed. I still have flashbacks to certain moments from that spring season. They are surprisingly full of joy, all muscle pain magically absent. I hung out in the back of the classroom, jumping and turning with the young men as they were put through their paces, laughing as I danced. How high could I jump? How many revolutions could I make in my own pirouettes? How did I look doing those jumps and turns which are usually reserved only for males? Mr. Jasinski invariably nodded his approval at my wild joy, smiling and laughing with me. What freedom I had through the discipline of ballet!

My last ballet class and my last company rehearsal remain clearly lodged in my memory. That evening I looked around and thought, *I don't belong here.* I had mentally moved on. I had made the decision to leave behind the world of ballet—that world of incredible beauty, of bleeding toes, of muscles so sore I wasn't sure I could get up in the morning, of brilliantly lit classrooms festooned with hanging garlands during the dark days of December, of colorful costumes, of stage lights, of moving, moving, moving, just for the joy of it all. I looked around and memorized the scene: the girls in their black leotards, pink tights, and black leg warmers, rising up on pointe to check their shoes while gossiping about the boys; the boys leaning back on their elbows on the barre in their white T-shirts and black tights, keeping an eye on those pretty girls; the pianist studying her sheet music in preparation for the moment when the artistic director would walk in and shut the door. One class and one rehearsal later, I walked out that door without a backward glance, knowing full well that this chapter of my life was irrevocably closed.

I had known for some time that I would be leaving. It was

time to fly the coop, and I knew without asking that my parents would not support me in New York, the epicenter of dance, while I continued to take class and audition. I also knew that while I was very well trained, I did not have the level of talent to dance with the two major companies, New York City Ballet and American Ballet Theatre, even though some of my friends in the company went on to do just that. There were a few other good professional companies in existence with whom I might have danced, but facts are facts: in spite of some physical advantages, my back was too stiff and my instep was not as highly arched as I desired. Even if I could have overcome these two hereditary physical impediments, my parents' opposition precluded any serious consideration of auditioning. And even then I was being pulled to a different life, a life of places to explore and people to meet. That was not going to happen in the narrow world of ballet, at least not for me. I left ballet behind.

I HAD GROWN up in and around theatres, and not just with the ballet. When I was eleven, my mother took me to Tulsa Little Theatre—now Theatre Tulsa—to audition for the role of a "royal child" in *The King and I*. "Where is your mother?" the choreographer said to me after the audition. I guided her to my mother, who was sitting in the last row of the house. "I want her to try out for the role of dancer," she explained. "Cheryl is too good a dancer to be one of the children."

After a month of nightly rehearsals, I learned to apply stage makeup to look as though I was from Thailand, still called "Siam" during the period in which the play is set. I had not yet joined the ballet company and had never worn any type of makeup in my life, and now, I was applying thick base, rouge, powder, eye shadow, eyeliner, lipstick, and body makeup. My fellow dancers instructed me, but they were never really pleased with my application; I was a child emulating dancers who were far older than I.

A few summers took on a pattern: spending every evening in June in rehearsal and every evening in July at the theatre in performance. A family vacation in August followed. Oh, to be so young, so privileged, so self-involved.

I did not fully appreciate what my parents were doing for me: driving me to the theatre every day at five (curtain was at eight) and picking me up at eleven for the two months of rehearsals and performances. On weekends, they drove me to cast parties after the show and retrieved me an hour or so later. Those summers were halcyon days: my stage makeup applied, my muscles warmed, my costume donned, our performance applauded.

During the school year I sometimes volunteered as a stagehand on Friday nights. I wore black turtlenecks and black pants and moved the lighter furniture around the stage during blackouts. On Saturdays, I helped the professional crew construct scenery. Sometimes, I would sneak up the ladder to the catwalk —a rickety contraption at best—which soared above the stage in the fly loft. I loved it up there. My parents would have grounded me had they known.

Occasionally, my future artistic director chose me to appear as a young dancer in various productions of Tulsa Opera, for which he was the choreographer. I draped myself about the stage in *Turandot* and came down some long, shaky wooden stairs in *Hansel and Gretel*, my arms outstretched like an angel.

Once I was accepted into the ballet company, I had classes six days a week, followed by rehearsals, performances at the large theatre downtown, occasional tours, and the odd opera, such as *Aida*.

I experienced years of happiness simply by being in a

theatre. I was usually the first to arrive, content to warm up in my leotard and tights; to apply my false lashes, heavy eyeliner, and lipstick; to assemble the required hairdo; and don the costume for performance. And until I turned sixteen, my parents drove, drove, drove.

My last summer musical with Theatre Tulsa, when I was twenty-one, was the show *Oklahoma* in which I was a lead dancer. The show followed the usual pattern of rehearsals for all of June and performances for all of July. On the night my fiancé's parents attended, the actress playing Laurey made sure that I caught the bridal bouquet, which I'm sure did not escape the notice of my future in-laws.

I married not long after this production, attended graduate school, moved to Virginia, and danced in a contemporary company. I taught school, and I taught ballet. I was busy, busy, busy, right up until the moment I had our first child, and even then, I stayed busy. Once we moved to New York, I taught dance aerobics in my building and started my research for the book *Gypsy Prince*, traveling to Lincoln Center on the crosstown bus several days a week. It felt wrong to just *be*, to throw myself into simply being "Mommy" for my child. I was supposed to do *Great Things!* It never occurred to me that perhaps I should slow down, enjoy the moment, and just appreciate that particular stage of life. I couldn't spend my time being outside with my son and later, my daughter, studying the shapes of the clouds. There was so much, I thought, that I needed to accomplish. So I kept right on accomplishing.

4

EPIPHANIES

Somewhere along the way, in the midst of all that *doing*, I lost myself, that small girl on the Belvedere who had her whole life ahead of her. Like the car, her hopes had been buried—or, perhaps, she had buried them herself. I had become a person who needed someone else's permission to dream. Why? What held me back? I could say it was my responsibilities, my volunteer work, my endless rounds of housework and homework with the children. I might blame it on a thousand things, but in reality the children eventually left home, and somehow, precious time had slipped away. I was just drifting along, held back by the emotional detritus of my childhood which ricocheted and reverberated through my days.

Eventually, I stopped long enough to listen to that quiet, deep, still voice within me, the one that spoke of possibilities, of a different sort of life. I was absolutely worn out by the expectations of others and with deadlines—deadlines for events, deadlines within organizations, deadlines for upcoming holidays, deadlines, deadlines, deadlines. At one point, I had seventeen post-it notes lined up on my mirror, in order, denoting major commitments over the next six weeks in which I was a major player. While skills such as mine were needed, I ultimately decided that someone else with those same skills could step up. I was *done*. I had rendered myself invisible, and I wanted to make myself a priority, to simply say, "I'm here, I exist." For many months, I had been longing, longing, longing...for something, but I didn't know what. I had been so attuned to others' needs and to my own need to achieve that I didn't really know what my true needs were. As the very wise Roman Jasinski once told me of the difficult periods in his life, "I needed to work on myself."

I found that I wanted to reacquire some fluency in French. It is the language of ballet, so I had been familiar with it since the age of four, and French had been a required course for me in high school. I had started taking classes in it again during my forties while researching the Jasinski book, only to drop them when my responsibilities became too numerous. French beckoned again in my late fifties, and so I again signed up for a class.

One day, my professor mentioned an immersion program in Quebec. *Quebec? In Canada? A French immersion course?* I had never considered such a possibility, but as I made the endless rounds of my life—everything predictable, static, and at times boring—the idea took hold. Like the heroine in Sonja Yoerg's wonderful novel *True Places*, I wanted to remember who I once was and to find the person I had become. Was I a wife? Yes. A mother? Yes. A volunteer at the ballet? Yes. But these things all involved *others*. Who was *I*, really? An artist? Yes, I used to be, as someone who enjoyed drawing. A researcher? Yes, I had done that, in the rarefied world of the Ballet Russe. A ballet dancer? Yes, but that was long, long ago.

I spent time considering what I might do during those weeks of freedom in Quebec. I could barely imagine time for myself with no demands save attending French class and completing homework. I inquired, enrolled, found an apartment, and made

The Girl on the Belvedere

airline reservations for Quebec City. And on the appointed day, I headed for the airport.

I was so impatient for the moment of departure to arrive and so terrified that someone would insist that I had to stay and complete some project and keep everything and everyone else on course. It was easy to imagine that someone would insist that I couldn't just up and leave for Canada.

When I first read the poem "Caged Bird" by Maya Angelou, I burst into tears. Not being someone who cries easily, I was forced to take stock of myself. I was happily married, had raised two wonderful children, and had discharged most of life's major responsibilities. Yet I had never dared to soar away, to "claim the sky." I had allowed my wings to be clipped. *Never again*, I vowed. *Never again will I sing of what might have been.* I was equating French with freedom, my escape from the cage. I was claiming this time in Canada as my own.

This was a course correction, a bold step. I hoped for a transformation, although into what, I was unable to imagine. "You can always just come home if you don't like Quebec," my kind friend Claire told me the day before my departure. While certainly true, that was not an option. I was going to spend half the summer in Quebec by myself. Period.

What is friendship? I've often wondered how we form attachments to one another. Do we choose our friends? Do they choose us? Does it depend on fortune, on fame, on culture, on kindness? Or is there an eagerness, a hunger, to *know*?

IMMERSED IN QUEBEC

5

INTIMIDATION

I plastered my face to the plane's window. Far below I could see a waterfall, green fields, small villages, and the mighty Saint Lawrence River. I was arriving in Quebec City, Canada, and no matter what the future held, here I was.

Worrisome thoughts whirled through my mind as we landed. What would I learn during this sojourn? What would I discover in this foreign place? Would I make friends from far away? Would my apartment, chosen online, be serene and welcoming? Would it be a gathering place on the weekends? Or would it be a place of lonely isolation?

In a sleep-deprived daze, I collected my baggage, cleared customs, and hailed a cab. I was a little surprised to see that while the signs were all in French, everything else looked just like the United States. However, as my taxi drew closer to the *centre-ville*—the city center—I noticed that the houses looked decidedly more French and less American.

My leasing agent met me at my building and carried one of my two overstuffed suitcases up to my apartment. I asked her about public transportation, and we immediately headed back outside. Walking up the street a bit, she pointed and said, "Go

The Girl on the Belvedere

through the gate." I saw an immense medieval-looking stone structure arching over the street, and I knew I wasn't in Oklahoma anymore.

Oklahoma. Land of blue skies, undulating hills, tallgrass prairies, and unhappily, tortuous summer heat. I'd been looking forward to the cooler climate of Canada, but shockingly, the air in Quebec was stiflingly hot. I'd donned a sweater, jeans, and a raincoat for my trek to the Frozen North, only to find it far from frozen. In fact, the heat and humidity were so high that I felt like I was back home. People on the street wore shorts, T-shirts, and flip-flops. What had I been thinking?

My apartment, though, was light, airy, and everything that I had hoped. It offered a respite from the unrelenting heat. As I opened the door, I could see a small entryway, a laundry closet, a bedroom, and a bathroom. There was enough seating for four in the living room, plus a stylish kitchen and a dining table. There were wood floors throughout. Through the many windows I could see two main streets, Rue Saint-Jean and Côte de la Fabrique. I knew from studying the map before my arrival that I was looking across the street at the Hôtel de Ville—city hall.

Once the leasing agent left, I stood in my beautiful apartment, alone, and thought, *What do I do now?*

I was intimidated. Despite having been on this earth for sixty-something years, despite extensive travel, despite four moves among three states, I was intimidated. I had moved through the defined, structured worlds of my parents' home, the college dorm, graduate school, and marriage. I'd been looking forward to being on my own, but I'd never been truly alone, until now.

My stomach churned as I stood there in that charming apartment overlooking Old Quebec. I decided to head out in search of a can of coffee and some cream for the next morning. I trudged one way, then the other, but to no avail; there were lots of restaurants, trinket shops, and boutiques, but nothing resembling a grocery store. I finally spotted some cans of coffee at the back of an ice cream shop. I entered and asked, in French, for the location of the nearest *épicerie*. The response came in perfect English: "There are two grocery stores further up Rue Saint-Jean after you go through the gate and cross the busy street." I thanked the shopkeeper for the advice, but I felt silly and out of place. *No one here understands my French,* I thought. *I'm just like any other tourist who butchers the language.*

I continued my way up the steep hill. I could hear laughter and applause and realized that I had arrived at the immense Château Frontenac. It was instantly recognizable as the most photographed hotel in the world. The area was dotted with street artists, musicians, magicians, singers, and crowds of tourists gazing at the Saint Lawrence River far below. I turned around and walked back toward my apartment, threading my way through the crowd. The sidewalk was as busy as those in midtown Manhattan. There were families strolling, people laughing, couples dining, young girls shopping. I was too tired and too unnerved to go any farther.

MY DAUGHTER, Stephanie, arrived from New York on the red-eye later that night. We stayed up late chatting, with Stephanie sitting cross-legged on the sofa in her pajamas and me in a chair next to the TV. Our conversation was interspersed with the sounds of laughter drifting in through the open windows. The *Festival d'été*—the summer festival—was underway, and the streets and outdoor cafés below were full of happy and animated people.

My daughter—long, lithe, and dark-eyed with flowing chestnut hair—is a true beauty. She is also compassionate, kind, intelligent, and a quirky comedienne (she took improv classes for fun). Stephanie had come to Quebec to assist me in settling in and finding my way around.

The next day, we wound our way up Rue Saint-Jean, the main street, for brunch. I ordered in French, and the waiter responded in English. *Is it my accent? My hesitancy? My grammar?* I wondered. My fear kicked in. *People don't understand me. I don't understand them. They find me ridiculous. I'm too old to do this. I'm going to get lost. I'm going to get sick. I'm going to fail.*

"Everyone answers you in English," Stephanie observed.

"I've noticed that," I said, smiling and hiding my embarrassment and dismay.

After brunch, we walked through the medieval-looking Saint John Gate to the open-air bus terminal. I needed to find my way to Université Laval, the home of my French course, and wanted Stephanie to go with me this first time, several days ahead of the program's start date. In a nearby tobacco shop I purchased a bus pass in French, but yet again, the attendant responded in English ("So that you will understand").

At the bus stop, I chatted in French with a tiny, elderly, well-dressed woman. At least, I think we were chatting. She responded to my simple questions in French ("Where is this bus headed? Does it go to Université Laval?") with a complete paragraph, a smile, happiness in her voice, and twinkly eyes. I understood the sentiment—kindness—but had no understanding of what she actually said.

The bus driver showed me how to use my new pass and spoke to me in French as though I understood. We rumbled down various streets, and after ten minutes or so, I started to suspect that I was on the wrong bus. Before leaving my apartment that morning, I had looked at a map and located the school, but the bus was taking detours around construction sites and seemed to be going in the wrong direction. I used my hesitant French to address the gentleman in front of me. "Does this bus go to the university?" I asked.

"Yes," he said in English, "your stop is just a little farther after you go through the village of Sillery." I was listening carefully and frowning in concentration, afraid of becoming lost, but he mistook my frown for a lack of comprehension. "Sillery," he repeated, "like the vegetable 'celery.' I'll ask the driver to help you." With that, he stood to exit.

A short time later, the bus stopped along a major avenue, and our driver turned and asked the other riders a question. A discussion ensued in rapid French, of which I understood not one word. After a few moments, everyone on the bus turned around and looked at me, all smiling and nodding. Our driver pointed at the bus stop, and Stephanie and I stood up.

"*Merci*," I said, with more confidence than I felt. I smiled and waved to everyone as we stepped down. We took a paved path through some trees onto the university grounds and wandered around, looking for my building.

"What's it called?" asked Stephanie.

"I can't remember. I forgot to bring the information sheet," I said, feeling foolish yet again.

The occasional passing student asked us in English—always in English—"May I help you?"

"No thanks, we're fine," I said again and again. How on earth could they always tell we were Americans, even when they did not hear us speak? Was it our clothing? Our shoes, that dead giveaway of American-ness in Europe? Our countenances?

We eventually did find my building, and then we headed back toward the bus stop. Along the way, we noticed some small animals foraging under a fir tree, and we stopped to watch them.

"What are they?" my daughter asked.

"Badgers, maybe?" I responded.

At dinner, Stephanie said, "You're going to be the subject of

The Girl on the Belvedere

the next Nancy Meyers film. Instead of *Something's Gotta Give*, it's gonna be called *Something's Gotta Be French*. Who do you want to play your role?"

"What? I'm not starring as myself?" I asked.

"Don't be such a narcissist," my daughter, the former casting assistant, said. "You can be on set every day to make sure the kitchen is correct."

Thinking of my disorderly kitchen at home, I asked, "Why the kitchen?"

"Because it's a Nancy Meyers film," she said. "You know, the writer-director of *Something's Gotta Give*? *The Holiday*? *It's Complicated*? With all those beautiful sets?"

"Oh, right," I said, remembering those movies' dream like homes and their stories about strong, beautiful, middle-aged women. I decided I would be played by Kristin Scott Thomas, since she's both gorgeous and fluent in French.

At three a.m., a drunken girl on the street below woke us. She was slim and pretty, dressed in a gauzy brown dress, and wandering from curb to curb, back and forth, up and down the street, yelling, "Alain!" "Alain! Alain! Alain!" "Alain!"

"I've heard this before—someone yelling 'Alan! Alan!'" Stephanie said.

"It's that squirrel on YouTube," I said. "The one on the BBC *Walk on the Wild Side* video."

We tried to go back to sleep, but soon after, another drunk, this one a young man, attacked a metal utility box again and again, hitting it, kicking it, and yelling something unintelligible in French. *What an unusual street,* I thought.

The next day, we wandered through the Lower Town with its trendy streets and chose a crowded corner café for lunch. I bravely used my best French accent and ordered, "*Une salade chèvre chaud, s'il vous plaît.*"

"A goat cheese salad," the waiter replied in English.

At this point, I was becoming frustrated.

Years before, I was seated in a café in Paris with Georgia, my co-author of *Gypsy Prince* when our server inquired, *"Bonjour, qu'est-ce que vous prenez comme boisson?"* [Hello, what to drink?]

I responded immediately with *"Un demi-litre d'eau minérale gazeuse, s'il vous plaît"* ["A half-liter of fizzy bottled water, please."]

After the ubiquitous *"Pardon?"* accompanied by the server's blank look, I repeated the phrase with what I thought was an exaggerated French accent. It was acknowledged with a quick nod of the head, a *"Merci,"* and *"Et pour le déjeuner?"* ["And for lunch?"]

After that, I learned to turn up the accent when I wasn't understood, which is what I just had done here in Quebec, but with no success. I was becoming more discouraged by the moment.

"Quebec looks like a Disney town, so pretty and perfect," said Stephanie as she looked out at the historic area, unaware of my growing uneasiness.

After lunch, we came across an office coordinating "ghost tours" and signed up for one on the spot. We chose the English-language tour, which was led by a large man in seventeenth century dress, with the booming voice of a trained stage actor. The guide continually referred to "Keebec," rather than "Quebec City" or the French pronunciation, "Kaybec." He took us through the Lower Town and then zigzagged up the steep streets toward the Upper Town. We stopped to rest as a group, cliff-climbing not being in our repertoire. I was so out of breath, I couldn't speak, and was dismayed to find that we were only halfway up the hill. A French-language ghost tour passed us while we were resting. The group leaders' faces were painted white, with black paint spiking down their faces. Their mouths were lopsided with painted red gashes.

The following day, Stephanie and I tackled the Upper Town.

We walked along the historic fortified walls, continually looking down, and calling each other's attention to the beautiful houses. We meandered along the boardwalk at Château Frontenac, watching the river traffic far below.

"This place is so charming," Stephanie said as we leaned on the cast iron railing while looking down at the Saint Lawrence. "Thank you for bringing me."

That night, we followed our noses into a popular restaurant and sat upstairs at an open window, watching the world pass beneath us. It was Stephanie's last night in Quebec, and while I was sad that she was leaving, I knew that it was time for her to rejoin the workforce and for me to immerse myself in the French speaking world.

6
EXHAUSTION

On Monday morning we were up at four a.m., and within half an hour, I had put my daughter into a cab so that she could catch the early flight back to New York. Then I returned to my apartment and prepared to storm the walls of the university, as I would every weekday morning thereafter.

Do I have my keys? Check. *My passport?* Check. *My wallet? My phone?* Once I was sure that I had everything I needed, I closed my messenger bag and, with my stomach roiling, walked out my apartment door and into Old Quebec.

I'd thought it would take fifteen minutes to walk to the bus station, but actually, it only took seven or eight. Just as I caught sight of the station, the bus pulled in, and thinking I was late, I ran like Yuri seeking Lara at the end of *Doctor Zhivago*. Out of breath, I climbed onto the bus and fumbled with my new pass. The driver once again had to show me how to use it.

The regular riders assembled over the next ten minutes—as it turned out, the driver had a regularly scheduled break at this station—and then we departed. Thirty minutes later, I descended at the university. It was pouring, and I arrived at the language building soaking wet, despite my umbrella.

I stood in line to pick up my information packet, understanding nothing that was said to me. I opened the first envelope, and it contained my *Carte d'assurance maladie et hospitalisation,* my health insurance card. Hoping I wouldn't need it, I tucked it away. I opened the next envelope, and was shocked to realize that I'd been placed in Level Five. *WHAT? LEVEL FIVE? Should I tell them that I've just finished French Three?*

Stunned into silence, I reported to my assigned classroom. A young professor entered, scribbled "9:30" on the board, and gave a short speech, of which I didn't understand one word. After that, he left, and our whole class sat quietly, awaiting whatever 9:30 would bring. I saw that it was only 9:15 and decided to get a bottle of water before we started the day. I asked a classmate where she had purchased hers, then darted downstairs to the cafeteria, bought my water, returned, and settled into my chosen desk just ahead of the entrance of our professor, a pretty, thirties-something blonde.

"My name is Aimée," she said in French, before launching into a rapid-fire soliloquy. I listened carefully, understood nothing, and retreated into silent panic. *What am I DOING here? WHY did I come? What made me think that I could EVER speak French?*

I had been afraid that this would happen. Before taking the online admission test, I had called the university with my concern that my results might seem better than my actual ability. I could read French, I could write it, but I couldn't speak it to save my life. It was lost somewhere in my head, rattling around.

I wondered if I should ask about my placement at the next break, knowing that I would be more comfortable at a lower level. I silently pondered my situation, since I understood nothing that was being said. I had already stopped listening.

Then I reminded myself that a linguistics major had once told me that ninety-five percent of all communication is non-verbal. I slowed my panicked, racing thoughts, breathed deeply, and tried to listen for clues. I began to understand about half of what the professor was saying.

"This week will fly by," she said, "and you will understand very little. But next week will be much, much easier, and you will understand more."

I took a deep breath and hoped that this was true. I decided to give *Niveau Cinq* [Level Five] a chance.

WE WENT to the computer lab to establish our university email accounts and receive our NIPs. *What's a NIP?* I wondered. Again, my comprehension utterly failed me. I had no idea what a NIP was. I didn't understand the French directions posted on the computer. I was totally lost. It did not help that it was a French keyboard, with the keys in different positions. After an hour and a half, I gave up and just hoped that since I had a smart phone and Wi-Fi in the apartment, I would be okay. It didn't occur to me that I would need a password for this account while in the language lab.

After this latest disaster had passed, I looked at the hand-drawn map posted in the lobby of the language building and followed the directions to the bookstore. It appeared to be across the street, but no such luck—it was the wrong building. A kind soul gave me directions to the student union and asked, in English, "Would you prefer to take the tunnels? It's pouring outside."

Tunnels? Did I hear that correctly? There are tunnels here? "Non, merci," I replied, thinking, *Great, another opportunity to get lost.* It would be the last week of class before I tackled the tunnels with friends who lived on campus and knew their way through the labyrinth.

Later, my books purchased, shouldering a bag now so heavy I was leaning to one side, I reported to the mandatory orientation, *l'assemblée générale obligatoire*. I understood perhaps fifty percent of what was said. They were speaking slowly, presumably for the lower levels, but I was grateful, even though I was in Level Five. I must admit that some of my confusion was due to the heavy *Québécois* accent that a few of the professors possessed. I wasn't surprised; I was in Quebec, a place where the inhabitants had been isolated from other French-speakers after the British defeated France and took possession of Canada. One would expect the language to change.

I wondered how the Level One students felt listening to this explosion of French. Thankfully for them—and for me—the professors eventually did turn to speaking English, the universal language, for the benefit of the lower levels, and I was relieved to hear my native tongue. I was exhausted, still jet-lagged after my three flights a few days before, and definitely overwhelmed.

After *l'assemblée générale,* they sent us upstairs to get our student IDs. While studying the sign posted in the hallway that explained where to form the line, I spotted a beautiful woman my age who also appeared to searching. I said "*Bonjour,*" hoping to make an acquaintance.

This lovely woman with gentle eyes and a smile responded in soft-spoken French, "Hello! My name is Celestina. What's yours?"

"Cheryl. Where are you from?"

"I'm from Santomah," she said. I wondered where that could possibly be. I had never heard of it. She continued, "And you? Where are you from?"

"Oklahoma."

"Oklahoma?" she asked, surprised. "How did you find this program?"

"Through one of my professors," I said.

"I've done something like this before," she said, "in France, through a college program in Vermont." She looked around. There was no one in line; the sign said the student ID queue would open at 5:00, and it was only 4:30. "I'm going to the bookstore," she said. "Want to go?"

"Already been," I said, fervently hoping I would see her, this kindred spirit, again.

I stood at the front of the line, waited forever for the desk to open, and then followed the directions in filling out my form as I listened to the person in charge. It was in French, of course, but this part I understood. It's universal, no translation needed. Predictably, my photo was even worse than the one on my driver's license.

As I finished, I turned around and glanced at the long line. Celestina, my new friend, was in line just a few places behind me. I waited for her to finish.

"I went halfway to the bookstore and decided to come back," she said in French. "Want to meet for lunch in the cafeteria tomorrow?"

"Yes," I said, checking my schedule. "12:30?"

She nodded and waved goodbye, and at last, the first day was done.

Arriving back in *Vieux-Québec* [Old Quebec], I caught a glimpse down a broad boulevard all the way to a small river and was charmed. I really, really wanted to succeed in this program and resolved to be back at it in the morning.

∼

The Girl on the Belvedere

ON THE SECOND DAY, I found that I did understand a little more, as promised, but only a little. Most of my fellow Level Five classmates chattered away in French and seemed to comprehend much more than I.

Many in this class were Canadian, but there were also some Americans, some Europeans, some South Americans, some Asians, and several from Mexico. We were truly an international crowd, though most of the class was young and taking this course for university credit. I quickly began to recognize faces and became friendly with young bright-eyed Anna from Germany. I was immediately grateful for her companionship, as I felt like the proverbial fish out of water. I met another young woman, Lucía from Mexico, who was very quiet, seemingly the more shy of the two. They began to seek me out in the morning, Anna and Lucía, both smiling and friendly, and I began to look for them each morning as well.

I usually joined Celestina for lunch in the cafeteria, and we would chat in French, fluently for her, stilted and struggling for me. She was patient and considerate and offered assistance whenever I laughingly threw up my hands in frustration.

"Do you have children?" I asked one day.

"Yes," she said, "and I have a baby grandson who lives near me. I miss him."

"How do you like to spend your time?" I asked.

"I'm a teacher," she replied. "I like to spend my summers studying French or Spanish."

"What is your native language?" I inquired.

"English," she said.

This took me by surprise. Given that I had never heard of her homeland, I had assumed that she was from some far-flung land—and people don't often speak English natively in such places. "I'm sorry," I said, "where are you from?"

"Santomah," she said, "but I was born in Puerto Rico."

And then it registered: she lived on Saint Thomas, one of the US Virgin Islands. *Duh, Cheryl. Duh. Will I ever understand this language?*

∼

ON WEDNESDAY of that first week, I arrived back at my apartment at 3:30, dropped my heavy bag onto the chair near the TV, and sat down on the sofa. But not for long. It was beautiful outside, and it dawned on me that I was in Quebec. It was time to go explore.

I grabbed my passport, my wallet, my keys, and my small shoulder bag. Still a little unfamiliar with my surroundings, I stepped onto the elevator and soon after, out onto my street. I intended to go up to Château Frontenac, but instead veered onto a side street, looking left and right at the small businesses and houses.

I turned left, catching a glimpse of a harbor below the ramparts, and as I descended toward them, a magical world appeared. I was in a residential area within the walled city, complete with ancient houses sporting gaily-painted front doors, many with historic plaques.

I simply wandered, my mouth slightly open in wonder. These streets were quiet, private; I could not hear any of the constant din of my street, Rue Saint-Jean. I turned this way and that, secure in the knowledge that I was still within the walled city. So long as I remained within it, I could easily find my apartment again.

I stood along the ramparts, studying the scene below, and recognized a few of the apartment buildings I had considered while searching online. I marveled at the view, taking in the

The Girl on the Belvedere

cannons, the old stone wall, the rooftops, the steep streets, and the harbor.

On Thursday, I was dragging and totally unnerved by the first group presentation, in which I had to introduce myself and explain my part of a PowerPoint presentation, which had been prepared by the others in my group. We had worked on it together in class on Tuesday, but I was intimidated and contributed little. These kids, all college students, were able to put the group presentation together while they chatted, barely needing to glance at the screen. On Thursday, right before class, I was bewildered. They had changed my part of the presentation, but had forgotten to tell me. I was so nervous, I simply read my notes—a big no-no—and had little idea of what I was saying. My head was spinning, and while I am not the type to admit defeat, I was very, very discouraged. In contrast, these youngsters spoke without notes, and effortlessly joked amongst themselves in French.

That was exactly what I wanted for myself: to be able to chat in French with others. I told myself that it was now or never. Just how many more grammar classes did I want to take? How many more textbooks did I want to complete? At this point, I wanted to enjoy my life, and I was in Quebec City because, darn it, *I wanted to speak French*.

On this day, back at my apartment, I found a letter from my landlord, written in perfectly understandable English:

Hi Madam

We are really sorry for the troubles of the air conditionning. We are waiting for the pieces. It will be in fonction next Monday or Wensday. I have bring you a small fan for the troubles and I give you a pass for the summer festival. The bracelet is good for all the show. We hope everything will be perfect for your confort. Thank you for your patient.

ALONG WITH THIS sweet note of apology for the lack of air conditioning was a brochure for the summer festival and an all-access pass in the form of an electronic bracelet.

The next morning, Professor Aimée taught us the phrase *nid-de-poule*, pothole, while speaking of the effects of Quebec's brutal winters. It literally means "hen's nest," which I found funny, though it aptly describes the shape of a pothole. Then I started thinking about the English word, "pothole," another funny, but apt, description. My French was full of potholes, and while some students may have felt like they were cruising in this class, I felt as though I was lurching along from one *nid-de-poule* to another.

"You need to ask me about vocabulary words you don't know. I am your dictionary," Professor Aimée said at one point, using her thumbs to point to herself. Of course, for me, that would have required formulating and asking questions in French, for which I did not have the confidence.

I tried to abide by the rules and looked around furtively whenever English accidentally slipped out, which was far more frequently than I cared to admit. And yet, despite my struggles, I loved it all. The students seemed universally engaged, and I rarely heard anything other than French.

Most of these students were *young*. In fact, there were so many young students that there was a separate activity group —*le club des maîtres* [the masters' club]—for those twenty-eight and older. *Twenty-eight?* I thought when I first heard the cutoff age. *Really? I don't even REMEMBER twenty-eight.* Our symbol was a picture of Yoda wearing white-framed 3D glasses—not a look I was aspiring to. There were far more *maîtres* in the program than I would have expected, perhaps fifty of us across all the levels. My classmate Robert, an American, lived in China where he taught English. My new friend Celestina, the teacher in Saint Thomas, aspired to doctorates in both French and Spanish. My young German friend, Anna, a year or so shy of thirty, was working on an advanced degree. We spoke French over coffee and cafeteria food and slowly learned about each other's lives.

There was a student lounge where one could sign up for field trips, check out the information posted on the bulletin board, and get a free cup of coffee. It was a lively place, with plenty of assistance available. The *animateurs* [assistants] were young, energetic, and happy to help. I steered clear of the lounge, though. The entire room vibrated with the energy of the young, and a Yoda with 3-D glasses didn't feel like she would fit in, even if she had been able to comprehend what was said to her.

AT LAST, the first week of classes concluded. Back on my street, I made a quick stop. The maple store, Délices Érable, offered the most delicious ice creams, pastries, and a plethora of maple products: candies, syrups, cookies, and butters. I could find maple syrup at home, of course, but any other maple product was elusive and exotic. Here in the capital of all things maple—the province of Quebec produces seventy-five percent of the world's supply—I was in heaven. At the end of this long first week, I decided that I would treat myself to something that had made me drool the weekend before: a large shortbread cookie with maple icing. I took it home, savored it, and promptly fell asleep.

I needed that sleep, as Billy Joel was singing that night at the

Festival d'été, on the historic Plains of Abraham, the field where the French lost their independence to the English in 1759. *La Conquête,* or the Conquest, part of the war known to Americans as the French and Indian War, looms large in *Québécois* ("kay-bay-kwah") history. Yet the Plains, while still a historic site, is now also the site of much joy, as it hosts the most important music festival in Canada, on the largest freestanding stage in North America.

When it was time to go, I checked the map and set out, walking toward the Plains through the tourists, townsfolk, and street artists on Rue Saint-Jean. I turned left and followed the old city wall, leaning forward into the steep incline and admiring the park-like street with its stately houses. I turned right onto the Grande Allée, passing through another medieval-looking stone structure, the Saint Louis Gate. Just ahead on my right was the magnificent Parliament Building, a Second Empire-style masterpiece. In front of it stood a glorious fountain, with benches all around, and stone frogs sending their spray toward tiered nymphs and cherubs.

As I left the Grande Allée, I could see that this beautiful street was full of restaurants and outdoor cafés, all filled to overflowing with festivalgoers. I joined the crowd entering the concert grounds, flashed my electronic bracelet, and was soon enjoying the music of Billy Joel. Later, on my way home, I lingered at the fountain in front of Parliament, watching the lights twinkle on the mountains beyond the Saint Lawrence River. This spot instantly became a favorite.

On my first Saturday morning alone in Quebec City, I decided to spend some time sketching. I never had time at home to sketch, despite the fact that I spent much time doing so in my youth. Out came my sketchbook, charcoals, and pencils, all so carefully packed. I spent several happy hours relaxing in this way before I decided that was time to be out and about. What I didn't realize at the time was that this would be my one and only chance to pursue this pastime, as my homework assignments would soon expand exponentially. My sketchbook would remain on my coffee table, along with a half-finished paperback, ignored for the rest of my stay.

I returned to the festival that evening, threading through the fantastic street artists. Clowns and musicians sauntered down Rue Saint-Jean, as did an angel and two gargoyles who towered above the tourists on stilts. This trio staged a fight, stopping abruptly to pose for photos. Street bands, sidewalk artists, stilt-walkers, and storytellers all had their place on Rue Saint-Jean.

I paused to listen to a fabulous band, Fanfarniente della Strada, self-described as a "spectacular and silly band" that conjured up "an irresistible urge to dance." Their outfits were part Bohemian, part Bavarian. The bandleader sported an orange shirt, brown jacket, plaid kilt, orange socks, and a captain's hat, with a fake parrot perched on his shoulder. When they broke into the song "Zaza," a cha-cha, half the crowd started dancing. I wanted to dance, too, but there I stood, still as stone.

On Sunday morning, I awoke and turned to glance at my husband, before remembering that he wasn't there. During the week, he was always up and about early. Same with Saturdays. But Sundays were generally much more relaxed. I felt his absence keenly.

John. Companion of my heart, father to my children. Physician by day, talented pianist and tennis player on nights and weekends, the person with whom I've shared adventure after adventure. As a physician's wife, I've spent a great deal of time on my own, but renting an apartment in a foreign city was far, far different from being apart for every-other-night in-house-hospital-call, or driving through the Virginia mountains for three hours to spend weekends together, as we sometimes did during those early years. We'd lived in three states in our almost forty years of marriage, owned three homes, had two children, and more pets than we could count. Recent years had brought more business travel for him and trips to New York to see our daughter for me, but I'd never experienced a weeks-long separation from my best friend. Generous and gentle by nature, John was not surprised when I announced that I was thinking of attending Université Laval. He merely raised his eyebrows. "Adventure" is a word he thoroughly understands.

The bells at the basilica began a Sunday-morning concert. Up the street, I could see Notre Dame de Québec, which was built in 1647. We have nothing like these bells at home, and I opened my windows to hear them more clearly. They were magical, otherworldly, sublime, and I could imagine them calling the faithful all those years ago.

I made my way to Paillard, a fragrant bakery just up the street. I bought two croissants, one almond and one plain, and back at the apartment, I made some coffee. We have croissants in Oklahoma, good ones, but none just steps from my door with age-old church bells sounding in the background. I was in heaven.

Later, while I was walking near Place de l'Hôtel de Ville, the square in front of city hall, the deafening bells started again, and I froze in place, leaned against a wall, closed my eyes, and just listened.

A clerk at the grocery store in the nearby neighborhood of Saint-Jean-Baptiste asked me something about my handbasket at checkout, but I couldn't understand what it was. *Should I take the basket? Am I supposed to put it away? Should I not be using it? Am I supposed to wear it on my head?* I wondered. Aloud, I said, "Répétez, s'il vous plaît." Repeat it he did, just louder and faster. *Perhaps it's not about the basket after all. Could he be saying paper or plastic?* I returned his questioning gaze with a blank stare,

The Girl on the Belvedere

mouth agape, eyes blinking. He finally took the basket and put it behind him, and I skedaddled, feeling like an idiot. My comprehension was still zilch.

That evening, the last night of the festival, I was about to unload the dishwasher before heading to the Bryan Adams concert when I heard my new favorite band through the open windows. I just grabbed my keys and headed out. This time, I watched the entire show, though I again stood stock still while others danced to "Zaza." When the band started marching up Rue Saint-Jean, I joined the crowd marching behind them. As they disappeared under the massive stone gate, the leader turned and waved the band's CD. Just like that, I handed over twenty dollars.

"*D'où est-ce que vous venez*?" he asked. ["Where do you come from?"]

"Oklahoma," I said, watching the surprised look my answer invariably elicited flit across his face.

Before he could even say "*Merci*," for my purchase, the angel and gargoyles on stilts were upon us, menacing the crowd. The gargoyles were chasing, people were running, women were screaming, yet everyone was laughing. The stilt-walkers turned back toward the gate, and the crowd followed, only to have them turn and chase us again. They turned a final time, disappearing through Saint John Gate, and we lingered, hoping that the gargoyles would chase us once more.

The weekend before, my daughter and I had blundered through an interactive street performance by a troupe wearing fantastical masks. "So French!" Stephanie had said. I wish now that we had paused to watch the silent troupe instead of blithely walking through them. She was now a New Yorker, as I once was, and as such, we did not stop for nonsense. I promised myself that from now on, I would stop for *all* nonsense.

On my way home from the Bryan Adams concert, I ran into

that silly street band again and listened to them play "Zaza" for a final time. They performed under an awning while the crowd stood in the pouring rain. As they marched away to Saint John Gate and disappeared under its arch, I felt curiously bereft. I stood in the middle of the street and watched them go, and I decided that from then on I would be a participant, not merely an observer.

7

EVERYDAY LIFE

The second week of my immersion program, *la vie quotidienne*, everyday life, kicked in. At 4:30, the first grey light snuck into my open bedroom window. The intersecting streets below were deserted at this early hour, save for the arriving trash trucks and street washers.

I made my coffee, and while it brewed, I turned on the TV and tuned into MétéoMédia, the French-language weather channel. I opened a living room window, and spread out my yoga mat. I was so stiff from all the walking and carrying my heavy book bag that I could hardly move. What seemed effortless in my twenties was an entirely different ballgame in my sixties. While watching the weather forecast, I considered the scene out the window and reveled in the view. I watched the early-morning sun glinting gold on the windows of the Hôtel de Ville and the Basilica. It was a daily show that was never the same.

I ate heartily for breakfast: quiche or sliced sausage, some cheese, some berries, and some coffee, thick with rich French cream. I didn't eat this way at home, but with the steep hills, the enormous concentration, and the long hours of homework, I needed sustenance. I was just praying that the famous "French paradox"—the rich, fat-heavy cuisine that supposedly does not cause weight gain—was real. But most importantly, I was happy, busy, and constantly in motion, my day filled with studying, attending class, and walking the ancient walled city. There was no time to worry, and I loved it.

I left my apartment at seven a.m. to catch an early bus and descended at school about forty-five minutes later. After a leisurely ten-minute walk alongside the edge of Université Laval's forest, I popped into the cafeteria to buy a bottle of water. I was in the classroom by 8:10, the first to arrive, save Robert—another Yoda, the American teacher who taught in China. We chatted in French, sometimes easily, sometimes haltingly, and always in the simplest language possible.

I SAT at a different table this week. Someone had taken Lucía's customary seat, and she and Anna shot me an exasperated glance and walked to a different table. Without a thought I gathered my belongings and joined them.

At this new table, we met another fellow student, Isaac from Montreal. We chatted about our backgrounds, and he mentioned that he had traveled to Israel several times with Birthright, the organization that promotes understanding of that country among Jewish youth around the world.

"My husband is from Israel," said Anna. "He's Palestinian."

"Oh, really?" Isaac responded in a friendly tone.

My thoughts flew to the current war. I'm sure I wasn't the only one thinking about that; there were sighs all around. I looked at the three people before me: Isaac, Anna, and Lucía.

Their shoulders were relaxed, their countenances peaceful, their eyes gently looking around, the way people do when they are thinking. There was no tension in the air, just the three young people and me likely remembering what we had seen on the news.

"This is his fourth war," Anna added. "His parents live in a mixed village in the north of Israel, but they can see the missiles flying back and forth."

I pondered this sad reality. There seemed to be nothing more to say, and we quickly turned our attention to Aimée, who was beginning the day's lesson.

AIMÉE, my professor of *grammaire* [grammar], taught us about the origin of the *Québécois* accent. It originally hailed from western France and remained isolated and somewhat unchanged after the Conquest by the British. The Quebec accent is very pronounced and nasal, with a broadening and lengthening of the vowel sounds. I had heard that the French accent in Canada was different, but I was not prepared for just *how* different. In the city center where I lived, it sometimes sounded more like a foreign language than it did French. As a result, I was struggling to decipher not only the French language, but also to discern meaning through the distinctive accent.

Comprehension came slowly. We listened to a song in class, "À nos actes manqués." Aimée asked us to fill in the blanks of all the verbs on worksheets containing the lyrics; I understood very few. I looked around and realized that most of the people in my class had filled in many of the blanks. I experienced a familiar sinking feeling; I'd traveled all this way, full of high hopes, only to find that my oral comprehension was almost non-existent. I loved the song itself, though. It had a hypnotic rhythm and infectious joy, and I wanted to get up and dance.

Each day, during our fifteen-minute break between classes, I headed down to the cafeteria to buy some decaf coffee, which wasn't available in the student lounge.

"BON-JOUR," the petite cafeteria lady boomed to each guest, wearing her habitual uniform of slacks and shirt, hair in a bun.

"BONJOUR, MERCI!" I boomed back, handing her some coins. I'd already become adept at counting Canadian change. I adored the fact that the one-dollar and two-dollar denominations came in the form of coins, not bills, and that there were no pennies; everything was rounded up to the nearest nickel. Having made my purchase, I rushed back to my classroom, with just enough time to stand in the hall and eat a small two-dollar bag of potato chips.

The phonetics professor, Sébastien, told me that my speech was very clear, but he worked unceasingly on my rhythm. I had never thought of language as having rhythm, but of course it does. We intonate, we inflect, we pause. The one word that gave me the most trouble? Video. I said it the American way, VID-e-o, instead of the French way, vee-day-o, with equal accents on each syllable.

I earned a *"Très clair!"* from Sébastien when I read aloud a nonsensical paragraph that I had been assigned. We spent time pretend-ordering four courses from a *prix-fixe* restaurant menu, trying to emulate Sébastien's verbal progression from soup to nuts.

"Je vais prendre les oignons français, le potage Crécy, le saumon à la québécoise, et comme dessert, le gâteau à la mousse au chocolat," I said. I'll take the French-style onions, the creamy carrot and vegetable soup, the Quebec-style salmon, and for dessert, the chocolate mousse cake.

"You don't sound like an American when you speak French," Anna said. "Your accent is very good."

AFTER OUR SECOND CLASS, I usually headed down to the cafeteria for the hot meal of the day. I sometimes had lunch with Anna and Lucía, sometimes met up with Celestina, and sometimes ate by myself, staring into space in a stupor, exhausted from that morning's mental challenges.

I had two afternoon classes, each of which met once a week. The first was *Danse*. It was led by two energetic young women, both talented dancers, who were teaching us to Salsa. I may have been a ballet dancer in my youth, but I knew where I belonged now—in the very back. I did not need to be noticed; I left that to the young dancers vying for attention and corrections. I was there simply to enjoy myself, and I did.

I watched the young women in front of me dancing their hearts out with the abandon of youth and recalled the days when the artistic director of my ballet company had told me to "Move! Move! Move!" Mr. Jasinski taught me to soar by putting his hand on the small of my back, assisting me to become airborne as I leapt across the floor. "I want you to know what flying feels like," he would say.

The first time I came to this dance class in Quebec, I was terribly late. I had lost the slip of paper containing the details of the time and place of this elective and had to go to the student lounge and ask for help. A professor looked it up for me with the assistance of a much younger fellow student who, seeing that I was bewildered, had offered to help.

"Go out those doors," the professor had said in French, pointing down the hallway, "and you will see the forest. Go past the forest and the building will be on the right."

I found the building, but had failed to ask the room number, and wandered around the seemingly empty building for a while, exhausted and close to tears. In desperation I asked a janitor if he knew where the dance room was, and he simply pointed. I was right outside it, but the door was closed, and it was unexpectedly very quiet. I opened the door a sliver, and an *animatrice* slipped out, asking "Why are you late?" I explained and entered, joining the others sitting on the floor.

There I was, a sixty-something amongst all the twenty-somethings. Evidently the class had begun with a verbal exercise on a topic related to dance. The students were reading and responding to questions on little slips of paper, and a discussion ensued right after my arrival. My ever-present fear, even in this most familiar milieu, was that I wouldn't understand what was being said, and this was indeed the case. I froze and tried to make myself invisible, lest I be called upon. *Once we stand up and start dancing*, I thought, *I'll be all right.*

However, once we actually did start dancing, I discovered that there was no hiding the fact that while I could execute the steps quite easily, I just looked *wrong* next to the young people. All my training was still there—my bearing, my coordination—but I just looked *wrong*. My body had changed over the years, and while I am still slim, I have taken on the hallmarks of one who is *plus âgée*.

This came as a shock. I was aware that I was in my sixties and that dancing was decades behind me. But I did not expect the mirror to be quite so brutal in its truth-telling. However, I am also a realist, and I made up my mind to, for once, simply live in the moment, with whatever joy it would bring.

My other afternoon class was an informal conversation class, this one also taught by young assistants. I didn't attend the first week, being shell-shocked and thinking that it was optional. I was wrong. Lucía and Anna dragged me along during our second week, and I initially felt so out of place that I had to force myself to sit still and not simply stand up and bolt from the room.

The three young *animatrices* leading the class gave us a variety of topics to discuss and then made the rounds, joining in our conversations and keeping us on track. I found that I was frozen and silent unless spoken to. I'm naturally a quiet person, but I was longing to jump in and take part with the others. I just couldn't for some reason. I was puzzled by this behavior and found myself thinking about my life in far-away Oklahoma. I wondered if it was only the foreign language that inhibited me or if it was a reticence that reached far beyond French, back to the fear of my childhood.

Taken together, my regular classes, extracurricular sessions, homework, and outside assignments made for a full week. Many days I stayed after class and studied with Anna and Lucía, but some days, I was just too tired.

The walk past the forest back to the bus stop always seemed interminable in the afternoon. My book bag managed to magically double in weight, my legs felt like jelly, and my eyes had that "I need a nap right now" feeling. I dodged the traffic turning into the university, made it to the traffic light, and hit the crosswalk button. The pedestrian is king in Quebec, but I was forever trying to beat the countdown on the "Walk" sign as I crossed the six lanes of traffic, always fearful of the large construction trucks idling at the red light. There were always so many of them, truck after truck, deadly in their mass and speed.

On my morning bus ride, I was always able to immediately sit down. On my trip home, though, the driver occasionally took off before I was seated. In those moments, I would lurch from side to side, trying to retain my balance. At age thirty, living in

Manhattan, I could easily walk down the aisle of a moving bus, leading a toddler with one hand and carrying his stroller with the other. What a difference thirty years make. Second languages do not come easily at this age, but falls certainly do.

Each afternoon, I struggled back to my apartment, dropped my heavy bag onto a chair, and took a short nap on the sofa. I awoke hungry and headed into the kitchen. For my first week or so, I'd have a slice of store-bought pizza or some quiche, but as time passed I switched to a handful of organic greens with some olive oil, some good French sea salt, and maybe a bit of brie. It was enough, and afterward, I studied a little before heading out the door for my nightly stroll. I quickly took to walking each evening along the ramparts, the defensive stone wall that separated the Lower Town from the Upper Town, to observe the kaleidoscope of color on the harbor as the sun *s'est couché*—went to bed. I frequently ended the evening at the Fortifications at Artillery Park, peering over the town's defensive wall, and watching the sun slip behind the clouds across the river.

THIS TIME of freedom from my regular routine slowly took on a shape of its own, and as it did so, I realized that my sought-after solitude was actually freedom from myself—from long-held thoughts, prejudices, and assumptions. I assumed nothing here; I was simply open to new experiences without thought as to how they might affect me. I just got up, went to class, studied, and walked the ramparts. And I found myself wondering, *When I leave Quebec and go back to Oklahoma, will I succeed in fuller self-expression, in fuller self-knowledge? Will I go home a more complete, self-actualized person?* I didn't know, but I suspected it would be a struggle.

Slowly, slowly, I began to understand the townspeople. For

The Girl on the Belvedere

the most part, they understood me, but it took me ten days to understand just a little of what was said in reply. It wasn't like we were discussing Sartre; these were simple everyday interactions. One thing was clear, though: these were very friendly people, and they were delighted when non-natives attempted to speak their language.

At one point, a young couple in a rental car stopped me on a back street. "Do you speak English?" the young man asked.

"Yes, where are you from?" I inquired.

"Uruguay," he said. "We are looking for the underground parking garage."

I gave them directions and cautioned them about the many one way streets.

English is the default language in Old Quebec, and the whole world—at least the whole young world—speaks it. The shopkeepers would always start in French, but would switch to English at the first sign of hesitation. And yet, *Vieux-Québec* has retained its French character and its French culture.

One evening, while strolling along the ramparts, I met an elderly woman who was leaning against the fortification wall, catching her breath. "*Bonsoir,*" she said to me.

"*Bonsoir,*" I replied.

"I've just come up from the market, and it's a long walk up with these bags," she explained in French, "and I have to rest. Are you lost? May I help you?"

"I'm looking for the best view of the sunset," I said.

"You have a little while," she said. "I'd go farther west, to the Fortifications. Where are you from?"

I told her that I was from Oklahoma and that I was attending the summer course in French at Université Laval. Once again, I noticed the surprised expression upon hearing my home state.

"I went to the university, too, while it still was located here in the Upper Town, before it moved out to the suburbs, to Sainte-Foy," she said.

I told her the story of my ancestor who had disembarked here at Quebec and how my family ended up as Americans. I also told her that by now, over two hundred years later, we have a very mixed ancestry.

When our chat concluded, she pushed away from the wall and picked up her bags to continue her ascent to the Upper Town. She said, "Your French is very good, Madame." I smiled and thanked her for speaking French with me.

I HAD BEEN THINKING about that particular ancestor ever since my arrival in Quebec. On Saturday, I had made my way to the museum at Artillery Park to learn where my great-great-great-great grandfather had first lived in the New World. He had been about twenty years old when he arrived with the British 62nd Regiment of Foot as a drummer, having left his Irish home at an early age.

When I arrived at the museum, I thanked the young receptionist at the desk for speaking French with me. I explained that I was a student at Université Laval and needed to practice. She seemed sympathetic, so I asked, "Are you a student, too?"

"Yes," she said, "I am, and in just ten days, I'm heading to Great Britain for my year abroad. I'm so excited."

I wished her great luck and much fun before turning to the reason for my visit. I explained, in French, that my ancestor had arrived here in Quebec in 1776, and asked where he most likely would have stayed. Did that building even still exist?

"Yes, it does," she said. "It's called the New Barracks."

Unfortunately, it was closed to the public, but the Dauphine Redoubt, a building with a similar function, was open. As I walked down the path toward it, I suddenly realized that I had understood the young woman's responses to my questions—not word for word, but enough that I understood the context and the meaning. At last, I was beginning to comprehend conversations on topics in which I was engaged.

As I looked around the barracks, I tried to imagine my ancestral grandfather in a similar spartan room. The conditions were rough: two men to a bed, a single fireplace for cooking and heat, a wooden table, stone walls, stone floors, and a stone ceiling. Was this truly a better life than the one he had left behind?

My ancestor, Joseph Preston Yadon, was sent to the New World to help put down the American Revolution. He arrived in the spring, spent the next year in Canada, and then served as a drummer in the First Battle of Saratoga in New York. Most of his company was killed, but he survived, was captured, and was force-marched from upstate New York to Virginia, where he was housed as a prisoner of war near Charlottesville. Two hundred years later, while newly married, I lived about a mile from where he had been held and often visited that site. I would sit in my car on Barracks Road, looking past the historic marker out to the empty field beyond, and wonder about his life.

My family lore states that the tall, red-headed governor of Virginia, Thomas Jefferson, paid a visit to the prisoners' barracks, looking for recruits. He particularly urged the Irish prisoners to switch sides. We do not know whether Joseph was recruited, released, or escaped from the prisoner-of-war camp, but he somehow made his way to Martinsburg, Virginia (now West Virginia), and enlisted in the Continental Army. Joseph now fought for his—and for my—freedom. He was again a drummer and, as such, was highly useful. The drummers were the Signal Corps of their day. He served his new country as part of the George Rogers Clark expedition to the Falls of the Ohio as a drum major; he was charged with communication among the troops during battles against the Native Americans allied with the British. After the war, he was honorably discharged, married, had numerous children, and enjoyed a long life in the new United States. I have for so long thought of him as my very distant grandfather, yet when he was here in Quebec, he was such a young man, with all his hopes and dreams still ahead of him.

I thought of those who followed. His children were raised on a mountain farm in Tennessee. His son was part of the migration to the West of that time, Missouri. A hundred years later, my father was raised on those original family lands in Missouri, picking strawberries at age ten to help put food on the family table. And then, just a generation later, there was me, a city girl, standing here in Canada, thinking of this patriot's arrival, in this place, Quebec.

I began to see Quebec in a different light. Despite still not understanding much of what was said to me, I now felt like I was a part of something far, far greater—my heritage, my birthright. One evening, as I sat in the shade of an oak tree in the Old Seminary, I felt the stirring of pride of place. This was where my family's story began. Did Joseph once traverse this same immense courtyard after his arrival in Quebec in 1776? Did he know that he might become an American? At age twenty, it's unlikely that he imagined a distant granddaughter walking these same paths and wondering about his life.

ON MY MORNING BUS, I sometimes wondered if Joseph had walked or ridden down some of the same sun-dappled maple-lined roads leading out of Old Quebec. One of these roads led to Sillery, a village two-thirds of the way to Université Laval.

The Girl on the Belvedere

Judging by its quaint appearance, I imagined that it was a wonderful place to live.

A young man boarded my bus every day in Sillery. He was always silent, looking neither left nor right, even though everyone else on board were all regulars, and most of us nodded to each other every morning. He wore black glasses, black slacks, a black T-shirt, black shoes, and sported a black backpack, black ball cap, and black earphones. He always sat in the back, even though there were many empty seats up front. *Why does he live here, in Sillery?* I wondered. *Does he have an apartment? Does he live with his parents?*

He always beat me to the buzzer for our shared stop, this Man in Black. Each day, we descended together at the main campus stop and walked stride-for-stride toward the university drive. We did not speak, not once, even though being from friendly Oklahoma, I had looked at him expectantly once or twice, intending to at least nod good morning. He always turned toward a campus bus stop as I turned toward the forest and my solitary walk.

On one day, I was so determined to beat him to the buzzer that I accidentally buzzed too soon and had to descend at the wrong stop. I felt his scrutiny and his surprise behind me as I descended from the bus, and I realized that he did indeed know that I was there. He just chose to hit the buzzer first and never speak. That day, I walked the rest of the way to campus, sure that the Man in Black was up ahead at our regular stop, watching me and wondering what the crazy *Anglaise* [English woman] was doing—why did she get off at the wrong stop, then walk? Didn't she know her own stop?

The next day, he beat me to the buzzer again, though my finger was poised just a millimeter above the nearest button. *Is he determined to race me to the buzzer?* I wondered. *Is he actually watching or simply in his own world?*

"Are you sure he's real?" my daughter, Stephanie, asked later, on the phone. "Or is he just in your head? Of course, he's real," she continued to herself, in full Harry Potter mode. "Why shouldn't he be real, even if he's just in your head?"

"Well, someone's ringing the buzzer, Dumbledore," I said, "even if he *is* just in my head."

AFTER MANY DAYS, I was finally *connectée* to Université Laval's Wi-Fi, could access my regular email while on campus, and could use the language lab. It had taken an additional half-hour and the assistance of two students. All of our exchanges were conducted in French, of course, which were difficult for me. I once thought that spellchecking a book on a Polish ballet dancer, whose name was constantly misspelled while he was living in France and working in a Russian company, was difficult. But I do not speak computer. I barely speak my own language on a keyboard, let alone French on a French keyboard. I'll take decoding Russian-to-French spellings of a Polish name anytime.

On the way home one day, I spotted a tour bus with a distinctive drawing on the side. I realized with a start that it was the same drawing that my son Bennett had copied with such finesse many years before in high school. It was an image from a long-forgotten magazine advertisement featuring a beautiful young girl in profile, with long wavy strands of hair streaming behind her. His copy is framed and hanging in my living room, a testament to the many talents of this young man, talents that he rarely has time to pursue. And now, twenty years later, this same image was on the side of a tour bus, a thousand miles away in Quebec. I texted him a photo taken through the window of my bus.

With his usual brevity, he texted back, "Strange."

The Girl on the Belvedere

Today, Bennett is a man of few words, a respectful son, a loving husband, and a doting father. However, I have jokingly said over the years—with some truth, alas—that he sent my hair colorist's children to college. As I watched that tour bus pull away, I pictured Bennett in my mind's eye, and in every image, he was laughing. I recalled Bennett riding his go-kart to Hooters; Bennett in a barn riding a bucking horse bareback, dismounting, saying, "That was fun," and doing it again; Bennett running from farmers' dogs. He was my wild child, my constant worry during his teen years, but he has matured into a truly responsible man. And he has lost none of his ability to entertain and surprise.

I missed Bennett, and I missed Stephanie, these two far-flung children of mine. I missed Bennett's wife, Sarah, and my grandson, the apple of his *grand-mère's* eye. I missed my husband, John.

NEARING my apartment on Rue Saint-Jean one afternoon, I saw a girl with emerald-green hair. I'd seen her before, this beautiful young woman, and I was fascinated by her. She was always eating ice cream, candy, or sweets, always sitting on the step of the same Rue Saint-Jean doorway. The first time I saw her, it was her hair that I noticed. Since then, I'd also observed her clothing —trendy—and her affect—happy. I was curious. Every person has a story. What was hers?

Rue Saint-Jean was a busy street during the day, but it became a pedestrian mall and popular gathering place in the evenings. Each afternoon, as I returned to my apartment, trucks began to park one behind the other, and the drivers unloaded tables and chairs for sidewalk dining. In time, the street closed, the artists arrived, the crowds gathered, and the festivities began anew.

Most nights, I could hear a young man playing the wooden spoons, a local tradition. It's a part of the aural background of Rue Saint-Jean. As I peered down at Spoon Man one particular evening, I happened to glance up at the traffic heading toward me. In the middle of the street was a woman in a motorized wheelchair, a huge bouquet of flowers on one side, darting this way and that, right and left, totally unconcerned about the cars and buses all around her. *Is she selling the flowers?* I wondered. Perhaps. As I watched, Flower Lady went from one side of the street to the other. She'd stop to chat and then race back out to rejoin the traffic.

Later, on the phone with my daughter, I described the woman and her behavior.

"Maybe the flowers are a decoy, and she's really dealing," said Stephanie. "I hear that in Canada, it's the older crowd who has all the connections."

"Well, what do you think she's dealing?" I asked.

"Speed," Stephanie replied, as I started laughing.

I also told her about the man who sang opera each evening under my window. It was never more than a few short phrases, and it was usually at the same hour. Whenever I heard him, I looked out each of my windows, but I could never spot him, even though I could see tourists snapping photos, their cameras pointed in his direction.

"Who do you think he is?" I asked my daughter. "Why does he sing the same song, night after night?"

"Remember, this is a Nancy Meyers film," she said. "He's singing the leitmotif of *Something's Gotta Be French*."

By the middle of the second week, school seemed to be getting a little easier, and I was not quite as worn out by the end of the day. I was growing used to the routine and the mental

The Girl on the Belvedere

effort. I still needed a nap upon arriving back at my apartment, and I had added an outright study session to my nightly homework. The days and evenings of study were demanding, and I had to remind myself every evening that I was here to learn a new language and that I needed to study. I still followed dinner with a stroll around the Upper Town if it wasn't raining, despite the increased workload. Time was flying by so quickly, I occasionally had trouble remembering the day of the week.

Our grammar teacher, Professor Aimée, had suggested that we read, read, read, if we wanted to become truly proficient. I took this advice to heart, headed to a nearby bookstore, Librairie Pantoute, and purchased a Harry Potter book. I had loved the series in English, so why not in French? As I exited the shop, I overheard the owner say knowingly to the clerk—in French, of course—"She's a grandmother."

AFTER THIS SECOND WEEK, I spent my entire Saturday in my apartment studying and doing homework, working from eight a.m. until eight p.m., stopping only for meals and the requisite nap. Was I making progress? I didn't know.

I heard Opera Man again that evening and went to the window. I couldn't see him, and none of the pedestrians even looked in the direction of his voice. Several people studied the instructions on a parking meter, and several others continued their conversations. I caught a glimpse of a retreating back after the music ended—white shorts, white T-shirt, dark socks, black backpack, headphones. Was this the mystery singer?

On Sunday, I had visitors: Anna from Germany, her husband Ibrahim from Israel, and my young friend Lucía from Mexico.

By now, Anna and Lucía were more than just my classmates. They were my constant companions and study partners. They were from different backgrounds, but shared the same traits: they were both quiet, gentle, and studious. We sat together in class, and had become good friends outside of it, despite the gap in our ages: I was sixty-one, Anna was twenty-eight, and Lucía was just nineteen. We conspired together, sometimes did our homework together, and complained about our workload together. Whenever a *travail d'équipe* [group project] was assigned, we looked at each other in silent agreement that our team was already formed.

I marveled at these two young women and their chosen paths. Anna was brilliant, holding a degree in math with a minor in chemistry, and fluent in English, having lived in England for the purpose of achieving fluency. In addition to her native German, her excellent English, and her conversant French, she also spoke Arabic and a little Hebrew. Spanish-speaking Lucía, equally brilliant, was also fluent in English, having moved to English-speaking Canada by herself at age fourteen for school. She was also very quick with French. Both girls enjoyed speaking English with me—off campus, of course—as it was their second language and my only true fluency.

Anna's husband, Ibrahim, was our unofficial fourth team member. He was here in Canada with Anna on their long-delayed honeymoon. Ibrahim did not speak French, but he seemed to be picking it up with the ease of one reared in a multi-lingual region. He was fluent in German and English as well as Arabic and Hebrew, with a smattering of Spanish and Turkish thrown in. Ibrahim was a medical student in Austria, now on summer break and carefree. On this particular Sunday, he was happy to help us with our assignment—or simply to assist in any way. He was a true old-school gentleman.

More than once, I wondered what my new young friends saw in me. Their ages—all three of them were under thirty—would not usually predispose them to deep friendships with people in

The Girl on the Belvedere

their sixties. Was it simply because I was an American? I doubted it. Perhaps it was because I was from Oklahoma, which is known for the open friendliness of its people. Of course, we were all strangers from strange lands here in Quebec; perhaps they simply didn't feel like they fit in with the other students. No matter the reason, I was grateful to have developed close friendships here in Canada.

I taught my young friends to say "y'all." "It's faster and simpler than saying 'all of you,'" I explained. They agreed and tried to teach me the German, Spanish, and Arabic equivalents.

"Everyone uses 'y'all' in English on Facebook," Anna added. All three pronounced it with the exaggerated tones of non-Southerners, but they continued to say it, laughingly, for the duration of the course.

I was becoming much more direct in my speech. I had no choice in French, being limited in my vocabulary and syntax, but I found myself needing to adjust my English as well. My friends did not understand all of my American slang, nor many of my cultural references.

As we studied that evening, I realized that we were facing week three, the week of midterms. *How can that be?* I wondered. *We've only been in class two weeks.*

We collectively wished that there was time to go out for a leisurely dinner, but my friends needed to go back to campus, as we all needed to write an essay, *une expression écrite*, which was due first thing in the morning.

As I escorted them out of my building, the bells at the basilica began their Sunday evening concert. "Just listen to that," I said.

"Listen to what?" Anna asked. "Oh, the bells? I hear those all the time at home in Germany," she said.

"Wow," was all I could say.

I accompanied my friends up Rue Saint-Jean, under the

stone archway, through Place d'Youville, and halted only at the six-lane Boulevard Honoré-Mercier. They crossed the busy street to catch their bus, and I turned back toward my apartment. I re-entered the walled city through the gate and sauntered down Rue Saint-Jean, stopping to listen to the street musicians, looking in a few shop windows, and inevitably settling down to face the dreaded essay.

8

DECISIONS

Week three began. It would be filled with presentations, exams, and essays. Stress *de plus en plus*.

While I wanted to go straight home after class on Monday and study, I had *Danse*. This time, the *animatrices* warmed us up with jumping jacks. I gamely gave it a try...and immediately reinjured my knee, which I had damaged in a bad fall on black ice. I had been at the Tulsa airport, having returned from California in footwear wildly inappropriate for an ice storm and went down into the almost-splits. Frankly, I would have been happier and less injured in the splits. Now, I realized once again that perhaps *Danse* was not the best choice I could have made, but as my artistic director, Moscelyne Larkin, always said, "Once a dancer, always a dancer."

This latest injury made me consider the next ballet season at home, which would include *The Sleeping Beauty*. During the last three Tulsa Ballet productions of this magical show, both at home and on tour, I had played Princess Aurora's mother, the Queen.

At my first rehearsal, I realized the full magnitude of this role. I would have to portray so many emotions in so many circumstances: the blessing of my newborn baby, the death threat against my little girl, that same girl's sixteenth birthday, the arrival of the dreaded curse, the princess's rescue by the prince, her marriage, and the relief of knowing that the future of the kingdom was assured. On that first opening night, I stood in the wings, thinking, *I can't do this! It's been too many years! I'll never remember everything!* But once I heard my musical cue, the training of my youth kicked in. I simply stepped out onto the stage with its bright lights and into the joy that awaited me.

Fifteen years and many portrayals later, I wondered if someone no longer able to do a few jumping jacks should really pretend to be the mother of a newborn. I was beginning to feel that this role, long my favorite, was no longer appropriate for me and that I should pass it along to someone younger. I didn't want to appear to struggle on stage, to just hold on by my fingernails. I wanted to rush forward to meet the next phase of my life, whatever that may be, with grace and confidence.

We women have so many roles in life. Child, daughter, sister; wife, mother, grandmother. Dancer, teacher, writer; archivist, researcher, historian. How do we proceed from one role to another? How do we know when it's time to let one go? I believe it's time to let go when there is fear, discord, or conflict—whether conflict of spirit or conflict with others. And how do we know when we have found a new role and are ready to experience something different? When there is peace, ease, joy, and a sense of belonging.

The Sleeping Beauty presented a difficult decision for me. I would be giving up a much-coveted, if late-in-life, character role, an important role that greatly explains and advances the story. It is always a privilege at my age to be asked to be on stage after so many years, and the dilemma did make me terribly sad. There might be other roles in my future, but there are no guarantees, whether on stage or in life. It would take me several months to finally walk into the artistic director's office and ask him to remove me from the lineup, and many months more before I could bear to watch my replacement glide across the screen on replays of the performance in the ballet building. Such is the price of freedom from the imprisonment of the past.

Walking home from the bus stop that Monday afternoon, my knee throbbed from the ill-performed jumping jacks, but I had a more immediate issue to worry about: the hours of studying that awaited me and the academic tasks that would define my third week in this program.

THE MOST UNNERVING exam took the form of an interview. Isaac, my tablemate from Montreal, was my partner. We were comfortable with this arrangement, as we already spent fifteen minutes each morning in quiet conversation. Isaac was my regular "Question of the Day" partner, the two of us responding to Professor Aimée's daily query, which was written upon the board. An example this week was: "*Avez-vous une cause qui vous tient à cœur particulièrement?*" ["Is there a cause that you hold particularly close to your heart?"] In many ways, we were as different as night and day. He was an English-speaker from an English-language university—Canada being bilingual, with almost everything divided into "English" and "French"—but his English was not in any way similar to mine. He had a distinct accent that I couldn't quite place. And Isaac was as voluble as I was silent. He had tremendous intellectual curiosity and constantly peppered me with questions about life in Oklahoma.

For our "interview" exam, Isaac played the part of a television journalist, interviewing me, the imaginary First Assistant Director of *Forrest Gump,* upon its twentieth anniversary.

We came up with this concept one afternoon when we met in our deserted classroom and simply threw around ideas. Isaac's intellect constantly astounded me. As we were coming up with interview questions, he would sit quietly for a few minutes and then announce each new question with such clarity and precision that it left me off-balance. I struggled to think of an in-depth response, and then further scrambled to phrase it accurately in French. We rehearsed our routine via FaceTime the night before our exam.

On the appointed day, we were supposed to speak without notes, but I clutched mine like Linus from *Peanuts* clutching his blanket, referring to them once or twice. I talked about the speech of the American South, and the fact that it is gentle, gracious, and slow when compared with that of the North. I talked about the South in fact being one of the characters in the movie, with its green vistas and soft skies. Halfway through, I realized that I was speaking about it with conviction and longing. As much as I had come to love Quebec, home is always home.

When our interview was over, we earned a verbal "*Excellent!*" from Aimée. I sighed in relief. For me, this was the most difficult task of this demanding week. It was even more unnerving than the hours of testing that still awaited me.

That night, I started preparations for the written grammar exam. I downloaded the song "À nos actes manqués" and translated it phrase-by-phrase so that I could make sense of it and have some hope of remembering the verbs by their meaning.

As I neared the end of this translation exercise, I was on the verge of tears. This marvelous song, despite its alluring rhythm, was about missed opportunities: sentiments not expressed, dreams not realized, our silences, our betrayals, our despair. I'd had no idea. I had loved this song, wanted to sing along with it, wanted to stand up and dance to it, but now that I fully understood it, I couldn't. I wondered how the artist was able to tackle this difficult subject and sing about it with such joy.

I needed some cheering up after this, so I located the "Zaza" CD that I bought on the street. I wanted to find the name of that wonderful silly street band from the summer festival: Fanfarniente della Strada. I downloaded two of their songs onto my phone's playlist. This band made me smile, and all thoughts of regrets and missed opportunities were temporarily forgotten.

As I HEADED out onto Rue Saint-Jean that evening, I saw the two young women who regularly played flamenco guitar. They drew large crowds and were paid well in tips—the best I'd seen, in fact. I dropped a two-dollar coin onto their shawl, having enjoyed their performances many times. Later in the evening, they were replaced by an accordion player who also sang. He, too, was excellent, and very much in the French style. This spot at a busy intersection was most likely highly coveted and lucrative.

I loved spending time in my local Jean Coutu *pharmacie* on Rue Saint-Jean. It was a regular drugstore with aspirin, toiletries, and prescriptions, but somehow, its huge sections of makeup, perfume, and personal products made it seem more glamorous than those at home. I frequently stopped in to try to make sense of the myriad moisturizers, to watch the pretty French-Canadian girls picking out the latest shades of nail polish, and to just look around.

There were two specialty crêpe restaurants on Rue Saint-Jean, both always full, always fragrant. The pub life was active, too, with many spirited nightspots filled with people drinking, singing, and simply hanging out. It all made for a busy, lively street. Tourists and townspeople alike walked down the middle of Rue Saint-Jean, stopping to chat, studying menus, and visiting the boutiques and shoe shops.

I met a neighbor one evening this week. I'd seen him before, parked on the sidewalk in his wheelchair, watching the goings-on of Rue Saint-Jean. I stepped into my building's elevator with him, and we exchanged pleasantries.

"Where are you from?" he inquired in French.

"Oklahoma," I said, preparing myself for the inevitable look of surprise. He raised his eyebrows, so I explained. "I'm a student at Université Laval, taking the summer course in French."

"You're a long way from home," he replied.

He turned out to be a lovely person, this man in a wheelchair, and we would speak several times during my stay. One day, several weeks in the future, I would be on the sidewalk, fumbling for my key in my messenger bag, when the door magically buzzed, allowing me to enter. I decided that this man must be my guardian angel, watching the street from above.

By Wednesday morning, I was exhausted. This was the middle week of midterms; I was now halfway through the course. That afternoon, with most of my exams behind me, I went to lunch with Celestina at the *Musée national des beaux-arts du Québec,* the National Museum of Fine Arts.

My friend Celestina was tall, dignified, and classically beautiful, with skin the color of burnished copper and hair worn in a chignon. She always had an encouraging word for me. She was studying at a more advanced level, *Niveau Six* (out of seven), and was patient with my halting French. We lingered and enjoyed ourselves in the restaurant, chatting about our separate lives over soup and salad, exchanging stories of our faith. I could easily picture her ankle-deep in the beautiful turquoise water of Saint Thomas, playing with her grandson, wearing one of her lightweight cotton dresses.

We enjoyed the overlook high above the Saint Lawrence River and marveled at the intricacies of the floral display in the middle of the nearby *rond-point*, the roundabout. We explored the nearby Avenue Cartier and stopped to look at housewares, where she told me about her house on the island. I could just see it—charming and elegant, like her. We went into an *épicerie* and admired the famous strawberries from the nearby island, Île d'Orléans, and into a bakery where Celestina bought some bread. I admired her easy conversation with the owner and thought, *Someday, Cheryl, someday*.

We then went our separate ways: Celestina back to campus, and me back to the *centre-ville*, the town center where I lived. I strolled along the beautiful Grande Allée, stopping to enter a decommissioned church that was, temporarily at least, an antique store. The air had turned clear and crisp; the sights were incomparable with the avenue's French houses and perfect flowerbeds. I thanked the heavens for this opportunity, for Quebec, and for friends like Celestina.

THAT EVENING AFTER DINNER, I decided to walk the length of Rue Saint-Jean, passing through the gate, through Place d'Youville, across Boulevard Honoré-Mercier, and into the Saint-Jean-Baptiste neighborhood, with its delicatessens and dry cleaners. This was Old Quebec's first suburb. As in most city centers, there was nowhere to park a car, but there were homes, apartments, groceries, bakeries, churches, and community colleges. This was the real Quebec, not the *Sex-and-the-City*-daydream tourist area where I lived. People here worked, shopped, commuted, dined, and worshiped. It wasn't fancy, but it was real; there were no touristy shops or trinket boutiques blaring *Québé-*

cois music, just restaurants and used bookstores for the locals, the students, the free of spirit.

On Thursday, we had a long lunch hour while waiting for our conversation class to begin. Anna, Lucía, and I bought our lunches and waited for Ibrahim, who was not taking any classes, to join us. We talked about our plans for after the immersion course.

Anna said, "I want to work for a large multi-national corporation after I finish my current degree."

"What's this one in?" I asked.

"International business," she said. "I'm staying here another semester, so I'll be in Quebec for a total of six months. I'll be taking four classes—two in English, two in French."

Lucía, also an international business major, said, "Well, I'm leaving for Europe next year, to spend twelve months there. It's a requirement, like this summer session here in Canada."

Lucía went on to tell us that just knowing Anna and me had changed her life. She had originally planned to remain in Mexico after graduation and begin working. "I want to help my people," she said, "but now, knowing the two of you, getting advanced degrees, writing books, doing so many things, perhaps I should live abroad while I can, gain some experience, and find out who I am before I go home to settle down."

Anna and I encouraged her to do just that. She was so young—just nineteen—with so much life ahead of her. This was a time for dreaming, for planning, for experiencing, and I hoped that this brilliant young beauty would take full advantage of it.

I was envious of these young women's freedom and their proficiency with language, which was so clearly neither a priority nor even a possibility for my generation. The term "study abroad" did not really exist in my collegiate years, but oh, how I wish it had. I envied them their youth, their sense of possibility, their wide-open view of the future. They were prod-

The Girl on the Belvedere

ucts of this new century and didn't seem to feel the constraints that young ladies of my era felt.

The concept of "Women's Liberation" was new on the scene when I was in college, and while we gave it great lip service, most of us had little idea of how to go about constructing meaningful lives on our own. The idea of "following your passion" was beyond our imagination. My parents advised me to "always have something to fall back on," not "find something that makes you happy." If I had, would I have found a way to dance in a larger company? Could I have become an artist? An actress? Who knows? Those doors were closed to me by well-meaning parents who were children of the Depression and intent on shooing me into a profession that offered safety.

I did teach, and through that "safe" job I supported my husband and myself. Was I happy? Not particularly. My happiest moments at the school where I taught in Charlottesville were during a one-semester course in dance. The course filled quickly, and it was the highlight of my day while it lasted.

Upon arrival in Virginia, I had looked in vain for an arts council hoping to work there rather than teach. There wasn't an arts council in Charlottesville so I founded one. *That* work did make me happy, even though it was a volunteer job. The arts council, plus the contemporary dance company, were the extent of finding something meaningful during my years of employment.

My Quebec friends Anna and Lucía had clearly considered what they excelled in, what drove them, and what they enjoyed. My daughter has done the same and is using her God-given talents in her job. In my next life, I will do the same.

In that week's obligatory conversation class, the activity was to tell romantic anecdotes about oneself and then engage in a game of "speed dating." I declined to participate, but the *animatrices* questioned my hesitancy—they didn't want to give me a bad grade for non-participation. I explained that I was almost sixty-two, had been married for forty years, and was a noncredit student, here at Université Laval just for fun. These young women did not yet understand that to be an older female in a classroom of twenty-year-olds playacting speed dating is to be invisible. For this, I was content to be an observer.

On my way home from the bus station that day, I saw the Girl with Emerald-Green Hair again and part of the mystery surrounding her was solved. She was wearing a shop-girl apron with an olive motif over her dress; she likely worked at one of the several olive oil stores on Rue Saint-Jean. Today she wore a multicolor floral dress that included the same hue as her dazzling coiffure. She was eating a baguette straight out of the bag.

I also finally identified Opera Man. He was wearing an "Italy" shirt, carrying a frozen coffee drink, and singing as he walked down my side street, headphones protruding from his ball cap. Mystery solved.

But that night, another mystery arose: I heard sheep bleating beneath my window. I jumped to my feet and looked outside, but saw nothing unusual. I could fully accept the fact that there were sheep walking along Rue Saint-Jean. After all, I'd seen and heard just about everything below me: screaming Argentinians in matching blue and white shirts waving their country's flag; Marie Antoinette on stilts; an old man, silver-haired, in coat and tie, riding on the hood of a car, holding a battered suitcase. So why not sheep?

By Friday, I was beyond tired and half-sick with a sore throat. I didn't feel quite right, but our phonetics exam was that day, so I gamely struggled to school. After sleepwalking through grammar, I reported to the language lab for the exam. I had twenty-five minutes to read, prepare, and record it.

After twenty-three minutes, I thought I was done and began

packing up. But then Professor Sébastien came over and asked where my recording was—did I know I had only two minutes left? Apparently, either it didn't go through or, as usual, I was flummoxed by the technology. I pushed the red button again and was off to the races. I finished with seconds to spare, and he verified that it did, indeed, record this time. I looked around and realized that I was the last to finish. Sébastien graciously told me that I could try again, if I liked, as I was *stressée*. Yes, I was definitely *stressée*, but I was also *teminée*.

I wished him a *Bonne fin de semaine* [have a good weekend] and headed out. I was *done*.

AFTER THIS DIFFICULT WEEK, with its round of papers, presentations, and exams, I was headed to Montreal for the weekend. My friends Anna and Ibrahim rented a car, and on Saturday morning, with Lucía rounding out our foursome, we set off. I felt a little feverish, with perhaps a slightly worse sore throat, but I would not miss this weekend for anything.

As we headed out, I struggled with my seat belt, and Lucía helpfully held the receptacle for me. It was a simple, kind gesture, but it filled me with horror and called to mind a similar incident during a short car trip with my mother and mother-in-law.

My husband and I were going downtown to see a performance of *The Nutcracker,* and our elderly mothers sat in the back seat, struggling with their seatbelts. We listened to the *click click click click click* of their efforts to buckle up the entire way, with the final *click* sounding just as we pulled into the theatre's parking lot.

Mirror, mirror, on the wall, I am my mother after all, I thought. Aloud, I said, "If you see me following a tour guide who's holding up his umbrella for a group of elderly people, please restrain me from joining them!"

"We're keeping you on a short leash," Lucía laughed.

Lucía and I chatted in French in the back seat while Ibrahim drove and Anna navigated. Lucía was amazed by my love of Mexican culture and cuisine.

"I've been to Mexico many times," I explained, "and grew up with the cuisine: tortillas, tacos, chile rellenos, mole..."

"Wow! You really do like Mexican food!" Lucía said with a grin.

"Oh, and huevos rancheros, guacamole, empanadas, pozole," I added.

"Okay, I'm making you an honorary Mexican!" she laughed.

"I love it all," I said. "At home we have it at least once a week."

I made her laugh even more when I told her that we called it "going out for Mexican."

I also told Lucía about my family's trip to Mexico City when I was young and about our guide, Rubio, who taught my brother and me to roll corn tortillas between our palms as we sat in a restaurant in the shadow of the pyramids.

"You really *are* Mexican!" Lucía said. "Please know that you have a home in Mexico." With that, she invited me and my husband to visit her parents in their village. I had no doubt that we would be welcome.

After about an hour on the road, Ibrahim asked, "Would *y'all* like to stop for a coffee?"

"Why not?" Anna said.

We stopped at a new McDonald's and relaxed for a bit. We had no cares and were not rushing toward our destination the way Americans do. Stopping for a coffee was a normal part of my friends' day, an experience to savor, *une pause* to catch one's breath. Tanked up with caffeine, we hit the road again, still marveling at the beautiful Canadian scenery.

In Montreal, after checking into our hotel, it was time to eat. While we were enjoying our alfresco lunch, a woman with an accordion set up shop across the street and placed her shawl on the sidewalk for tips. She was very good, this diminutive woman with crooked teeth and gypsy clothing, singing mournful songs. It was a scene straight out of Paris. She had chosen her site with care and winked or smiled every time one of us looked in her direction. I left the obligatory tip. I loved these street artists and the way they enriched my everyday life here in *La Belle Province*, the beautiful province, *Québec*.

We headed to the Old Port and had to raise our umbrellas against the sudden rain. We waved farewell to a departing cruise ship, yelling *"Au revoir,"* along with everyone else on shore. We discovered the pocket parks that exist throughout this sophisticated city and stopped in several of them long enough to look at the fountains, the reflecting pools, the monuments. We visited Old Montreal, the section of the city formerly contained within the now-nonexistent fortifications.

So much of Montreal is old by US standards, as it was founded in 1642. Many of its streets are pedestrian-only, with colorful storefronts and restaurants sporting tables shaded by umbrellas along the sidewalk. It is bilingual, with French the dominant language, but most Montreal natives are happy to switch into English at the first sign of tourist confusion.

It's a lively city of cobblestone streets, coffee, croissants, and a few kitschy boutiques selling Canadian hockey sweatshirts and other souvenirs, but it is also a modern city with skyscrapers, traffic, department stores, and large crowds. Its architecture is not as *cohérente* [consistent] as Quebec City's. *Vieux-Québec* is protected as a UNESCO World Heritage Site, whereas Montreal is, in our *hôtelière's* words, "a mini New York."

Eventually, we found yet another small, charming park and decided to rest in the shade. These green leafy parks, crafted so well by the French-Canadians, are conducive to conversation and reflection. This one was a long rectangle with a center path, benches, and the requisite monument. The rain had passed, and the evening was luminous. I did not want to leave.

"Anyone hungry? We'll treat everyone to an ice cream," said Ibrahim as we left the park and started down Rue Saint-Paul, Montreal's oldest street. We walked past the many restaurants on Place Jacques-Cartier, and spotted a Ben & Jerry's. Then, with ice cream in hand, we retreated to yet another tiny green park and relaxed, chatting like old friends, without a care in the world.

Ibrahim told me about his family in Israel, his medical school in Austria, and his soon-to-be-adopted country, Germany. "I love Germany," he said "and after I finish medical school, I'll be able to join Anna there."

When we had finished our ice cream, we slowly strolled back to our hotel, looking in shop windows, admiring the sunset, and exploring the parks along the way. One park had an art installation in the form of a maze, with large windows along its many walls. There were tourists and families here, with children running, laughing, and climbing in and out of the openings. I took a photo of my friends as they stared out of one of the concrete circles. To this day, they are perfectly framed in my memory: Anna, Ibrahim, Lucía, forever frozen in this moment, my friends from across the globe, in this city foreign to us all.

Late that night, I heard the telltale thud of fireworks, part of the Montreal Fireworks Festival, *L'International Des Feux Loto-Québec*. I was treated to an hour-long display through my hotel window, which only added to the ambience of this most international city.

On Sunday, we set off to Olympic Park, site of the 1976 Summer Olympics.

"The elevator to the top of the Olympic Tower is too expensive," Anna said. "It's the tallest inclined tower in the world, and I'd like to go up, but it's just too much money."

"I agree," said Lucía, "and I want to buy some gifts for my sister."

Without another word, we women took a detour into the gift shop and spent most of our time there looking at key chains. As we were paying for our merchandise ten minutes later, we saw Ibrahim hurrying in through the exterior doors, a worried look on his face. He must not have seen us enter the gift shop, and had been searching for us ever since. He'd only been married for a few months and did not yet realize that groups of women can communicate telepathically and make beelines for stores without announcing plans to do so.

Later, we explored the Latin Quarter and found our way to Boulevard Saint-Laurent for lunch. Ibrahim spied a Lebanese restaurant, and we decided to indulge in his Middle Eastern cuisine. He chatted easily with the owner in Arabic and ordered us a feast. The food was delicious: chicken *shawarma* carved from a spit, *hummus*, *tabbouleh*, *falafel*. We sat near an open window and watched the passers-by with their raised umbrellas. Ibrahim taught Lucía and me how to scoop up the delicacies with pita bread.

We finished the day by heading to the park on Mont-Royal, the mountain that looms over the city and from which Montreal takes its name. "Want to get a coffee here in the park?" Ibrahim asked.

"Sure, why not?" Anna responded.

We sat down at a picnic table with our coffees and chatted. We were delighted by a toddler chasing a squirrel around a tree while we visited with her French-Canadian family.

"This is how I like to travel," Anna said at one point. "I like to sit and have coffee and visit with the locals, not run around and try to see all the tourist things. And by the way, Cheryl, we'd like to meet your daughter, Stephanie, when we go to New York, and maybe have a coffee with her. Do you think that's possible?"

"Sure," I said. "She'd love it." I texted Stephanie on the spot and asked for permission to give out her contact information.

Back came an instantaneous "Yes!" Oh, the marvel of modern communication.

At six p.m., it was time to head back to Quebec City. We got lost on one of the exits from a bridge (Montreal is an island), ended up in an unmarked neighborhood, and needed to consult our smartphones.

"Don't tell anyone that I got us lost!" Ibrahim said, laughing.

Once we found our way back to the Trans-Canadian Highway, we noticed a low bank of clouds on the southern horizon.

"Wow," Lucía said, "those clouds are really beautiful."

I looked at the density, color, and shape of those beautiful clouds with dismay; I could tell that they were boiling to evergreater heights and would bring a severe storm. Sure enough, we soon encountered a horrible rainstorm, complete with heavy wind and lowering black sky. Mesmerized and trapped in the small car, I stared out at the whipping trees, the flattened grass, the shaking highway signs. I was frightened and trying not to show it. Ibrahim could not see where we were going, as the windshield wipers were totally unable to keep up with the deluge.

We had to exit the road twice, and the second time, we parked at a gas station. I felt vulnerable in the small rental vehicle and asked if anyone could pull up the weather radar on their phone, since mine wasn't loading. I wanted to know if we should go inside, head in a different direction, or move on. Silence descended on our vehicle, and the Mexican, the

German, and the Israeli turned and looked at me—the American, the Oklahoman—like I was crazy. But I had decades of experience with severe weather and knew my storms. I could tell that this was the real thing.

The next day, I found out that it had been hailing up ahead in Quebec City. Hail is not a good sign for someone who grew up in Tornado Alley in Oklahoma. I was not so crazy after all.

9

REFLECTIONS

I dragged myself to school Monday morning. We didn't get back to Quebec City until eleven, and I was exhausted and sick. My pre-Montreal malaise had become a full-fledged cold, complete with a cough and fever. And in those pre-COVID days, there was no question of staying home when ill; there was simply too much information presented every single day.

I was handed my grammar test results right away. The comprehension portion had lowered my overall score, which was no surprise, but I still managed to get an eighty-four percent. I was thrilled. Having decided over a decade ago, at age fifty, to study French again, I was initially a very serious student; only straight A's would do. Happily, I had relaxed a bit since then and realized that I was not competing with anyone. I was taking French exclusively for my own enjoyment. An acquaintance once told me that while he was serving in the military, his commanding officer taught him the phrase "Perfection is the enemy of good enough." His C.O. was correct; there is no perfection when learning a second language at my age. A grade of eighty-four was more than good enough, and for the first time, I felt sure that I was in the right class.

The Girl on the Belvedere

I dragged myself back home after an exhausting *Danse* class and stopped in at the grocery store, as I was out of food after my weekend getaway. I paused to listen to yet another fabulous band—the African Festival was now underway—memorized some verbs, did some laundry, and then slipped off to buy Victor Hugo's *Les Misérables* in French at Librairie Pantoute, assuming that I would someday finish *Harry Potter*.

That night, facing the last of my midterms, the dreaded *Compréhension orale*, I tried to study the videos upon which the take-home test was based. My cell phone refused to open them, though, so the next morning, I caught an early bus to the university so that I could have a little extra time in the twenty-four-hour language lab.

The first computer did not recognize my password. The second computer did not have attached headphones, and the wires were immoveable. I didn't want to risk the video blaring into the room and disturbing others, so I moved on. The third computer opened, but said I needed to install Flash. I shut down the program, installed Flash, and realized that it was now time for class.

I explained to Emmanuelle, my professor, why I wasn't done with the test. She understood and didn't mind, especially since I was a non-credit student, but she wanted me to turn in the test that afternoon. After my grammar class, I headed to the language lab, installed Flash on yet another computer, and tried to decipher the video. When I had finished, I set out in search of my professor to hand in my test, but I couldn't find her. I knew that she had an office somewhere in the building, but of course, I hadn't quite understood her directions.

I bemoaned my fate to Stephanie over the phone that afternoon. "It was a comprehension test," I said. "My comprehension is so bad that I didn't even understand where to turn it in! It was due this morning, and the professor gave me an extension, but I still have it because I didn't understand the directions to her office! I'll never understand this language! How do you pass a comprehension test when you can't comprehend anything?"

"*Le Catch 22,*" Stephanie said.

I turned in my test the next morning, but it was now officially late and would be downgraded as a result.

THAT EVENING, as I stared out of my window at the passing show below, I saw a bicyclist holding onto an open-air tour bus, catching a ride downhill. As the street gradually quieted, a number of bicycles suddenly appeared, all going in different directions. I headed out into this scene, watching as delivery bikes, mini bikes, and racing bikes sailed past. I thought about the many unusual sightings here in Quebec, like these bicycles, as I made my way up to Parc Montmorency, overlooking the Saint Lawrence River.

Standing near the cliff, I looked down at the ancient Lower Town, then up at a luminescent pale-blue sky with pink streaks. A large cloud bank was moving in, and it would rain tomorrow, but for now, it was perfect. The river was calm, and its deep shade of blue-grey complimented the mountains in the distance. The air was cool and clear, with a breeze coming off the river. I turned to leave Parc Montmorency and drifted toward the ramparts, nodding at a man walking his two dogs. I glanced at the row of cannons, stopped to read the plaque on a monument, and gazed across the street at the Séminaire de Québec.

I loved the terrace at Château Frontenac with its spectacular view, but I could hear the distant cheering and clapping of the tourists even from here in this quiet park. I preferred the peace and quiet of the ramparts, where I saw few people as I made my nightly rounds. Everyone was strolling, and no one was rushing

The Girl on the Belvedere

or applauding. At most, people were engaged in quiet conversation.

I turned around and gazed up at the original Université Laval before starting my leisurely stroll home. As always, I was torn between staring down at the harbor or walking the streets lined with stately historic homes. The evening light played on the rooftops below, on the barges in the river, and on the village of Lévis across the Saint Lawrence. I tried to memorize this scene; I knew that my precious days of solitude were diminishing.

I stopped and looked down the length of Rue de la Vieille-Université, which ends at an old building that arches over the street. I continued along the ramparts and then turned my gaze to Rue Hébert, longing to walk its quaint deserted length. This town was so lovely; there's a reason it's a World Heritage Site. I took one last look at the pink-dappled sky and the lights winking across the river, then turned toward home.

I reflected on my time here in Quebec. For many weeks, I had done exactly as I pleased when not in class. I walked in the evening, I ate when I was hungry, I watched TV occasionally. I had not gotten much sleep as there was always something that beckoned—a sunset, a half-remembered beautiful building, Parliament lit up in all its glory, a sunrise. And yet, I had experienced a deep, deep rest—visual, mental, and emotional. I had not realized until now, in this time of peace and reflection, what a toll modern life takes, even on one as happily situated as I.

Back in my apartment, with my windows open, I heard a large group of young chattering Germans walk by. Passing in the other direction were half a dozen or so young Asian people. French, Spanish, English, German, Chinese, Arabic, Japanese— all languages are heard on Rue Saint-Jean. *Tout le monde*— everyone—turns out for Quebec.

Later, in the darkness of my bedroom, with my window

open, I received a text message from Anna, with an attached video. I watched it on my phone. It featured a segment from the animated film *Up* and was accompanied by a French song titled *"On va s'aimer encore"* ["We will always love each other"]. Anna, with most of her life ahead of her, proclaimed it "cute." I felt my eyes fill with tears; most of my life was behind me. I looked out the window at the darkened street and marveled at the brevity of life. I thought about my grandson with his tiny, happy face, always toddling around and expecting to be cuddled and kissed. How sad that those years end so soon, that we change so quickly as we are buffeted about by circumstance.

THIS FOURTH WEEK, we experienced "24 Hours in French." I'd heard people talk about it and seen something in the weekly university newspaper ("Take up the challenge! To live an entire day in French is far from being an easy experience!"), but I hadn't paid much attention. I was sitting at my desk one morning when Anna came in wearing her usual outfit of jeans and a flowing black top. Her hair was loose, her makeup natural, her smile warm and genuine. She was wearing a lanyard with a "*24H en français*" card attached. She asked if I was going to participate, and I said, "Sure, I'll go get my card during break."

"No, no, you need to go right now! They are closing the desk in five minutes!"

Without her insistence, and ability to always anticipate my lack of comprehension, I would have missed out on this bit of fun.

I hurried to the tent outside and signed a pledge that I would speak nothing but French for twenty-four hours. This was easier said than done, of course, but I loved it, and made more progress on this day than any other.

The only time I broke into English was late that night in my apartment, when someone buzzed me on the intercom while I was on the phone with my husband. He was struggling to understand what I was saying—he spoke very little French—but he understood my startled "Hold on! There's someone at the door!" in English. *Who is buzzing me at this hour?* I wondered. I wasn't expecting anyone, and everyone I knew was on campus this evening.

"*Parlez-vous anglais?*" [Do you speak English?] I said into the intercom, too tired to engage in French with a native speaker over a garbled connection.

"*Non,*" came the response.

"*Au revoir,*" I said, letting go of the buzzer, certain that whatever the request, it wasn't for me. I returned to my conversation in French with my husband.

My daughter called a bit later, and after a few sentences she said, "Let me guess: you're speaking only French today."

Stephanie speaks Italian and studied film in Italy during her semester abroad. My husband and son both speak Spanish. I'm glad they speak those languages, for I will not. French will be my one and only foreign language. At least, I hope it will be, someday.

The next day, back at school in Quebec, I learned that while I had done well on the phonetics test, I had bombed the comprehension test. I wasn't surprised. We all have strengths and weaknesses, and my strengths seemed to be grammar and pronunciation, while my greatest weakness was comprehension. I was pretty sure that between my poor comprehension and the professor's downgrade for my test's tardiness, it was the lowest score I had ever received on anything.

That night, I walked to the fortifications to watch the sunset, ignoring my lingering cold and cough. My days in Quebec were precious and finite, and I did not want to miss a thing.

I arrived at the town wall near the New Barracks and watched the sunset, with its spectacular shades of magenta, azure, and violet. Did my distant grandfather Joseph stand in this very spot and stare at this same sun? The air gradually changed from crystal-clear to soft and seductive, and another of my forty-five days in this charming city slipped away. I had begun to memorize the sights and sounds of my evening strolls. Quebec now felt like home, and the memory of my life in Tulsa had receded. I knew that the halfway point of my stay had occurred a week ago, and with just seventeen days left in Canada, I was already grieving. I could feel my time of absolute freedom fading with each day, and I was afraid that I would not be able to reproduce it at home.

In my apartment that night, I opened my window, and the ambient noise of the street drifted up: dogs barking, spoons clacking, horses clip-clopping, conversations, cars, skateboards, buses, the sounds of people enjoying the most beautiful city in North America. I didn't feel like a tourist; I was working far too hard for that, and the regular act of schlepping groceries home harkened back to my New York City days. Even so, I resolved to see the city afresh and to recapture my early amazement and awe.

After class on Friday, Anna and I headed to PEPS, the enormous sports complex at Université Laval, which I had never seen. I was always content to follow my friends around campus; they lived in the dorm and by this time knew what was worth a visit. There was a wonderful sporting goods store within PEPS, but I settled for purchasing an oblong scarf from the logo shop. Anna and I then headed back to the student union to grab a sandwich.

"Will Ibrahim be joining us for lunch?" I asked.

"No," Anna said. "It's Friday, and he's at the mosque. He said to tell you hello, and that he will see you tomorrow night."

The Girl on the Belvedere

Home at last after this long week, I opened my window wide so that I could gaze at the last of the afternoon sunlight playing on city hall. I was fixated on the approaching end of my stay, and I wanted to memorize every moment. I was a happy and engaged student during the day, but in the evenings, I frequently felt some unidentifiable emotion welling up. Tears formed for no discernible reason. *Is it the language?* I wondered. *The culture? The friends that I have made but must leave behind? The sheer beauty of this marvelous place?*

I DECIDED to spend the evening in the Lower Town. I moseyed along this street and that, chatting with the shopkeepers, taking my time. I tried on a few things and settled on a grey wool top, which the *vendeuse* [shopkeeper] assured me had just come in for the fall and was from the shop's *Nouvelle Collection*. "This was recently designed and made in Quebec," she said in French. Shopping along a cobblestoned street, speaking French, choosing locally produced designer clothing—all was magical to me.

The *Plein Air* Festival was now in full swing, and I strolled through that, too. The white tents along the Saint Lawrence River were filled with artisanal goods, and the weather was sunny and cool. Everyone looked happy. It was Friday, the weather was perfect, and there were all manner of good things to eat, drink, and purchase. Quebec City is such a festival town, with a new *fête* opening almost every weekend. I was delighted to enjoy this one.

On my way home, I found a low wall upon which to sit and rest before climbing the hill. I gazed up at the fortifications, which are so impressive when seen from below. Sitting there, on the harbor side of the old wall, gazing up at the New Barracks, I again wondered about my ancestral grandfather's life. *Did Joseph stand near here and whisper pretty French phrases to the local girls? Was he frightened when he marched off to battle? Could he imagine the possibility of his capture and his forced march to Virginia, and all the twists and turns of his future life?*

As I sat there, a young man with a backpack suddenly came toward me, eyeing my purchase. I shifted it away from him, and he veered away from me without a backward glance. It was the first time anyone had seemed even remotely threatening, and the total lack of a crime report on television had lulled me into a false sense of security. I felt very, very safe in this city—everyone had told me that it was safe—but I needed to remember that there's always an exception.

Back in my apartment, I looked out the window and saw a young American couple exploring Rue Saint-Jean. I knew they were American, because I had walked up from the Lower Town behind them. They had been pulling their suitcases, presumably from the train station, and went into a hotel red in the face and gasping for air. It looked like such a short distance on the map, but it was almost straight up.

I finished the day in my living room on the sofa, enjoying a *chocolatine* from Paillard. It's called *pain au chocolat* in France and *chocolate croissant* in the United States, but it is delicious in any language. I sat in the semi-darkness, my window open, surveying the never-ending parade of people on Rue Saint-Jean. A helicopter flew overhead, and I immediately looked up. I had been here for a month and just now realized that I had neither seen nor heard planes overhead. The skies above the old town were empty save for the sun, moon, and clouds.

On Saturday, I was up early, as usual. Anna and Ibrahim were coming over that afternoon, Anna to study with me, and Ibrahim to prepare dinner in my kitchen. We had coordinated

The Girl on the Belvedere

our ingredient lists, and I planned to head to InterMarché, the grocery store, on this morning.

The first French-language tour guide of the day was below my window telling his group about the McDonald's up the street, and I went to the open window, interested. He was partially drowned out by Opera Man making an early appearance, but I caught something about signage in the Old Town, an explanation of the four city gates, and the possibility of rebuilding the two city gates that had been lost in the past.

I made my way to the grocery store. On Rue Saint-Jean, near the gate, I noticed three people carrying signs that said, "*Câlins gratuits!*" ["Free hugs!"]. They looked like tourists, not residents, and I found the whole thing very odd. *Why are they giving free hugs? Couldn't they just hug one another? Why are their hugs free? Are they on special for today? What do they usually charge?* Ignoring their invitation, I kept moving. I was on a mission.

The checkout lady who used to gossip across the aisle about me, the *touriste*, to the other checkers now accepted me as a regular. She made small talk with me in French as she scanned my items. I bid her, "*Merci, au revoir,*" and headed back out. I wished that I had one of those rolling carts for the street like those in New York City; my load was so heavy that my shoulders ached immediately.

As I walked back along Rue Saint-Jean toward the gate with my bulging plastic bags, I saw that the Free Hugs People had increased in number, rather like the birds in Hitchcock's movie. They spotted me and attacked. One large lady planted herself and her sign directly in my path, with another right behind her. There was nowhere to go; the Huggers were hogging the sidewalk. I lowered my head, increased my speed, and charged directly ahead. The first Hugger got out of my way. The second muttered an insincere "*Bonne Journée*" ["Have a good day"] as she stepped aside to avoid a collision. I noticed another Free Hugger across the street, closing in on another innocent citizen. *Who were these intrusive people?*

After stowing my groceries, I set out again, this time to shop for trinkets. I wanted to find some matching items for Anna, Lucía, and me that said, *"Je me souviens"* ["I remember"], the official motto of Quebec. There were lots of tourist items with catchy phrases, but only *"Je me souviens"* would work for me. I settled on refrigerator magnets, with the words *"Québec"* and *Je me souviens,"* plus drawings of the Saint Louis Gate and Château Frontenac against the blue and white flag of Quebec.

By 4:30, my apartment was clean and even somewhat cool on this warm day, and I'd set out the Camembert and crackers. Anna and Ibrahim were on their way, bringing chicken, rice, and yogurt. Ibrahim was also bringing, as a gift to me, his mother's recipe for falafel. It's a favorite dish of mine, and Anna said that Ibrahim's is the best.

An hour later, Ibrahim called Anna and me into the kitchen. He was concerned that the oven was not heating correctly, as the chicken was not cooking properly.

"What temperature are you using?" I asked.

"175," he said.

"Ummm," I said, "let's try 350. This is an American range. The temperature is measured in Fahrenheit."

"Oh!" Anna exclaimed. "I bet that's why our frozen pizza wouldn't cook the other night at the dorm." They looked at each other and laughed, shaking their heads at their mistake.

The meal—fragrant chicken stuffed with seasoned rice—was wonderful, and the company was even better. I loved these two people with their blended heritage and large worldview. I realized that, because of them, I now watched the nightly news differently, seeing it from perspectives other than my own.

After our leisurely dinner, a thunderstorm suddenly illuminated the town from one direction, while fireworks over the river lit up the street from the other. It was raining, and the air was fresh and cool as my friends set off into the night.

They loved my apartment, as did I. It was small—just a little larger than our former one-bedroom in Manhattan—but nicely laid out. I liked the compactness and the ease with which I could straighten and clean. It made me realize how few clothes I actually wore and how little space I actually needed. I was perfectly at ease here, perfectly secure.

In the middle of the night, I was startled awake by the sound of screaming. I rushed to the window, heart racing. Below was a gaggle of girls, all shrieking, as though a rock star were nearby. Suddenly, they formed a flying wedge, began chanting some sort of cheer, and pumped their fists as they marched up the street.

As usual, the skateboarders appeared next. They generally arrived in the middle of the night, after the street was deserted. They sailed down the hill to pick up speed, then coasted uphill toward Saint John Gate.

Then the spoons started up again. I couldn't locate the person who was playing them. Was it the usual young man or the old man in the beret, who had appeared more recently?

Those spoons were background music, and a constant presence, like the voices of the tourists and the rumble of the buses. Saturday nights were always noisy, and I'd come to accept that, but on this night in particular, I got precious little sleep.

SUNDAY DAWNED CLEAR AND COOL, and I heard Opera Man stepping onstage early. I watched him walk up the street in his uniform of shorts and T-shirt, today completely in white, even his shoes and socks. This time, he led two young children, one in each hand, up Rue Saint-Jean. And he was singing, singing, singing, always singing.

At 9:15, the bells at the basilica begin the first of their Sunday concerts. I put down my notebook, closed my eyes, and just listened. They sounded for ten solid minutes, giving me a respite from the assignments ahead.

I ditched my homework after several hours and walked up the hill to sit in the shade at city hall to listen to the midday bells more closely. The little park was busy, with some people sitting on benches and others in the bleachers usually reserved for the acrobat shows. As the sounds faded away, I knew with certainty that this was the last time I would hear the entire concert at such close proximity by myself, undisturbed. My husband would arrive the next weekend, and he would share the experience with me.

Several hours later, having finished my written assignments, I feasted upon the remains of the previous night's dinner, then headed out to walk the Upper Town's quieter streets. I reached the top of the Cap Diamant, the uppermost area of Quebec City, and then descended into the Governor's Garden, which was guarded by tall houses and small hotels. I stopped to read the obelisk honoring the opposing leaders of the battle that resulted in the Conquest, the English General Wolfe and the French General Montcalm. I stepped onto the Dufferin Terrace at Château Frontenac, where I spent many minutes studying the majestic river. I chose a bench and listened to a female street artist singing "Time to Say Goodbye," the song made famous by Sarah Brightman. It was my last Sunday on my own, and the combination of the talented *chanteuse,* the river, and the view of the Château left me a little teary.

As I listened, I thought about "À nos actes manqués," the song about regrets and missed opportunities. Studying the lyrics had brought to mind things I hadn't wanted to think about. At this point in my life, there were so many things I would have liked to do over. Why didn't I sit on the floor with my young children more often? Why didn't I stare at them and memorize their little faces? Why didn't I stare at the face of my young husband and memorize his? Why didn't I spend more time with my parents? With my husband's parents? Why didn't I make more time for friends? Why didn't I spend more time petting our parade of animals? I didn't have a single regret about anything material or work-related. In fact, I didn't even think about those things at all.

When I arrived in Quebec, I was in a rut and knew it. The busyness of everyday life had shielded me from unhappy thoughts of my past, but it had also dulled me and kept me from life's possibilities. But now, here, I was free. I was free to experience life as it happened, with no expectations to restrict me or weigh me down. I began to see my life as a whole, rather than in segments.

I thought about my children and the fact that they are truly good people. I reflected on the fact that I had insisted that they choose a line of work that was fulfilling and would allow them to discover and develop their own unique talents. I made it clear that the role of "mini-me" would not be tolerated. My shortcomings as a parent are legion, but in that one area, I claim success.

I thought about my husband, our happy forty year marriage, our continued sense of adventure, our common goals for having fun in our looming retirement.

And I thought about my friends here in Quebec: Lucía, Celestina, Anna, and Ibrahim. These were true friendships, based solely on commonalities, affection, and easy camaraderie. There were no worries about offending each other despite our disparate backgrounds and no expectations other than the enjoyment of each other's company.

Coming from a chaotic and restrictive childhood, joy was an emotion I didn't always recognize, but now, I began to understand the joy present in a song about paths not taken. This was my life, in total. I had experienced fear, yes. Sadness, yes. I had missed many opportunities, yes. But overall, I'd had so much happiness and so many blessings. It was simply my life. It belonged to me, with all of its myriad moving parts. I owned it.

∼

CONVERSATIONS WERE BEGINNING to unfold around me. On my way home from the Château, on the ramparts, I listened to a young father admonishing his child to not climb on a cannon, as it was dangerous. I had walked several blocks before I realized that they had been speaking French and that I had understood every word.

I ran into Flower Lady, who was parked on a corner, surveying the street. I was surprised to see that the flowers were attached to her wheelchair and that they were artificial. She wasn't selling them at all. *Who is she? Where does she live? What does she do beyond racing up and down the hills of Quebec City in a motorized wheelchair?*

I loved my sightings of these characters here in Quebec: Flower Lady, Spoon Man, the Girl with Emerald-Green Hair, the Man in Black, Opera Man. Why? Why did they fascinate me so? I think it was due to their complete freedom, their ability to live life on their own terms, and not worry about what others thought of them. I hoped that I could pinch off just a little bit of their magic and simply be *me,* once I was back home.

This Sunday evening, as I was doing homework, I paused to listen to the basilica bells ringing at six o'clock on the dot. It wasn't the full recital, just a simple sounding, but it went on for a full five minutes. *How I will miss this,* I thought.

Our phonetics teacher often talked about *la prosodie*: the rhythm of language. With my window open, I realized that there was a rhythm to the life on Rue Saint-Jean. There was always

Québécois music playing, always the rumble of tour buses, always the hum of indistinguishable conversations. It was a noisy place. Would I be able to sleep without the constant cacophony, accustomed as I now was to sleeping with my windows open? Would I remember it?

10

SEE YOU LATER

I was up at five, as usual, to begin my last week of class. I was giving a presentation today as part of a *travail d'équipe* [team effort], but was only a little nervous. By now, we'd done so many that they no longer held any true terror for me. Today, I would be talking about job opportunities for the mentally handicapped, and as a former special education teacher, I could speak on that subject with authority. I still had to refer to my notes, but my rate of speech had picked up. All went well with my presentation. I was content.

With hardly a breath in between, I was off to *Danse*. I'd never really relaxed in this class, even though it was familiar territory. This week, though, I felt a subtle shift within myself. There was always an opportunity for conversation at the beginning of class, but thus far, I had remained silent, never volunteering, speaking only when spoken to. Now, I discovered that I had lost my fear of speaking up. As I made the rounds of the class, moving from individual to individual, I chatted with each without shyness or concern about correctness. This time, rather than learning a new dance, we were asked to devise comedic skits. One of the young women in my group had a great idea, and I quickly

The Girl on the Belvedere

sketched out some easy choreography for the four of us. For me, it was as simple as breathing. I suddenly realized that I loved the girls in this class, these young dancers from all over the world. At last, I was enjoying chatting with them in French. The sketch was fun and funny, and we got the warmest applause and most laughter of any group in the class. Then we switched gears to focus on our Salsa routine, which we would be performing on Thursday. The class was exhilarating, exhausting, and our last one.

The next morning, Tuesday, there were just four days of classes to go. I had a comprehension test, but there was no formal preparation this time—we were going to watch some new videos and answer questions. Instead, I resolved to simply enjoy my bus ride to the university. The air was fresh and clear, and the sun was shining. The regulars on the bus slowly assembled: the thin woman with the ball cap who sat behind the driver, the fashionable woman with cropped red hair and an ankle bracelet, the tall blonde with the coffee. On Avenue Honoré-Mercier, we picked up the largest crowd of the morning, most of them destined for the same workplace, *Régie de l'Assurance maladie* (the government health insurance agency). Soon we were rolling down Boulevard René-Lévesque, a main artery heading west. I looked down a side street that descended toward a favorite church, Saint-Jean-Baptiste, marveling as always at the steepness of the street and the beauty of the church's spire.

We crossed Avenue Cartier, a major shopping street, and I vowed to go there on Saturday, before the arrival of my husband and friends from home. It was a little bit of a hike from my apartment, but *ce n'était pas grave*—it didn't matter. My program ended on Friday, and Saturday would be a free day, with homework no longer a concern.

We turned down the Grande Allée, that most beautiful of avenues, and sailed past Battlefield Park with its stately Museum of Fine Arts and cannon-lined walks, where I watched the usual band of military men, all trim and tan, running along the paths. Across the boulevard were spectacular houses and beautiful apartments. The entire Grande Allée was tree-lined, flowered, grand indeed.

We passed Parc du Bois-de-Coulonge, a densely green park, and turned toward the village of Sillery. It was a pretty neighborhood with a small business district. I thought of it as a place where my husband and I might live if we settled here. It was just ten minutes from town, a leafy oasis with handsome houses adorned with flowers. We were not considering a move to Canada, of course, but it was fun to daydream.

The Man in Black ascended in Sillery, which reminded me that the university would soon appear. We exited the village and in another half mile, there it was—a veritable forest on the campus of Université Laval. We approached the bus stop, and the Man in Black beat me to the buzzer, as he always did. We descended in silence, *c'était normal*.

I passed the impenetrable forest, walking slowly along Avenue des Sciences-Humaines. The foliage was green, dense, and cool—a delightful respite from the stone and concrete of the *centre-ville*, the city center where I lived. Looking into that sun-dappled expanse, with its meandering paths and benches, always eased my mind and gave me peace first thing in the morning. I paused to imagine this forest in winter, and while I would appreciate the beauty of a snowy scene, I knew there was a good reason for the six miles of underground walkways on campus. This girl from the Southern Plains needed the sun. I didn't ski and no longer ice-skated, and I feared my life would be greatly restricted here in the winter. I was much more suited to life in the sunny southwest.

I stopped to watch a badger rooting underneath a tree, in the same exact spot where my daughter and I had stopped to watch two of his friends. It seemed like a lifetime ago that we had explored the campus ahead of my first day of class.

I arrived at school early, as usual, and sat down outside the cafeteria with a cup of coffee to review my notes before the comprehension exam. My professor of grammar, Aimée, stopped by to chat, and I caught perhaps ninety percent of what she said. I really liked Aimée as a professor; she was exacting and unrelenting in her quest to impart knowledge, but never condescending. She wished me *bon courage* on my comprehension test. I was going to need it.

My heart pounding, I entered the classroom and sat down to take my test. The first video was difficult, as the speaker rushed his words and had a heavy Quebec accent, but the second was easier to understand. I did my best and prayed.

Later, as I headed home, walking down Rue Saint-Jean, I saw a skateboarder with a cigarette dangling from his lip as only the French could manage, sailing down the street. I saw the Girl with Emerald-Green Hair. It had been a week or two since I last saw her, and her brown roots were showing. She looked tired, this gorgeous young woman. After five weeks away from home, I was sure that I looked exhausted and that my roots were showing, too.

IT WAS PERFECT, this final Tuesday evening of my solitude. Soon, I would return to my regimented, predictable life. I would undoubtedly spend far less time deciding what I wanted to do each day and far more time on those chores that kept my life in order.

I decided to visit the beautiful fountain at Parliament. As I made my way up Rue d'Auteuil, a young man sailed past me on a skateboard. His pants were baggy, his underwear was showing, and he was bare-chested. His two dogs, both on leashes, were pulling him up the steep incline. This street was as steep as any in San Francisco, but those dutiful dogs pulled, pulled, pulled.

I sat on a bench at the top of Rue d'Auteuil and gazed at the sun-dappled houses on the other side of the street. When I was young, I could never understand what "old people" were doing when they simply sat and stared. Now, I understood. Life continually flows by, and the first two-thirds of it pass almost unnoticed, so busy are the years of education, working, child-rearing. The empty nest brings happiness as well as heartache, plus an ability to hyperfocus, yet also to detach and observe. By now, I had probably occupied every bench in the Upper Town, spending time simply sitting and sitting, staring and staring.

Once through Saint Louis Gate, I entered Esplanade Park, then turned to face the Fontaine de Tourny. It was situated such that, from my perspective, the watery tiers of stone cherubs and nymphs were centered against the backdrop of Parliament. The grounds were ablaze with flowers, and I circled the gardens. I turned to look back at the fountain, whose spray now appeared outlined against the brilliantly lit walls of the Fortifications. It was pure magic.

The bell on the Hôtel du Parlement struck eight. Another day was slipping from my grasp. How could that be? The fountain sprayed, the Quebec flag fluttered atop Parliament, and soon, I would see them no more.

I hoped, as I stared at the gloriously illuminated capitol building, that I would remember these carefree, evocative evening scenes. I am a deeply visual person, and the beauty of Quebec fed my creativity and restored my spirit. I wanted to retain as much of it as possible. I had become more observant as the weeks passed, and had settled into my routine, calmed down, and now marveled more than ever at the loveliness of this place. Leaving the Parliament on this evening with its amazing sights was difficult.

I turned toward the fading sunset. The mountains in the distance glowed purple and lavender. Perfect wisps of aubergine floated by in an apricot sky. I started toward home, but found that I wasn't ready to leave this dreamy scene just yet. A creamy yellow moon hung in an indigo sky above the old fort, the Citadelle, and I turned toward it, into the quietude of the highest point in Old Quebec. The houses here were tall, gracious, charming, and oh-so-French. Church spires towered over the many blocks. Here and there neighbors visited, some setting up card tables in the street for their shared bottles of wine. People walked their dogs and did their dishes, the clanking reverberating from open kitchen windows.

I stumbled upon a hitherto unseen park, Parc du Cavalier-du-Moulin. At the entrance, an elderly, perfectly coiffed woman cautioned me, "Don't go into the park! It's late, and there are two young men loitering there." We spoke in French for perhaps ten minutes about the park, about Université Laval, about Quebec, and all over again, I was entranced by this beautiful city, its enchanting people, and its glorious language. I headed for home, this time for real.

WEDNESDAY CAME ALL TOO QUICKLY. I arrived at my seat at 7:55 that morning and started a half-hour review of the entire course. Anna soon arrived, she of the smiling eyes and flowing hair. She took out and arranged her materials—pencils, pens, highlighters, a ruler—like the former math major she was. I'd never seen such beautiful notes. Lucía arrived soon after with gifts; she had handmade Mexican rings for both Anna and me. They featured delicate grey and mauve beaded daises. I put mine on, and it fit perfectly.

After class, I shared a quick lunch with my friends in honor of Ibrahim's twenty-eighth birthday. *So young!* I thought. Afterward, I had a review session with Anna and Lucía before heading home. Quebec City's Fireworks Festival was beginning, and the streets were packed, but I would be staying in tonight, studying.

In my apartment, I looked out the window and saw Flower Lady. She was wheeling her way up the sidewalk, then switched to the street. Her wheelchair picked up speed as she ascended the hill. She was fearless, and fast. She passed the cars and buses, butting into line and cutting across lanes of traffic if it gave her even the slightest advantage. At last, she disappeared from sight near the basilica. "Granny on the loose!" as Stephanie would say.

Just as I settled down to study, I heard Opera Man singing his opening three phrases. I went to the window, and since I had now seen him many times, I was able to pick him out him right away. Tonight, he was wearing a red satin jacket, a royal-blue "Italy" shirt, a matching ball cap, pale blue shorts, black socks, and black shoes and was carrying a celery-green backpack. I scurried from window to window, following his progress up the street. He usually fell silent for a bit at my corner, but not tonight. I heard him singing as he continued up the hill toward City Hall. I had always assumed that he lived on my street, but perhaps not.

The tour buses—mainly the red double-decker, open-air variety—were out in force tonight. They arrived in packs from both directions, and I fully expected there to be yet another traffic jam where the road curved and narrowed beneath me. I stared unabashedly at the tourists. They were almost at my third-floor level as their buses climbed the hill, but they rarely

The Girl on the Belvedere

saw me. They were too engaged in the circus below them on Rue Saint-Jean to look up.

On occasion, in the evening, I would stand in front of my apartment building, where street artists with spoons or guitars or accordions sometimes played. I would look up at my open windows and think about what brought me to this place: my deep love of the French language and culture. I was so comfortable on this street, in this walled city, Quebec; in this country, Canada, a country of two cultures and two languages, united by the vastness of its landscape and the immensity of its sky. I had found so very much to admire here: the architecture, the forests, the people—always the people.

This week, while sitting on a bench beneath my window, I watched the crowd, which was full of locals in seventeenth-century period dress. This was a little unusual, even in this historic area. The latest festival, *Les Fêtes de la Nouvelle-France*, was underway, celebrating four hundred years of *Québécois* history. I chuckled when I noticed some women in full period dress sipping Starbucks, their companions eating hamburgers from McDonald's, and all of them stepping onto an electric bus.

On Thursday, I gave Anna and Lucía the "*Je me souviens*" refrigerator magnets. They exclaimed over them before we turned our attention to the toughest exam of the course: grammar. It covered everything we had done, and Professor Aimée's expectations were high. She had already informed us of what was, and was not, acceptable for students at Level Five, and the "unacceptable" list was long. I'd studied hard, but there simply was not enough time to absorb this amount of information. However, my comprehension had improved, which I counted as a victory.

My other test, the oral comprehension exam with Professor Emmanuelle, actually proved to be easier. The test itself was a nice surprise, because it simply took the form of a conversation with my two best friends in the program, talking about careers past (me) and future (Lucía and Anna). I was relieved.

I was eating lunch with Lucía, Anna, and Ibrahim when I saw Celestina enter the cafeteria. I waved her over, made introductions, and invited her to join us. Celestina said a prayer, and we bowed our heads, all of us being people of faith. I realized yet again how blessed I was, to be sitting with friends from around the globe—from Germany, from Mexico, from Israel, from Saint Thomas. All of us were so similar, our needs and wants so much the same.

AFTER LUNCH, I rushed home to my apartment for a few hours to prepare for the other part of Professor Aimée's grammar final, which would be a simple conversation with her, without notes. After dinner, I put away my books, changed clothes, and headed back to campus for *"Le Spectacle"*—the evening of song, dance, and videos for which our *animatrices* had been preparing us, the talent show at the end of the Intensive. I was not performing, having begged off; I had attended every rehearsal and knew the salsa routine, but had decided to leave the stage to the young.

I took a slow bus back to campus, chatting with the driver about how much I enjoyed this drive, with its beautiful avenues and the forest at Université Laval. The evening light reflected differently on the scenery along the route, more golden than in the mornings, and the parks were aglow. The village of Sillery had come to life with dog-walkers and bicycles, and its village center was busy with pedestrians crisscrossing the main street. The forest at Université Laval did not disappoint. The evening light was flickering through the trees from the other direction, and I remained amazed at its density, its freshness, its magic.

I took a seat in the auditorium and was immensely pleased

when my fellow dancers, sitting *en masse* in the audience before the show, called me up to sit with them. The show was fantastic, with singing, dancing, and student-made videos in between the live acts. I waved at Ibrahim, who joined me, and we saved seats for our favorite two performers, Lucía and Anna. We cheered for Lucía and the rest of my *Danse* class in the Salsa number, and later for Anna, stunning in her black dress, her group singing the French version of "All That Jazz." I spied Celestina on stage, singing with her own group. Afterward, she stopped by to give me a gift, a book that was meaningful to the two of us, with the inscription "*Pour Cheryl—Merci d'être si gentille avec moi. Que Dieu te bénisse.*" ["Thank you for your kindness to me. May God bless you."] Oh, how I would miss my friends.

One sensational song, "Elle Me Dit," had half the audience dancing in the aisles. "Danse, danse, danse," the song cajoled. We were all singing along, but again I continued to sit, like a stone. Why? Would they stop the song and stare in amazement if I got to my feet? Would one more person dancing crazily in the aisle cause the world to come to an end? This immovability of mine would be one of my few regrets from my time in Quebec.

After the show, with its attendant rounds of congratulations and laughter, I exited the theatre with my three young friends, said goodnight, and turned toward my bus stop. I was amazed to realize that they were all following me; they insisted on waiting with me, refusing to let me stand at the bus stop by myself this late at night. Again, I was touched by the thoughtfulness of these young people from different cultures, all united by cores of dignity, goodness, and compassion. It dawned on me that the crazy quilt that was my life was stitched together by such moments; once again, I felt the joy that emanated from the song "À nos actes manqués." I understood the line, "*À tout c'que j'ai pas vu, tout près, juste à côté*" ["To everything I didn't see, so near, right next to me"] more completely. *Please, God, let me notice such things from now on, and let me be touched by them,* I prayed.

The next day, I gazed at the morning sun dancing on the forest's leaves for the last time. I headed to my building and paused in front of it to reflect on the first time I had seen it, with Stephanie. The bus had let us off in what had seemed like the middle of the forest, I couldn't remember the name of the building, and it took forever to find it. I remembered entering and orienting myself in advance of the first day, locating the classrooms and the cafeteria. It felt like a lifetime ago.

And now, five weeks later, it was time to face my last two exams. My first was grammar, simply a conversation with Aimée. I had no idea how I had done the day before on the written portion or how I was doing now. I didn't really care; I just relaxed and enjoyed myself. I was becoming a regular French chatterbox.

Then came the final exam in phonetics, where I recorded several paragraphs. At this, the eleventh hour of the eleventh day, my password was finally accepted on my first try and the program opened without any problems. I practiced and then recorded my paragraphs. Two girls in my class stood by to make sure that I sent it in properly. Bless them. I had almost mastered technology at Université Laval, thanks to the help of so many young students along the way.

With their encouragement, I clicked on the French version of "Send," and just like that, it was over. All of it. I went into the hallway, looking for Anna and Lucía. I saw several small groups of students exchanging email addresses, everyone looking slightly stunned at this sudden turn of events. One moment, we had been frantic, studying, comparing, cramming, reviewing. The next moment, we were done, and there was nothing left to do. Nothing at all.

Several of the younger students surprised me by asking for

my contact information, and one of them surprised me further by telling me that I'd been an inspiration, saying, "When I'm your age, I want to do what you're doing: study a foreign language, take an apartment in a foreign city." I was truly touched; I'd never tried to be one of the gang, to horn in on their activities, to impede or interfere. And yet, they held me in high esteem. I was moved, and promised to follow my young friends on their various social media.

I wandered outside, remembering that I wanted to take a photo of this place where I had invested so much time, energy, fear, and joy. I ran into Celestina on the steps, and I took a picture of her. Someone else snapped our picture together. I thanked her for the gift she had given me and promised to keep in touch. We hugged.

"*À la prochaine*," she said.

"*À la prochaine*," I echoed. Until next time. She walked away, melted into the departing crowd, and was gone.

Professor Aimée had reserved a room for our class at the pub in the student union. As we gathered, Professor Sébastien, our witty phonetics teacher, sat at one end of the table while Aimée sat at the other. We asked them more personal questions than we could in class, and we all ended up staying far later and longer than any of us intended. Almost the entire class turned out, and no one wanted to leave. We took a group photo with Aimée, and then suddenly, this intense experience really *was* over. I said goodbye to my brilliant friend Isaac from Montreal, who had been my "Question of the Day" partner. I said goodbye to all the others with whom I'd shared so much. "*À la prochaine*," I said, again and again. "*À la prochaine*." When I'd said all there was to say, I turned, exited the pub, and made my way to the grand foyer.

I took a moment to reflect while waiting for my two friends. I'd had so many fears in the beginning: fear of looking ridiculous, fear of not fitting in, fear of not understanding or being understood, fear of getting sick. What came true? All of it.

But what did I learn? I learned that it is possible to face down your fears, one at a time, simply by putting one foot in front of the other, by being determined, and by not losing sight of what is really important. Did I do poorly on a few tests? You bet. Did people at the grocery store make comments that they thought I couldn't understand? Yes. Did my young fellow students wonder what I was doing there? Undoubtedly. Was I myself? One hundred percent of the time.

I once read that if you have a second language, you should use it for problem-solving; the lack of facility cuts out the excess chatter in your mind. Here in Canada, I had existed for five weeks without that chatter. For better or for worse, the real me was present in Quebec, stripped down, simple, complete.

So what took the place of my fears? My friends, my acquaintances, the people I met along the way. The sights, the sounds, the beauty. Those memories were now mine, forever mine, and they were life-changing and life-sustaining.

MY TWO FRIENDS met me in the foyer, and someone took our picture as we stood together under the flag of Université Laval. Lucía was coming into town with me now, and I would see Anna the next day, but when I climbed onto that bus, I would be leaving an entire world behind, a world I had come to love, to treasure.

Lucía and I boarded that bus, and it was so crowded that we had to stand for a while. This driver was a wild one, and we giggled as we pitched back and forth. We eventually found two empty seats and laughed out loud as we lurched forward and slipped sideways.

The Girl on the Belvedere

In town, we shopped for trinkets in the *Haute-Ville*, the Upper Town, with Lucía buying this and that for family and friends. She had been to Old Quebec quite a few times—enough to know her way around—but I was certain that she had not explored the glorious Parc du Cavalier-du-Moulin, given that I walked Old Town every night and had just recently stumbled upon it. I decided to take her to it.

We exclaimed over the beautiful homes at the entrance, and then entered to walk along the ramparts. This place was designed to be the fallback position in battle. If all else failed, this small fortification sitting in the uppermost part of town was where everyone would retreat. Now, it provided a very different type of retreat from the hustle and bustle of the *Haute-Ville*. Lucía and I stood in silence on the walled promontory and regarded the homes and churches below. We said nothing, simply taking it all in, memorizing the moment.

From there, we made our way to Parc Montmorency, which offered my favorite view of the river. We spoke of the uniqueness of Quebec as we gazed at the historic district below. "Quebec reminds me of San Miguel de Allende in Mexico," Lucía said, "but Quebec is perhaps more beautiful. I don't want to leave."

We sat in Chez Temporel enjoying our *Tarte au Sucre* [French-Canadian Sugar Pie]. It was pouring outside, but here in this tiny bistro, it was warm, dry, and cozy. We sat with our bowls of *café au lait* and *chocolat chaud* [hot chocolate], tearing into our shared piece of pie. At times, we sat in silence, not wanting to finish, not wanting the check, not wanting to admit that we would part very soon. And so, we sat.

Lucía was such a beauty, this "Little Mexican" as she called herself. She was all black eyes and long lustrous long hair, demure in her cardigan and jeans and with a ready smile. She was loved by everyone. My heart was breaking at our inevitable parting, and while I knew I would see her again, I also knew it would not be anytime soon.

The rain had stopped, and the evening shimmered with that silvery light I had come to love. We strolled along the ramparts over the harbor, walking toward the New Barracks, and I showed her where my ancestor had likely lived. We turned and made our way to the Augustine Monastery, where we peered inside the ancient walls through a gate. Finally, we went to my apartment, where we sat and chatted.

Lucía had an early flight and needed to get back to campus to pack, but we were dreading the moment of our parting. I walked her up Rue Saint-Jean. At the gate, she turned and hugged me. "I thank God that I met you and Anna and Ibrahim," she said in her beautiful textbook English. "I'll never forget you, Cheryl, and you'll always be an important person in my life. I'll always remember you, and I'll always remember Quebec."

"I'll miss you so much," I said to this young woman, who was so wise beyond her years.

We were too emotional to say much more, so we clung to each other and cried instead.

"*À la prochaine*," she finally said.

"*À la prochaine*," I replied.

With that, she suddenly let go of me, turned, and walked through the gate, not once looking back. She was gone.

ON SATURDAY MORNING, I made my usual trip to Paillard for a coffee and croissant, *à emporter*—to go. I spoke to them in French, and they responded in French, *c'était normal*. I brought my breakfast back to my apartment, cranked open the window, and listened to the bells.

The Girl on the Belvedere

I heard Opera Man and saw that he was wearing orange shorts, a red jacket, black socks, and black shoes today and was carrying a grey backpack as he trekked up the street. He sang his way up the hill, but then stopped suddenly, crossed the street, stopped an old man, spoke to him while poking him in the shoulder four times, then proceeded up the street again. I could still hear him singing, faintly, as he disappeared from view. For the first time, the thought occurred to me that perhaps he sang for tourists at the Dufferin Terrace near the Château.

Later, I mentioned my thought to Stephanie. "Mom! *No!*" she responded. "Can you imagine an opera star from the Met walking down Fifth Avenue in socks and sandals, poking people?"

As Opera Man vanished from my view, I looked at the clock. My husband was boarding his plane at that very moment. I was sure he would text me from the gate, per our custom, but I received nothing. I called him instead, gave him directions to my apartment, and wished him "*Bon voyage.*"

I was speaking Franglais, and I knew it. I was determined to speak only English with my husband and our Oklahoma friends, who also were arriving today. I was equally determined to speak only French with the *Québécois.* But it's never that easy.

Years ago, my husband and I were asked to help arrange a meeting in Montreal. The local florist with whom I worked had been born in Spain, educated in Canada at a French convent school, and learned English from television. I asked her what language she spoke with her friends, and she said, "All three. Whatever expresses it best." At the time, I thought she meant that she actively *chose* the language. Now I understood what she really meant: whatever pops into your head is what you say.

Sometime in these last few weeks, I had lost my ability to speak only in French or only in English. I now spoke Franglais. One evening, while on the phone with my husband, I was telling him about the many tour buses visible on the street below. "Another festival just started," I said, "and a *bateau de croisière* must be in town."

"What's that?" he asked.

I absolutely could not remember the English term I was looking for and said to him, "You know, the big boat with all the people who are traveling."

"Cruise ship?" he responded.

"Yes! Cruise ship!"

Franglais.

On this beautiful Saturday morning, I set out for my last solo adventure, a shopping excursion on Avenue Cartier. I walked along Boulevard René-Levesque, the bus route. I'd often thought of the parallel Grande Allée as the pretty street, and René-Levesque as the commercial street. Today, to my surprise, I discovered cool green *allées* of trees for pedestrians and stopped to snap a photo of my favorite church, Saint-Jean-Baptiste, far below on Rue Saint-Jean. I'd admired it every day from the bus and wanted to remember it. Avenue Cartier, my destination, was a good half-hour away on foot, but my clothes were baggy, my legs were strong, and I was content to walk. The French paradox had turned out to be true, at least for me, in this time and place.

I purchased a dress and a sweater and had wonderful conversations in French with the shopkeepers. I stopped at an outdoor café for lunch along Avenue Cartier and tried to follow my husband's progress across his three flights. I needed Wi-Fi to do so and asked the *serveuse* for the restaurant's password; by now, after all my difficulty at school, I certainly knew how to ask for a password. Unfortunately, I didn't understand her response. To be fair, the *mot de passe* turned out to be in Italian, not French.

I texted my husband to wish him a safe trip on his second flight, and included our daughter in a three-way conversation, as is our custom. My husband responded almost immediately with a weather report. He's not exactly a nervous flier, but he's always aware of the flying conditions and the type of equipment he's flying on. I grew up flying beside my father, who taught me not to worry. He often admonished me when I was very young, "Don't be frightened. The pilots want to get there, too."

Stephanie and I are merciless when it comes to teasing John about his preoccupation, and today was no different. "Fly safe!" she texted in the group chat.

"Well, he's in charge," I texted, giggling out loud, "but I'm a little worried. Visibility is only one hundred thousand miles, the pressure is one million millibars, and the fuel's a little heavy."

"Well, I checked the G26 radar, and all seems fine for the F55 routes, but tell him not to jim-hickey," Stephanie said.

I laughed out loud at my daughter's response, not caring if I was overheard by the other patrons or the café's waitstaff. "I'm a little worried about the low ceiling," I added. "There seems to be gum stuck on it."

"The airline is trying to save money with that gum; it keeps everything smelling fresh. They brought that idea over from the other airline during the merger," she quipped.

John piped in, "I'm in charge of the tower."

"God help them," I said. "Are they diverting all traffic?"

"He's been taking classes, Mom, it's okay."

"They were ONLINE classes, Steph," I texted. "It's not okay."

"Shutting off the phone now," John said.

I had to tease him one last time. "Autopilot inflated?" I asked.

After lunch, I returned to the walled city by way of a street near the Plains of Abraham. It was quiet, tree-lined, and elegant. I walked through the Plains, next to the glorious Saint Joan of Arc Garden. This day was the most beautiful since my arrival. There were clear skies, a slight cool breeze, and sharp shadows in the gardens. It was picture-perfect.

I was disappointed to learn that my husband would not arrive in time for dinner with Anna and Ibrahim. His second flight was delayed in taking off, and he had missed his final connection. Now, he had to take a later flight.

Back in my apartment, I packed up my books. I left my tiny French-English dictionary out on the coffee table, but that was it. There were no projects to complete, no websites to check, no dinner to prepare. From this moment on, I was a tourist like any other.

Anna and Ibrahim joined me for a stroll and a Lebanese take-out dinner, which we ate while sitting on the steps of the Fortifications and watching the people on Rue Saint-Jean. We headed to Château Frontenac and beyond to the Dufferin Terrace to stake out a spot for that evening's fireworks. These fireworks over the river are a summer tradition, and they produce a carnival-like atmosphere and huge crowds. We watched the entire show and then ambled down to my apartment to wait for my husband's call. They waited with me, Ibrahim in a chair and Anna curled up on the sofa, twisting her hair from time to time, serene. I gazed at this pale-skinned, raven-haired, dark-eyed Snow White beauty, sitting, smiling, perfectly at ease. Why, oh, why, didn't we do this before, like the girlfriends we were?

Many times, we sat at my dining table, working, planning our projects, and studying. We were busy, always busy, and there never seemed to be time to just exist, to sit happily in companionable silence. It was another small regret from my time in Quebec.

My phone rang, and the spell was broken. My husband had landed, and there was now an air of expectation, rather than contentment. My friends stayed a few minutes more and then departed for the dorm at Université Laval.

John, my sweet husband, arrived eight hours later than

The Girl on the Belvedere

planned. He exited the taxi, grinning. After depositing his suitcase in the apartment, he insisted on strolling for a bit. Up to Saint John Gate we went. We turned around, passed the apartment going in the opposite direction, and walked halfway up the hill before the fatigue of travel set in and demanded that John rest.

The next day, we greeted our newly arrived friends from Oklahoma, Claire and Michael, at their hotel in the Lower Town, the *Basse-Ville*.

"The walls in this building are three feet thick," Michael exclaimed. He was an eternal student of history, and was delighted by this detail. "Where is your apartment? Do you live within the walls?" he asked.

"Yes," I said, "I live within the walls."

Later, we walked toward Saint Louis Gate, and Claire stopped at the sculptures commemorating the highly secretive meeting between Roosevelt and Churchill in 1943, during which they first discussed the planned invasion of France. "History was made here," Claire said. "This is a remarkable place, like a little Paris. I'd recommend a visit to Quebec to anyone."

In the evening, Anna and Ibrahim joined us for dinner at an Italian restaurant near my apartment. The three men—two physicians and one medical student—discussed medicine, while we three women chatted about Anna's life in Europe.

After dinner, I introduced John and our Oklahoma friends to the Upper Town, including the glorious Parliament and its adjoining park. It happened to be the night of a "super moon," which cooperated by rising in a clear sky over Saint Louis Gate. It was a photo-op made in heaven.

When we all agreed that it was getting late, Anna, Ibrahim, John, and I escorted our Oklahoma friends to one of the staircases leading to the Lower Town. Leaving them to find their way back to their hotel, the four of us walked toward Saint John Gate for our goodbyes. Anna and Ibrahim were leaving for their own vacation, a quick tour of the Northeast. It would be their first time in the United States, a true honeymoon.

As we approached the gate, I stared at Anna, trying to memorize her face.

"Oh, please don't look at me like that," she said, trying to keep the moment light. I had asked her earlier how her parting from Lucía had been the night before. "Bad," she said. "Really, really sad."

The moment arrived. How could I have known Anna for only five weeks, and Ibrahim only four? While I would stay on in Quebec with my husband and our Tulsa friends for another week, the departure of Anna and Ibrahim signaled that my journey to Quebec was ending. I was so terribly, terribly sad to see them go. We looked at each other. This energetic, educated young couple suddenly fell silent, and we embraced.

"See you later," Anna said.

"*À la prochaine,*" I responded.

And with that, they walked through Saint John Gate. There was one last turn, a final wave, and they were gone. It was over.

11

AU REVOIR

A week later, on my last evening in Quebec, John and I walked through Artillery Park, and I turned and stared at the New Barracks for the final time. It contained parts of my ancestor's history, his beginning in the New World. His story had been lost to time, but now his very distant granddaughter had uncovered it.

We watched the sunset for a moment, and realizing that the angle of the sun had begun its inevitable slide toward autumn, I said, "The sun *se couche* earlier tonight."

"Huh?" John asked.

Franglais, I discovered, just slipped out, despite my five weeks of intensive study of French. *Will I ever be able to keep these two languages straight?* I wondered for what felt like the millionth time.

The morning of my departure dawned grey, rainy, and cold. A chanting religious procession passed beneath my window, but other than that, Rue Saint-Jean was empty. We turned my keys over to the leasing agent, got in a taxi, and left *Vieux-Québec*.

The airport was, well, an airport, familiar territory, but with signage in French. My last meal in Quebec, at the airport, was an egg and grilled cheese sandwich, cooked to order, and delicious. We boarded, we taxied, we ascended. There were the deep green fields, the small villages, and the blue swimming pools dotting the suburbs. Just as we soared over the Saint Lawrence River and turned back toward Old Quebec, the plane pierced the clouds. I was on my way home.

The next day, the Oklahoma skies were clear and bright. In my pajamas, I took my coffee out to the back patio to survey my kingdom. The foliage was lush and dense; the grass a brilliant green, though a different hue from that of Quebec. The morning sun streamed across my fountain through the neighbors' magnolias and turned the clinging ivy into a gently waving pattern of light and shadow. Overhead, a half moon was suspended in the early morning brilliance.

I sat with my cup of coffee. My husband brought out the newspapers, but I could not make myself read them. Instead I grabbed my phone and chose "À nos actes manqués" from my playlist. The dog trotted up, her nose wet from seeking interlopers in the azaleas.

I thought about Quebec and what it had meant to me. My goal had been to speak French more fluently than when I arrived. Mission accomplished. But what else had I learned from the experience? I thought about Université Laval, about the *animatrices* teaching us to dance, sing, and speak casually. I thought about the forest. I thought about my morning bus, its driver, my fellow passengers. I thought about the New Barracks. I thought about Rue Saint-Jean, my apartment, the gate. I thought about my professors—Aimée, Sébastien, Emmanuelle. But mostly, I thought about my friends—Lucía, Anna, Ibrahim, Celestina.

"Zaza" started up its cha-cha on my playlist. I stood up and motioned for my husband to do the same. He did, though he raised his eyebrows. I looked down at the dog, who raised hers as well. I looked around. Hummingbirds hovered, hydrangeas bloomed, trees swayed, "Zaza" played.

And I danced.

IMMERSED IN PROVENCE

12

TRANSITIONS

After two years, I was ready to return to an immersion course. I wasn't tilting at windmills this time; I'd realized that no one wanted to hold me back. In fact, everyone offered encouragement when I mentioned that I was going, that it was time to tackle a new challenge.

This was a revelation to me. All I needed to do was state my position, and while people might have been surprised or thought privately that I was a little crazy, they accepted it, *voila*.

Quebec had changed me. I had more confidence, more belief in my own uniqueness. I had come to recognize that our differences are what give an added "*je ne sais quoi*" [a certain something] to our lives. I was anxious to experience a different culture again, to take in the colors, the scents, the quality of light, not to mention the people—always the people. I wanted to push myself further, to see more, to do more.

I was braver now in general, and just a shade less intimidated by others. I cared *less* what other people thought and *more* about who was doing the thinking. I made an effort to spend more time with people of substance and emotional stability, people who had an attitude of *joie de vivre*. I let go of people who had an agenda that went along with their friendship.

I no longer cared whether I pleased people on matters of importance to me, but I still had difficulty voicing my opinion. The lessons of my childhood remained with me: don't rock the boat, stay silent, and above all, "Be nice to everyone." Those sentiments were all rooted in fear. Even though one can decide to leave those ill-advised lessons of childhood behind, there is always room for improvement. I am a work in progress and always will be.

At Université Laval in Quebec, I had learned much, both about the French language and about the Canadian way of life. I had expanded my knowledge of French, of course, but experience had taught me that there is always more to learn. Cultural clues are not always easy to decipher, and I was quite certain that I would always make many mistakes, both in the classroom and outside of it. One thing had changed, though: I was not particularly worried about my level of French anymore. I was more relaxed and more open to the process of learning.

In the two years since Quebec, I had taken French Four, then repeated it at a different college, followed by the fifth and sixth courses. Had my French really improved all that much in Quebec? I didn't know. Local language courses are so different from immersion programs.

I had to accept a huge limitation in my quest for fluency: my life in Tulsa took place in English, except for my two French classes per week. I spoke English right up until the moment I passed through my classroom door. I switched back to English when class was over. I was pretty sure that I knew more French than I had before I went to Canada, but I wanted to find out how much more—or how much less.

I found myself being forced to consider why French was so

important to me. Why did I put myself through this difficult subject? Few people speak French here in the southwest; the Spanish culture is much more prevalent. One can hear Spanish at the mall, in the grocery stores, and certainly in the many Mexican restaurants. I rarely heard French except in my Tulsa Community College classroom or at Tulsa Ballet whenever I passed an open studio door on the way to the archives. The names of ballet steps are in French, so I heard that language whenever a ballet combination was being announced.

I still found French impossibly beautiful and I felt I had a natural talent for its accent and vocabulary. Perhaps my love of French had come down to me through a distant French grandmother who had emigrated to the United States. I grew up enjoying butter and granulated sugar on my pancakes rather than syrup, much the way the French enjoy their *crêpes*. Over time, I also realized that my Ozark family's odd way of phrasing things had a distinctly French style and cadence. Perhaps the language was simply in my blood, a part of my heritage that I wished to recover.

Regardless, it was time to continue my exploration of this language and culture, and I knew where I wanted to go for this latest experience. The course that I had chosen was in France, on the Mediterranean, much farther away than Quebec, and with fewer safety nets.

A good friend of mine had spent some time in Villefranche-sur-Mer, at the Institut de Français, one of the best French language schools in the world. She was quite fluent, and had been placed in the advanced class. She encouraged me to go, regaling me with tales of the beauty of Villefranche and the excellence of the program. *Perhaps if I go to the Institut I'll be able to speak French like her*, I thought.

Coincidentally, a dear friend invited John and me to the celebration of her recent marriage. It would take place at a luxury

The Girl on the Belvedere

hotel in Versailles, just prior to my course. How could I resist? Of course, I would go!

I wondered how on earth I had become an intrepid solo world traveler, someone who thought it would be fun to travel to France to attend a French immersion course on the Mediterranean *by myself*. When did this become normal for me? I had the passing thought that this—*this*—was what I had really gained from my time in Quebec. While I had grown up traveling, those expeditions were always chosen and planned by my father. Even as an adult my travel destinations were largely selected by the realities of my husband's profession, as our trips often coincided with medical conventions. These were sometimes in glamorous locations, but his itinerary decided so much for us. Rare were the occasions when I announced a destination to which I would lead and others would follow.

All that had changed with my adventures in Quebec. Now, I made inquiries about the Institut, decided I would go, and informed my husband. When my friend invited us to Versailles for the wedding celebration, I accepted for both of us on the spot. Happily, my husband is always up for an adventure.

He did look a little surprised when I announced that I would probably also travel to Germany to see three of my friends from Quebec— Lucía, Anna, and Ibrahim—after my French course, before returning home. We had stayed in touch via texts and photos these past two years, and we had made tentative plans to reunite in Mannheim.

That child on the Belvedere would *never* have made such an announcement. She was a "good girl," someone who accepted whatever life meted out. Thanks to her parents' emphasis on education, she knew that she had a promising future. But she was also content enough—or intimidated enough—to let that future happen, rather than chart her own course.

And now, all that had changed. From this point on, I would determine my own future, thank you very much.

13

STRUGGLES

The flight to Paris was uneventful. I eventually drifted off to sleep, and awoke somewhere over the English Channel, approaching Charles de Gaulle Airport, after a smooth flight. Thunderstorms had delayed us in Dallas. This was not an unusual occurrence in our part of the country, but I was amazed that after buckling in, settling down, and hearing the announcement of the delay, everyone on board was calm and accepting. People read, chatted, and slept. Despite the constant drone of combative reality TV and national news programming with its parade of argumentative people, we Americans are actually a well-mannered and generous nation.

My husband would be with me for the first two weeks. We would go directly to Versailles for the wedding celebration, then enjoy a week in the Loire Valley, which we had long wanted to explore. Then he would drive me to Villefranche-sur-Mer, just outside of Nice.

SECURITY WAS heavy at Versailles in the summer of 2016, which makes a certain sense in this uncertain age. The hotel itself was gated, and there were several security guards stationed at the barrier. One had a large mirror on a pole, which he used to look at the undercarriages of entering cars. There was also at least one security guard per floor in the hotel itself, guarding against the unthinkable. The Euro soccer championship was being played in France, and after the *Charlie Hebdo* attack, the Bataclan nightclub attack, and the Stade de France stadium attack, everyone was on high alert.

While we waited to check into our Versailles hotel room after our long flight, a soccer team from Northern Ireland sat down next to us. Evidently, they were staying at our hotel during the European Championship. Families stopped by to chat with the team, and children sat on the arms of chairs and sofas for their selfies with the players. My husband couldn't stop staring, and I offered to take his photo with the players. I told him to pose on the arm of the sofa like one of the children. He laughed, but declined. He has always been easily star-struck.

We were shown to our room at last, and being true Americans, we flipped on the television while we unpacked. We were greeted with terrible news from Orlando: there had been an attack on a nightclub, and many people were dead or injured. After Oklahoma City, after Boston, after San Bernardino, after Fort Hood, and certainly after 9/11, we should not have been surprised, but of course we were. We were deeply shocked.

I tore myself away from the terrible news, unpacked, and prepared to start my sojourn in France. I reminded myself that I was in France for a wedding celebration and an immersion course and that nothing should deter my joy at being back in this beautiful country. I was determined to enjoy my two weeks of vacation with my husband before he drove me to Nice and flew home. My course at the Institut was a full four weeks, and

The Girl on the Belvedere

once again, as in Quebec, I wanted to solidify and use whatever knowledge I had.

Of course, tearing myself away from the news was easier said than done. As I write this five years later, I still vividly remember the sequence of events that day: walking into the room with our bags, looking around the very French room with curved windows, glancing out the window at the sculpted green view below and at the famous chateau of Versailles itself just up the hill, and then, turning on the TV. In that moment, something about this whole trip changed.

We think we can tear ourselves away from tragedy that does not directly affect us. We think we can compartmentalize terrible news, but consciously or not, it takes a toll. That day in Versailles, that moment when I first heard about the deadly attack in Orlando, lives on in my memory. It's likely that it always will. Why is that? Why do the terrible moments remain, but not the small joys of our lives?

LATER THAT DAY, my friend Anna sent me a text from Germany regarding my travel plans after the course: "Good morning, Cheryl, hope you had a good flight! I hope that your plans for the end of July haven't changed." Her text was in English, as we had quickly given up on texting in French. English was simply easier for all of us.

"I'm still planning to visit you in Germany, as we discussed," I texted back. "However, my best friend Marjorie will be joining me. I hope that's okay! Marjorie and I have been friends since we were teenagers. She studied ballet in Cannes and has been longing to return to the Riviera. I would love to see you while I'm so close! It's been awhile since we talked, and I wasn't sure what your situation was. I didn't want to presume."

"I really hope you will still visit us next month, I don't want to miss that chance since you are so close! Will you come by train?" Anna replied.

"I'm afraid a train from Nice would take too long, and I'd rather spend the time with you. I'll start looking at flights." I was relieved that our plans to reunite were confirmed.

"Just let us know when, and we will be there," Anna said. "We look forward to getting to know Marjorie! And for now, enjoy your time in Villefranche! Our warmest hellos and hugs to John."

Lucía, my other dear friend from Quebec, was now studying German, and lived in Heidelberg, near Anna and Ibrahim, so I hoped to have the good fortune of being reunited with all three of them at the same time. It had been two years since that course in Quebec where the four of us were thick as thieves, and now, I felt the same insecurities creep back in: *I'm thirty years older than these kids. Will we regain our easy camaraderie? Or will we revert to being the strangers we once were?*

ONCE THE WEDDING celebration was over, John and I set off for our sojourn in the Loire. Then, when the time came, we turned south toward the Riviera.

We were used to driving long distances in the US, but after several hours, the driving became difficult, the mountains tall, the highway twisting, and the traffic heavy. Trucks and cars wove all around us on this busy *autoroute*, which climbed and descended the foothills of the Massif Central, the mountains in the Rhône-Alpes region of eastern France. "I must really love you," my husband said, frowning in concentration. He occasionally shook out his hands to keep them from cramping while he gripped the steering wheel.

We were already exhausted when we arrived at the turnoff for the *A8 Autoroute*, which parallels the Mediterranean Sea. We were supposed to turn in our rental car 100 miles up ahead at the Nice airport, which seemed relatively close on my GPS. However, traffic was impossibly heavy along the Côte d'Azur, the French Riviera. We struggled toward Nice in Friday-evening bumper-to-bumper traffic.

The GPS doesn't always tell the whole truth; we found the airport with no difficulty, but missed several of the turns into the rental car area. When we finally did arrive, we were driving the wrong way on a long, narrow one-way street, my husband sputtering curses.

John and I spent two days in Nice, touring, eating, relaxing, and resting. The Promenade des Anglais, the long sidewalk along the beach, was wide, and gloriously pretty with palm trees and benches. We strolled, we sat, we stopped for gelato. I slept soundly at night, trying not to think about the challenge that lay ahead. I knew that I was privileged to even have such a challenge.

On Sunday morning, still at the hotel, I received a text from Lucía.

"Hi dear!" she said, her usual greeting.

I was glad that Lucía was checking in with me; seeing her after a month of French class seemed very far in the future. I told her I was getting ready to take my apartment in Ville-franche and I would be in touch. She wished me luck at school and signed off.

I put my phone in my purse and packed my large suitcase, leaving behind a small overnight bag for my last night in Nice. We called for a taxi and gave the driver the address in Ville-franche-sur-Mer where I would pick up the keys to my apartment. Over Mont Boron—the hill that separates the city of Nice from the village of Villefranche—we went. We located the address easily, and I ran inside, leaving my husband to hold the taxi. Then, keys in hand, I gave the driver my newly acquired apartment address, and we set off to find my home for the next four weeks.

∼

IT WAS VERY dark inside the apartment when we arrived. I had requested a good view—it was the only thing I had asked for—and with high hopes, I walked over to what I imagined were the hurricane shutters I had seen frequently on the Côte d'Azur, the "azure coast." There was a button on the wall. I pressed it, and the shades rose. My husband gasped.

Below, I had a 180-degree view of the sparkling bay and the Mediterranean, framed by palm trees, cedars, and terraced hills on each side. Immediately below was the village of Villefranche, both ancient and modern, with terracotta homes and multi-story apartment buildings. We stepped out onto the balcony, stunned into silence.

"Why don't you sit and enjoy the view while I unpack," I suggested, knowing that this glimpse would be John's only chance to experience the glory of Villefranche. I would be able to sit on this balcony for hours at a time during my month here, watching the comings and goings of the sailboats, yachts, and tenders that silently whisked cruise ship passengers back and forth to the port of Villefranche. But for my husband, this was it.

I turned, went back inside and looked around. There was a small kitchen, which was open to the tiny living room, complete with a table and four chairs, a worn yellow sofa, and a TV on the wall. My bedroom had just enough space for a double bed jammed against a small window; I would need to stand to one side while opening the closet door on the other side of the bed.

I unpacked, squeezed my suitcase into the space at the foot

The Girl on the Belvedere

of the bed, and walked back into the living room, only to find my husband watching French TV. He had tuned into a sporting event, one with which he was totally unfamiliar: *pétanque*, a combination of pool, horseshoes, and lawn bowling. I had played it before and enjoyed it—the teamwork, the skill, the joy of camaraderie—but on television, it reminded me of American TV golf, with the same hushed voices, the same groups of men standing around watching little balls, the same hushed gallery that erupted into occasional applause, the same slow-motion replays showing the same throws over and over. To me, it was the French TV equivalent of watching paint dry. "*Incroyable! Magnifique!*" the announcer said.

"Why are you watching *pétanque*?" I ask, bemused.

"But these are the *masters* of *pétanque!*" my husband declared staunchly. He was evidently a new aficionado of the French national pastime.

What is it with men and sports? I wondered. *Evidently, any sport will do.* Aloud, I said, "I'll need some groceries and some water. We passed that little grocery store up above us. Shall we walk up?" I asked, diverting my husband's attention from the screen.

"Sure," he said willingly, leaving the unfamiliar game of *pétanque* behind.

Up, up, up we walked in terrific heat, only to find the store closed.

"Well," I said," at least I know the way now. I'll come back tomorrow."

On the way back down the hill to my apartment, a car passed, the driver tooting his horn and shaking his fist. I was alarmed for a moment until I saw the wide smile on his face.

"Oh!" I said. "I think France must have won the soccer match this afternoon." It reminded me of being in South Bend, Indiana, when the University of Tulsa defeated Notre Dame at football. The TU fans were jubilant, with much cheering, flag-waving, fist pumping, and horn honking. Some things are universal.

We decided to descend into the village for dinner. As we passed my new apartment along the way, I told John that I wanted to go back inside one more time, so that I could practice the complex entrance ritual: the electronic traffic gate, the building code, the tiny elevator with its outer door and inner compartment, the triple locks on my apartment door, the electronic controls to the hurricane shades. Once I had repeated everything on my own, I was ready to depart for the night, certain that I could manage everything by myself in the morning. I was so grateful to have my husband with me as I settled in. Despite my love of France, it was still a foreign country.

We continued down, down, down into the village, found a pizza restaurant, and sat outside. The restaurant, Le Serre, was not quite open yet; it was only six p.m., early by European standards, and the cooks and waitstaff were enjoying their own dinner. They brought us sparkling water to sip while we waited. After we enjoyed our pizzas, we walked through the colorful village for a bit, then found the taxi stand near the Hotel Welcome, and returned to Nice.

The next morning, my cab arrived, and I climbed in with my small bag. I waved a teary goodbye to my husband, who stood on the sidewalk and would soon catch the train to Paris for his flight home. I was sad, but pulled it together.

Class would start in one hour.

I ARRIVED at my apartment a mere fifteen minutes later; Villefranche is just a few short miles over the *colline*—the hill, or, for this girl from Oklahoma, the mountain—that separates it from Nice. I left the taxi and found my way into my apartment. When I raised the hurricane shutters, I found that a huge cruise ship was in the hazy harbor below. I immediately snapped a photo; this was certainly not a sight I saw every day on the Arkansas River.

At 8:25, I headed over to school. It was just across the street from my apartment, and was fronted by a paneled green metal fence atop a low stone wall. The tall green gate—between two stone columns, one side with a sign, security pad, and a speaker—was open, and a kindly gentleman pointed the way to a common room. I passed the wooden front door flanked by tall blue Provencal pots containing ficus trees, and walked along a stone path fronted by terra cotta jardinières with evergreens underpinned by red petunias.

At the end of the walkway, I went down some stairs and into the common area. The room was painted white, with terra-cotta-colored tile floors and a view of the sea through its many windows. There were eight tables, with eight chairs at each. The tables were pre-set with carafes of coffee and pitchers of milk, along with yogurt, bread, butter, cheese, and jam. At one end of the room were tall shelves with all manner of plates, bowls, and serving pieces. At the other end were doors to a lattice-covered patio.

I sat down next to a beautiful young blonde. We smiled at one another and were soon chatting.

"*Français? Anglais?*" I asked, wondering what language she would like to speak and not knowing whether she spoke either of the two at my disposal.

"English," she said. "My French is terrible. My name is Therese." "What's yours?"

"Cheryl," I said. "I'm from the United States. Where are you from?"

"Norway," she replied. "I teach at a university there."

We poured ourselves some *café au lait* and helped ourselves to breakfast while we chatted. Others soon joined us, introductions were made in English, and then we all fell silent, intimidated by what the day would bring.

The head of the school interrupted our collective reverie and announced that we would now take a test to assess our level in French. He spoke in English, and explained that this would be the only day we were allowed to speak anything other than French and that English was the one language that most people had in common.

Then the exam papers were handed out, and the French test began. The most difficult part for me was the listening test, which was designed to determine whether we could distinguish different sounds in French. I had a sinking feeling during this particular exam. At my age, it was becoming difficult for me to hear English, let alone to distinguish among similar-sounding words in French.

An hour later, we were instructed to go up to the Grand Salon, to await our individual oral exams. Mine went poorly, which was fine with me. I was hoping to be placed in the intermediate level so that I could fully assimilate what I already knew.

We waited in the Grand Salon for everyone to finish. It was a large, beautiful room, with huge arched windows and a pair of French doors leading out to a balcony edged with a carved marble balustrade. Gardens cascaded below us, and in the middle distance, there was the sparkling bay of Villefranche-sur-Mer, with the deep blue Mediterranean beyond Cap Ferrat. It was mesmerizing.

At last, all the tests were complete, and we were dismissed to lunch in the common room, which proved to be the first of many three-course feasts. First, there was a salad with tomato slices, corn, soft lettuce, a crispy Parmesan wafer, and an excellent vinaigrette dressing. Next came platters of roasted chicken with mushrooms, zucchini cups with carrot puree piped on top, tiny roasted fingerling potatoes, and *haricots verts*—tiny green beans—along with some buttery sauce for the chicken. For dessert, there was crème brulée. Then espresso, tea, or *café au lait*. Everything tasted fresh and real, not processed.

Lunch was followed by several hours of practical information, rules and regulations, all given in English. One man raised his hand and said he didn't understand a certain point, and the director effortlessly repeated it in German.

FINALLY, the day was over. I joined some new friends and walked up the "hill" to the grocery store at the top. I purchased some necessities—coffee, cream, lettuce, yogurt, honey, almonds, cheese, olive oil, bottles of water—and retreated down the hill to my apartment, carrying my heavy load. I had to purchase my paper grocery bags, not knowing to bring my own. Not once in this month would I remember to bring reusable bags with me. So very American.

Back home, I texted Stephanie and my daughter in law Sarah a photo of the Mediterranean taken from my *terrasse*, the balcony. "Pinch me!" I said.

I told them that the school was right across the street from my apartment on a two-lane switchback road ascending a mountain. I described my breakfast and lunch, and told the girls that both meals were provided on campus. "In the US, we talk about what we shouldn't eat, but here, they talk about what they *get* to eat. And it's very, very *biologique*—organic. What a refreshing attitude." I also gave them the bad news: if we were caught speaking anything but French, we had to pay two euros per infraction.

THE NEXT MORNING, our test results were announced. Names were called, starting with *Debutant I*, those absolutely new to the language, the true beginners. This was followed by *Debutant II* and *Intermediate I, II,* and *III*. I sat, waiting for my name to be called. It wasn't. When they announced "*Avancé I*," I thought, *Okay, here I go. I can live with Advanced One, rather than Intermediate*. But they did not call me.

Finally, the director said to the nine of us who were left, "*La Crème de la Crème, Avancé II.*"

Oh no, I thought, *Please God, no, not the highest class.* I threw a panicked look at a new acquaintance from Switzerland, Susi, who threw it right back. Her name had also been called for *Avancé II*. Lost in a fog of advanced confusion, we followed our professor, Luc, out the door of the common room, up the stairs, through a garden, and up a few more steps to a remote classroom on the grounds.

Our classroom was located on the upper level of the gardens. There was a terrace just outside the classroom surrounded by flowering shrubs. The blue bay of Villefranche sparkled far below the terrace which sported a ping-pong table that was in constant use between classes. There were matching potted trees outside the detached restroom pavilion, which had one of those graceful iron and glass awnings that the French do so well. All the doors and windows on this level had white *volets*, those marvelous louvered shutters one can close against the night or against the elements. Outside our classroom, one could hear the noise of the neighboring sprinkler systems set against the constant background din of the scooters and motorcycles going up and down the switchback avenue.

There were nine of us in the class:

Henry, the baby (the "*benjamin*") of the class, nineteen years old, brilliant, with four languages to his credit, and a student at Harvard.

William, a young investment banker from London, handsome, funny, and as unfailingly polite as any Southern gentleman.

Emily, from Seattle, a lawyer specializing in women's rights, working on yet another degree, with aspirations of eventually working in Geneva.

Susi, a dental technician, my new acquaintance from Switzerland. She was positive, mature, funny, and our beacon when the ship needed to be righted.

Neill, a retired investment banker from Edinburgh, droll, the oldest of the class, edging me out by two years, and an inveterate traveler with immense intellectual curiosity.

Fiona, from Dublin, a young film major, excited by the possibilities that stretched endlessly into the future.

Katherine, Canadian, a U.N. lawyer working in the Congo, self-described as "worn out" by its danger but exhilarated by its challenges.

Therese, the gorgeous blonde from Norway with whom I sat the first morning. In addition to being a university professor, she was also a former elite ice-skater and competitive pianist.

And Luc, our professor, who constantly cracked the whip, even on the first day. He led us through the Socratic method of learning with a dry sense of humor, and left us nowhere to hide from his incessant questioning.

In this class at the Institut, Luc's French was rapid, although he claimed that he was not speaking as rapidly as he did with his fellow Frenchmen. We were discouraged from taking notes, as this method was almost entirely oral—a departure for me and a very difficult one.

Somehow, I made it through the first day almost entirely in French. And then the second. And then, the third. I say "almost" because my *Franglais* habit persisted. At sixty-three, my vocabulary recall was slowing in English; in French, it lagged far behind.

Lunch was a little stilted in the beginning, as we had to converse entirely in French; one seat at each table was reserved for a faculty member. The first course was salad or soup, usually pre-set when we arrived. The lunch ladies would then roll in a cart with the second and third courses, one at a time, and the professor would serve, asking for our plates individually: *"Shayril"* [Cheryl], *voulez-vous des carottes? Du bœuf?"* ["Would you like some carrots? Some beef?"] And later, "Some dessert?" Finishing with, "Some coffee?"

The coffee was strong, and at lunch, I took it black, in the French manner. Lunch was late, starting at 1:15 for those of us in the advanced class, and I was mindful of the caffeine. At first, I asked for *"Un demi, s'il vous plaît,"* indicating the *demitasse* size rather than the giant cup used at breakfast for *café au lait*. After a few evenings with way too much caffeine coursing through my veins, though, I started to say, *"Un demi-demi, s'il vous plaît,"* a half *demitasse*. I had no idea whether this was a real term, but it worked.

We were finished by five, both mentally and physically. Most of us did not stay to chat; we headed to our individual apartments. When I arrived in mine, I would throw down my bag, raise the electronic shades, and immediately sit down on the balcony overlooking the harbor of Villefranche. I did not move from this spot until six, when dinner and homework beckoned. Once I completed the requisite two pages of work, I would shower, put on my pajamas, and head back out to the darkening *terrasse*.

My view of Villefranche was so beautiful that it almost defied description. I sat on the balcony every night until 9:30 or 10—at this time of year, in July, it was still twilight—and watched the waves cross the bay and gently rock the sailboats, the pleasure craft, and the yachts. The rotating lighthouse beacon intermittently reached across the harbor, but the cicadas sang constantly as the frogs commenced their nightly chorus. As it began to grow dark, the lights across the bay began to twinkle, reminding me that the day had come to an end.

I have always been in awe of summer nightscapes. I love how moonlight projects patterns through branches and leaves onto the ground below, the moon itself standing above in stark white contrast to the cerulean sky. I love the sight of white cumulus clouds scudding across navy-blue starlit heavens. I love the sound of cicadas chirping their peculiar rhythm, tree frogs adding their songs to the choir, and the whispering sigh of a hot breeze. I love the stillness, the darkness, and magic of summer. Each night, I breathed deeply, memorizing the moment, and then went inside and lowered the shades.

Every morning, we began class with a song. Luc would hand out the lyrics, and we would listen to it and then give our opinion of the song, supported by our reasons for liking it or disliking it. All in French, of course.

One day, he asked about our favorite French artists. "Jean-Jacques Goldman," I said, thinking of that marvelous song I had learned in Quebec, "Á nos actes manqués."

"Jean-Jacques Goldman?" echoed Luc, eyeing me quizzically. "That's an unusual choice." He did not explain why he thought that, and of course I was too intimated to ask him. I assumed it was because Mr. Goldman and I are roughly the same age, and the musical artists named by the other students tended to be rap artists or at least very young performers.

Some days, we were quizzed about current events. One

morning at the beginning of my first week, I said, "I heard on television that there were two hundred people killed worldwide last week by acts of terror."

"Two hundred?" asked Luc, confirming my number.

"Yes," I said, "two hundred."

He shook his head but did not comment.

A part of me wondered why I had become so fixated on terror attacks as of late. After all, my stay here in France had been so quiet, so full of joy. Was it because I was older now and more mindful of the uncertainty of life? I had children and grandchildren, after all, and each time I heard of another attack, my mind flew to those precious babies: mine—alive and healthy —and those reported as lost. I tried to put such morbid thoughts out of my mind and find more pleasant news to discuss in class.

This experience was so different from the one in Quebec. There, I had been full of personal anxiety and uncertainty. I was working hard here in France, just as I had in Quebec, but I was not so intent on *achieving*. I knew that with hard work, the knowledge would come. I was more settled here in Villefranche, more accustomed to letting my experiences influence me without thinking about *how* they should affect me. This was a very good school in a very beautiful place, and I thanked the heavens each day for the agreeable circumstances that had led me here.

All day long, no language other than French was allowed. We constantly greeted one another with, "*Bonjour, ça va?*" ["Hello, how's it going?"] Even the Level One beginners picked up the phrase quickly, and greeted everyone accordingly.

During breaks, students checked their cell phones quietly, or studied the latest handout. Sometimes I simply sat and looked at the bay, or walked along the garden paths, glancing at the flowers, the palm trees, the cedars.

I heard the constant hooting of an owl, both at school and

above my apartment. The birds set their alarms for five a.m.—well before sunrise—and did not quiet until well after dark, when the swifts made their nightly swoops and the doves cooed.

My mornings began to take on a rhythm. I could hear other people's electronic *volets* being raised near me as I raised my own. The cool fresh air came rushing in as I sipped my coffee while seated on my yoga mat, relaxing more than stretching. The sun, barely visible at this point, illuminated only the ships far out to sea, plus a few of the hilltop houses that dotted Cap Ferrat across the bay.

ON ONE MORNING during this first week, a dove landed on the very top of a fir near my balcony, cooing incessantly. The church bell in the village below chimed seven. It was time to rise from my yoga mat and start the day.

I flipped on the TV to catch any last-minute news items for the "current events" discussion in class. There was nothing noteworthy, except for a commercial for *Krave* cereal by Kellogg. It featured a pole-dancing piece of cereal dressed only in a red thong. She—he?—captured the audience of chocolate squares, using a straw to slurp them up. *Voila,* the cereal was now chocolate-flavored! I was pretty sure that I would not be reporting on this pole-dancing cereal in class, nor did I expect to see this particular commercial at home. It was *way* too French.

On Tuesday night of this first week I had to make the trip up to the Casino Shop to buy the groceries I had forgotten the evening before. I walked, of course, and met my new friend Suzi outside her apartment along the way. She was kind enough to carry my four large water bottles back down as far as her apartment. What a genuinely nice person.

I later pointed out to Stephanie some details of the photos I had sent her earlier: the olive grove beneath my balcony, the Rothschild Villa across the bay, and Cap Ferrat, the peninsula that literally is the end of the Alps where they plunge into the sea. I also complained to her that English was never allowed, not even at lunch—a professor sat at each table and led the conversation.

On Wednesday evening, I decided to go down into the village and was almost hit by a scooter in doing so. I was crossing a street when the scooter roared around a blind corner, missing me by inches. I continued my way down into the village, intending to go all the way to the harbor, but I only made it halfway before realizing that if I went all the way down, I would have to climb all the way back up. It was just too daunting, and I was just too tired. I reluctantly made my way home, realizing that I would not be going for long walks every night as I did in Quebec.

When I got back to "Scooter Corner," where I was almost run down, I paused for a few minutes and determined the safest crossing pattern. It was an intersection where three sides stopped and the fourth did not. *Kitty-cornered*, I decided, *is the safest way to go. And at a jog.*

That first Thursday night, we went on a coastline cruise to Monte Carlo, in Monaco. I had not been there for more than a decade, and was happy to see the Casino and the Opéra de Monte Carlo, which share the same beautiful building. I had researched the life of Mr. Jasinski there, and my co-author Georgia and I have many happy memories from that trip. I was frankly amazed to be back once again, if only on the harbor side, gazing up at this famous building.

"I did some research in the Casino a long time ago," I mentioned casually to the professor who had accompanied us.

"Really?" he said. "On what?"

"Ballet history."

He nodded. "I thought you were a dancer. You walk like a duck."

I chuckled to myself and shook my head. Even fifty years later, I evidently still walk with a pronounced turnout. I gave up caring long ago.

As I gawked at a huge yacht carrying a helicopter in the Monte Carlo harbor, it began to rain. I scurried inside, and watched the coastline fly by through my window as the captain gunned the engine and hightailed it back to Villefranche.

It was pouring by the time we stepped off the boat and onto the quay, and Susi offered me her umbrella for the steep ascent back to my apartment. "I have an extra," she said. "I have this one, but my husband has two. He's joining me for dinner in the village."

I trudged back up the hill, getting soaked in spite of Susi's umbrella and prayed that I would not be struck by lightning.

The next night, Friday, there was a dance at the Institut.

"Are you going?" I asked Susi during a break that day.

"I think so," she said. "We may as well. We're here." She shrugged.

"Okay," I said. "I'll go if you go."

"I've taken Salsa lessons," she said. "So why not?"

We met outside the school at the appointed hour, punched in the code, opened the gate, and descended the few steps to the villa that served as the school. There was a veritable feast set up for us in the common room: beautiful salads, platters of meats and cheeses, savory *tartes*, and mounds of tiny desserts.

Soon, the dancing began. Susi was proficient in Salsa, and I could fake it after all my years of training. We laughed and acted like the kids we once were; gone was the hesitancy that marked my presence in Quebec. I danced full out, with joy, "like no one is watching" as they say.

I noticed that some people around the room were indeed

watching me dance. I didn't care. I just wanted to *move*. I danced the salsa, the cha-cha, the twist, whatever and however I wanted. I laughed with Susi the entire time, and again, I thought that this—*this*—was what I had learned in Quebec. I had lost my inertness, my time as a stone statue on the sidelines. That young child who had been embarrassed to be heard singing, who had burned with shame when she made a mistake in ballet class, was now fully present in this moment, and loving it. She was growing up.

The DJ announced a game of freeze, where we danced until ordered to stop, changing partners all the while. I was happily dancing with a young man from China when an older middle-aged student bumped my partner out of the way during a freeze, thereby disqualifying all three of us.

"Who *is* that guy?" I wondered out loud, annoyed.

"Oh, he's an American," Susi said, having attended a previous session, and knowing all the gossip. "This is his fourth summer at the Institut, and he really likes the young ladies. They call him "The Playboy."

I was hardly young, but I supposed I should be flattered, even though I was actually rather miffed at being disqualified through no fault of my own.

We stayed to observe a game of musical chairs, and then Susi and I danced our way out of the room, backwards, laughing and giggling like schoolgirls. Our first week was finally over.

The next morning, Saturday, there was a tour of the village. I walked down to the market, which was in full swing, to meet the group. We gathered in front of the tourist bureau and walked down to the old fort, the Citadelle, where we divided ourselves into two groups—those who wished to hear the tour in English, and those who wished to hear it in French. I chose French, and was very pleased that I was able to follow it quite easily. It was a real change from two years before in Quebec.

We followed our guide around the small town and ended up at the village church. Afterward, I mentioned to a few classmates that it might be fun to grab some lunch together, and off we went back down to the seaside, to a restaurant that would become a bit of a hangout. I ordered an omelet, which was excellent, but I was surrounded by five women eating *moules*—mussels. To this Oklahoma girl from the land of hamburgers and barbecue, the briny smell was overpowering. The others were in heaven with their *moules*, but it is one delicacy for which I would never acquire a taste. After lunch, I walked up, up, up to my apartment and slept the entire afternoon.

Upon awakening, I found that I had received a text message from Anna, in Germany: "Hi, Cheryl, how are you doing? Did you already look for a flight to Germany?"

"*Oui*," I responded. "I've looked at flights, and there are some good ones, but before I book, I want to make sure that this is absolutely okay with you. This is your vacation, and I want you to spend it in the absolute best way."

"Sure, I want you to come!" Anna replied. "I'm taking my vacation that week because you are coming and I'm looking forward to seeing you!"

"Okay!" I said. "I'll try to book tomorrow. Can't wait!"

I sat on my balcony that shimmering evening, gazing at the hillside town, at the infinitely blue Mediterranean, and at the azure sky, wondering how the Americans in the Sixth Fleet felt when this was their home port in the mid-twentieth century. When it grew dark, I went inside and lowered the electronic shades just enough to give me privacy while still allowing fresh air to flow through the tiny slats.

Late that night, I was awoken by someone pounding on my door, screaming. I knew no one in this building, so who could it be? I ran to the door, and looked through the small viewing lens, but there was no one there. The sound of shattering glass frightened me, but still, I saw nothing. Then there was more shouting. Finally, I saw the source of all this commotion: a young man was pounding on the door across and down the hall, almost obscured by the elevator. He was answered by the muffled voice of a frightened-sounding young woman inside the apartment.

The young man's voice receded, and I realized with a start that he must have opened a window to the wide ledge that ran alongside the entire building: both the stairs and the elevator were in front of me, and he had taken neither. I rushed to my bedroom, heart pounding, crawled over the bed, and shut the window. I could hear him out on the ledge, not far away. Suddenly, everything went quiet. *Did he climb into her apartment? Did he fall?* I stayed awake for a long time, but heard nothing more.

The next morning, Sunday, I heard a knocking on the young woman's door, but this time, there were men shouting, "*Sécurité!*" The woman did not open the door, but she did conduct a teary-sounding conversation with them, too rapid and too muffled for me to understand.

Later, as I exited to go to the grocery store, I peered around the corner of the elevator. Next to her door was a large framed panel, once made of glass, and now covered in plywood after the young man had broken it. All seemed calm, but I was still wary and looked around before calling the elevator, afraid that the screaming young man would reappear.

I trudged up the mountain to the Casino store, as I was already out of everything. I was worn out from the week and would soon learn to do my shopping on Saturday so that I could rest all day Sunday.

That evening, on my *terrasse*, I regarded the Mediterranean, resplendent in its bluest blue. The village lights below me and the string-of-pearl lights along Cap Ferrat gave off a golden glow, their reflection wavering in the bay. The old houses glowed terra cotta, reflecting the sun's fading light as well as the incandescence of the village. A crescent moon rose over the ancient fort high above me to the right. Its walls seemed to be lit as if by magic, golden against the fading blue sky. A cruise ship, illuminated with strings of white lights, silently glided across the mouth of the bay, slipping out of sight on its way past Nice to an unknown destination. I hoped that those on the ship were enjoying their cruise, but I would not trade places with them for anything. I loved this *terrasse*, that sea, this view, that sky. I wished that I had a month of Sunday evenings instead of just three.

14

CHALLENGES

The second week was much like the first. Each day began with a challenging morning without note-taking, which made studying in the evening very difficult. I could never remember what we had studied or the answers I was supposed to give to Luc's incessant questioning. I came to dread the oral quiz we took every morning.

Each day, around 11:30, Luc gave us our guide sheet for the language lab. We would go over it and practice a few examples: verb tense piled upon verb tense, pronoun upon pronoun, noun upon noun. I could do this with ease on paper, but in this totally oral language lab, I was completely lost.

Most days, I wondered, *What on earth am I doing here? I'm way too old to hear something one morning and remember it the next. Why don't they let me write it down so that I can at least study it at night?* I was beginning to doubt that I had made any progress at all in Quebec or in the years since. I definitely thought that I was in the wrong class. The shame of my childhood came flooding back when I couldn't keep up. Sometimes, a question asked of me made total sense, and I could formulate the correct answer. During those brief moments, I was on top of the world. But I quickly realized that most of my classmates were much more fluent than I. And much younger.

Lunch was always welcome, though afterward, I found that I sometimes wanted to skip the practical class, where we discussed daily interactions. Unhappily, I sometimes have migraines, and I would have more during this four-week period than at any other time in my life. The intense mornings of oral work, followed by the incomprehensible oral lab, wore me out, every single day. When a migraine threatened, I just wanted to sit outside and write, which relaxed me. I found that the rest of the day went very well for me if I could just sit quietly for a time on such days.

On the second Tuesday evening of my session, the school had dinner at Le Serre, that wonderful pizza restaurant where John and I had dinner the night before his departure. Susi and I sat with a couple from Nigeria who were moving to the Ivory Coast, or Côte d'Ivoire. The wife was in the classroom next to mine, and I had visited with her over lunch several times. Her husband was a banker and always on his phone during breaks. He was in *Débutant I,* for absolute beginners, trying to learn some French before taking up his new job. It was obvious that he and the other beginners were making progress in this intense school. He listened attentively, and while he did not have the ability to communicate at our level, he clearly understood most of what we were saying.

On Wednesday, I sat outside near the lower gardens during a break, looking out at the bay and the Mediterranean beyond, which was a blinding blue. Each level of the garden contained lavender, roses, geraniums, and flowering herbs. A slight breeze ruffled the evergreens in the *Provençal* pots and the roses flanking the villa's back doors. Lazy bees buzzed among the lavender, whose scent reached me across the walkway. I could hear the cicadas making their lovely sound, reminding me of high summer at home. There was a stone water fountain with a spigot against the wall in this lower garden, where one could fill a bottle with cool water.

A young professor, Chloé, stopped to visit with me and asked what I was writing. I told her that I was working on a book. I was a little surprised at how rapidly the words tumbled from my mouth, how rapidly I was able to speak. It was a definite change. *Perhaps I'm learning something after all!* I thought. *I completely understand her, and she understands me!*

We agreed—Chloé was also a writer—that it was easier to write when the muse was present, and that the muse was always present here in beautiful Villefranche-sur-Mer. The gardens, the breeze, the scents, the sea—every aspect was inspiring. And it was so gratifying to have a relaxed, easy, fluid conversation with someone in French. I had not been able to do that in Quebec.

On Thursday, the locals were abuzz. France would be playing Germany in soccer that evening, and everyone was talking about it. *Allez les Bleus!"* [Go Blues!] we called to each other all day.

I watched the televised match. France won, and the village below erupted in honking, screaming, and blaring music. The next morning, everyone was smiling...except for one of the young professors, a favorite, who had a hangover and was not able to report to work until the afternoon.

This week, it was business as usual in class, with a single addition: we were each required to give an *exposé* [report]. It would last twenty-to-thirty minutes and had to be done without reading, and with minimal notes. William, the banker from London, was chosen to go first, and he spoke about Brexit. The referendum had just occurred, and he was very worried about his professional and financial future. Therese talked about Norway; Susi, about Switzerland; and on it went.

On Friday, during the last period of the day, it was my turn to give an *exposé*. Most of my classmates assumed I would talk about ballet, but no. I was going to speak on "the Tornadoes of Oklahoma." I drew a regional map of Tornado Alley on the dry-erase board. I gave them a quick lay-person science lesson about the causes of tornadoes. I showed them photos of tornadoes on my phone. And I shared two personal experiences with tornadoes—one humorous, the other more serious.

When I was through, my classmates had many questions. Fiona, the girl from Ireland, asked, "Why would anyone want to live there?"

I must have scared them, so I rushed to reassure them that tornadoes are very rare. At any rate, I was glad to have this task behind me.

On my way out the door, Professor Luc said, "Very good report."

Susi and I dragged ourselves out of the villa grounds, exhausted after our second week of school.

"What are you doing tonight?" I asked.

"Nothing," she replied.

"*Moi non plus*"—me neither—I said. "Want to go down to the village for dinner? It's Friday, and I don't want another plain salad at home."

"Sure!" she said. "Let me change, and I'll meet you at your apartment gate in forty-five minutes."

"*Parfait!*" [Perfect!] I replied.

At my apartment building, I held my electronic key up to the keypad at the large traffic gate, but nothing happened. I tried again. Nothing. I started to panic. This was the start of a three-day weekend, a short respite from school, and I couldn't access my apartment. If it were just for one night, I wouldn't have worried; I'd have simply waited for a car to enter, walked through with the driver, passed the evening in my apartment, and let the school handle it the next day. That, however, was impossible; I would need to go in and out of this gate many times over the next three days.

I rushed back to school and was relieved to find the director still there. I explained the situation, and he gave me another key. Back I went to my gate, but again, nothing happened. I returned to school, and this time the director came with me. Still nothing.

As we stood there, a car arrived, and a young man emerged from it. He saw our predicament, walked to the far end of the gate, reached through, released something, and manually opened the large gate. "This happens every so often," he told us in French, "and you can either open it by hand or wait about twenty minutes for it to reset."

I thanked the director and walked into my complex with this young apartment-dweller. He turned into my building with me, used his own passkey, and opened the door for me. "You're at the school," he observed while calling the elevator, "and I'm guessing you're on my floor, three?"

"*Oui,*" I told him, "*le troisième étage.*"

We exited the elevator on our floor, and to my surprise, he said *"Bonsoir,"* while opening the door across the hall. Evidently, this was the door-pounding, glass-shattering, ledge-climbing, screaming drunk from last weekend. He was now perfectly sober, perfectly polite.

Susi and I walked down to the waterfront, with no specific destination in mind. We came across half our class seated along the water at the bar of the Hotel Welcome. They waved us over, and a new tradition was born.

After drinks on the harbor, we walked up to the pizza restaurant, Le Serre. We took a long table—there must have been ten or twelve of us—and squeezed in together. I was so happy in this moment. I was here with friends from England, Scotland, Switzerland, Ireland, Canada, and the United States.

I was talking animatedly at one point and accidentally flung my fork to the floor. There was no hope of retrieving it—I was wedged into the middle of the group against the wall—and I looked up, hoping to catch the eye of a server.

"What do you need, Cheryl?" kind William, from England, asked. "A fork? I'll get you one." He immediately hopped up, without my having to say a word.

I wish I had been the kind of person that night who deserved his kindness.

Sometimes, the weakest part of one's character surfaces when one least expects it. My long battle with cynicism-disguised-as-humor erupted at this dinner, and I regret it still.

I thought I was saying something funny, but while it was a quick comeback to another's comment, it was unkind. I saw the look on my classmate's face, and hastened to apologize and say that it was a joke, but it stung him nonetheless.

I had learned cynicism from my father, but that was no excuse. *I, and I alone, am responsible for my behavior. I am an adult. Why can't I act like one?* The recipient of my comment may have long since forgotten the incident, but I cannot. It lives on in my memory, and I cannot think about this nice person without remembering the shame I felt in that moment. And this was *real* shame for saying something so unkind.

Later, as I walked up the mountain with my friends, I was concentrating so hard on this seemingly impossible climb that I didn't stop to reflect until later what had transpired. It had been a joyous evening with new-found friends, though marred by two wounds—one self-inflicted and, most unhappily, one inflicted upon another.

Once home, I heard on the French evening news that there had been an attack on the American police in Dallas. I wasn't sure which country was more unsettled at the moment: the US with its constant conflicts, or this country with its multiple terrorist attacks in one year.

In light of the distant American news, I felt very safe in France and very far removed from the turmoil of the United States. There was a large police presence here, which was only heightened by the occurrence of the European Championship in soccer. I was curious as to what I would find when I visited my friends in Germany.

My family had been worried about me traveling in Europe by myself, but now so much of the violence on the news was occurring in the United States, not in France. In truth, there had been a constant drone of violence in the United States over the last twenty years: school shootings, movie theater shootings, mall shootings, and religiously motivated terrorism. To me, it was all terrorism. Hate is hate, no matter what the supposed source of discontent.

I should have been deliriously happy. I was in France, I had an apartment on the Mediterranean, and it was high summer in an area known for beautiful weather. And yet, I was periodically gripped by fear. I was afraid—unreasonably—that I would be killed by an act of terror while in Europe.

I call my fear "unreasonable" because I had looked at the statistics. There are so many more causes of death all around us —car accidents, falling off ladders, slipping on ice during the winter, the many natural causes associated with old age—other than terrorism. Before I left the United States, I heard a report on the radio that during the summer, ten people would be killed every day by inattentive drivers texting or talking on their cell phones. That's almost one thousand Americans in a single summer. So why did I feel as though there was a target on my back? It was illogical, but I suppose that one of the facets of terrorism is surprise and shock. Or perhaps my fear was simply

The Girl on the Belvedere

a deep-seated holdover from the fear from my childhood—that general malaise, that uneasiness, that suspicion that the other shoe was always about to drop.

Yet, in spite of my unreasonable and illogical fears, I was actually very happy here. The sun, the cuisine, my friends, and the marvelous views of the Mediterranean all brought me such joy and peace. I was living a fantasy life, and I was trying to memorize every moment of it.

THE NEXT MORNING, Saturday, I met Susi in front of my apartment for our trek down to the village. We were meeting Katherine and Emily at the train station. I was anxious to see the station; I'd only seen it from a distance. It hovered above the beach, just under the road to Monte Carlo, with purple shrubs spilling from its old stone walls.

To my surprise, up close, it was quite worn-looking. It needed a fresh coat of paint and had just two machines to dispense tickets. Susi was kind enough to buy my round-trip ticket, as she could see that I was hopelessly confused by the machine. We were going to Antibes, an ancient fortified city an hour away by train.

At school, we had been instructed to not speak French this weekend and to just relax. Now, I found that I was speaking English the way I probably spoke French, saying things like, "I think maybe she go to Antibes with us?" "What time the train is coming?" "I have hunger now for breakfast." *What is going on here?* I wondered. *I know that language constantly seeks to become shorter and more direct, but must I go backward in my own tongue?*

The day was extremely hot and very bright, and soon, we were seeking out a café in the Antibes village center. Afterward, we found our way to the covered food market and tried some *socca*, the famous chickpea flatbread baked in a wood-fired oven right in front of us. We bought olives, spices, and dried fruit. The fruit vendor kept talking, talking, talking, while adding more dried cantaloupe to the bag on the scale, perhaps thinking that we wouldn't notice.

Susi spied some beautifully ripened local cherries. She told the vendor—in very good French—that she would like to buy a carton.

He silently handed her a cherry to sample.

Maybe he didn't understand her, I thought. *She wants to buy an entire carton.*

She said, "*Merci*," and then repeated, "I would like to buy a carton."

He definitely heard her that time, I thought.

He handed her another sample.

She stated again, louder this time, "I would like to buy a carton."

He gave her a third sample, without speaking.

Is he hiding something? I wondered. *He had to have heard her that time.*

The elegant Frenchwoman standing next to Susi said, "SHE WOULD LIKE TO BUY ONE OF THESE," as she picked up a carton and banged it down on the counter.

The vendor placed the carton on the scale. "Twenty-six euros," he said. Seeing the shocked look on Susi's face, he said, "I told you."

What?

Silently, with a look of disbelief, Susi handed over the money.

We never did figure out what was going on with that vendor. Could he tell that she was not a native speaker? Did he just want to wear her down so that he could overcharge her? If so, it worked. Perhaps there was a cultural clue we were all missing?

We would never know. But for the rest of the afternoon, Susi laughingly asked us, "Who would like a cherry? They were only twenty-six euros."

We lingered over lunch for two hours, enjoying our various courses. I tried a dessert I'd read about, but never made at home: *Île Flottante*, or Floating Island. Soft clouds of meringue rested in caramel sauce and were topped with ice cream, and I was greedy in my enjoyment.

We wandered into Librairie Masséna, a branch of the Nice bookstore Professor Luc had told us about. We flowed in and out of boutiques. I purchased sandals and a navy and white striped dress, while my friends bought linen dresses and similar sandals.

One train ride later, we descended back in Villefranche. We stopped in a small grocery store for supplies and yet more bottles of water, before sharing a taxi to our apartments at the top of the "hill."

On Sunday morning, I sat on the *terrasse* in my pajamas with the sun shining on my shoulders and savored my coffee with rich French cream. I looked around and surveyed my temporary home. The bay of Villefranche sparkled below me, full of sailboats, yachts, and pleasure crafts. The Mediterranean lay just on the other side of that verdant spit of land known as Cap Ferrat. A large ship of some kind traversed the path of the sun as it exited the distant port of Monte Carlo, a black shadow against the shining pathway. There was a light breeze. I could hear the constant call of doves above the roar of the scooters and motorcycles climbing and descending my switchback road.

This Sunday, I did not venture out. It was a real relief to forgo makeup and obligations, and just enjoy a quiet day to *faire la lessive*—do the laundry—study, and reflect.

I hung my wet clothes on the drying rack on the balcony, knowing that they would carry the scent of sunshine once dry. It reminded me of the clothing of my youth, when my mother would hang the wash on the clothesline near her lilacs and hydrangeas, under the clear blue skies of Oklahoma.

Sitting here in Villefranche a lifetime later, I vowed to purchase a drying rack at home to use on my patio in the abundant sunshine. I wanted to scent my clothing with something natural, rather than artificial.

ON THIS NIGHT, France was playing Portugal in the Euro 2016 soccer final. The sounds of honking and screaming drifted up from the village below. Someone nearby alternately played fragments of a tune on his trumpet, then tooted it in joy, like a car horn. As game time approached, the noise from the village intensified, while out on the deep harbor of Villefranche, all was calm. Most of the weekend sailboats had departed.

Here is an image from that night that has stayed with me: The red moon rises far out on the Mediterranean, and the river of shimmering rouge races toward me across the sea, over Cap Ferrat, and across the bay of Villefranche.

I stared at this amazing sight as the evening deepened—captivated, immobilized, and stunned—until water and sky were inky blue. The now-white moonlit path across the water was broken only by the lights on the cape and the boats moored in the bay. I wanted to sit there all night, but I had school early in the morning. I took one last look at the magnificent view spread below me and glanced far out to sea, committing this starlit night to memory. Reluctantly, I went inside and lowered the shades.

By now, I knew that France had lost the final soccer match; nothing drifted up from the village. There were no cheers, no horns, no trumpets.

15

TRAGEDY

The next day, Monday, the third of the session, was a day off for the entire school, a break from classes. Instead, we had the option of traveling by bus to St. Paul de Vence, a cobblestoned *village perché*, a perched village, sitting high above Nice, filled with shops and restaurants. Once there, I immediately spotted a large canvas bag and handed over my credit card, the whole time chatting with the owner and answering her questions about the Institut de Français. Susi found a *crêperie* with delicious selections perfect for lunch. Back on the bus, we made our way to the Matisse Chapel in Vence, the artist's homage to his newly discovered faith. We finished our day at Tourrettes-sur-Loup, an austere but architecturally lovely perched village. Susi and I left the walking tour as she had been hit with a migraine, the unhappy affliction that we shared. We sat in the shade of a large tree in the town square and enjoyed our cool drinks.

On the way home, I sat behind Chloé, the young professor who was also a writer. Looking out the window, I thought about the many books I had read on the occupation of France during

World War II. I asked Chloé about Provence during the war, and she explained that while it was within the Non-Occupied Zone, it was also the center of the Resistance. One of the reasons why the Nazis eventually occupied Vichy France was to snuff out those actively opposing them. I brought up the subject of the *"collaboration horizontale,"* the accusation against the women who had consorted with the Nazis. I'd read that many of them were actually working for the Resistance, relaying pillow talk to their cells, and the professor confirmed it.

"If I had been alive at that time, with children," I said, "and my husband was a prisoner of war or away fighting or dead, I don't know what I would have done."

We both fell silent.

As I watched the hills of Provence fly by, I thought about it. Would I have stood by and watched my children starve? Would I have "collaborated" to save their lives? I will never know, but I do know this: none of us can say for sure what we would do until we are actually placed in that situation. Judging others is easy. It's difficult to comprehend all that France had endured during the last century, or know how we would have reacted, had we been there.

Once back in Villefranche, Susi and I ventured into Picard, the frozen food emporium. This was nothing like the frozen food sections in grocery stores at home. Here one could find crispy croissants and coffee éclairs, chicken Kiev and exquisitely prepared vegetables. Susi and I wandered the aisles and picked up a few items to get us through the rest of the week. Then we headed into the Petit Casino grocery store next door for more water before sharing a taxi to our respective apartments at the top of the hill.

Tuesday found me waiting outside my classroom in the shade of an oleander, surrounded by begonias and geraniums, with the intoxicating rose-like scent of plumeria floating by.

These terraced gardens were a marvel to me. They were private, scented, heavy with bloom, and a delightful respite from the unrelenting sun of Provence. They cascaded down the hill from the villa that serves as the school, with benches and chairs interspersed among the plantings. As much as I love Oklahoma, it was these gardens that I would think about during the dark days of January, while staring across a parking lot at other downtown buildings from my classroom window in Tulsa.

I LOST my temper one day, which was highly unusual for me, when one of my classmates gave a very biased political report on capital punishment and directly criticized Oklahoma's policies. I certainly don't mind if people have diverse opinions—we are all different—but criticism of my state, from a non-American, I would not tolerate.

My classmate had started the argument right after introducing her topic with a pitying face, saying, *"Je suis desolée, Cheryl, mais Oklahoma..."* ["I'm sorry, Cheryl, but Oklahoma..."]

I startled the class by yelling in response, *"Je ne suis pas desolée! Je ne suis pas desolée!"* ["I am not sorry! I am not sorry!"] All of my queenly ballet training, with my ramrod-straight back and my chin in the air, was on view as I looked down at her over my long nose.

The room grew very still as I explained, loudly and with passion, still sitting up very straight, with hauteur, why I felt the way I did about the policy of my state—the bombing of the Oklahoma City Federal Building, which killed 168 people. I have mixed feelings about capital punishment, but I was deeply shocked and very disappointed that a classmate would turn her *exposé* into a personal attack.

Maybe it was a blessing that I lost my temper. For too many

years, I had remained silent and avoided conflict, even while I raged inside. I had always buried my true feelings just as deeply and as imperfectly as the Belvedere was buried. *Maybe I ought to lose my temper a little more often*, I thought. *I've had enough of fearing what others might think.*

After class, Susi and I walked out together. Once we were clear of the gate, I turned to her, and asked, "What just happened back there?"

"It's over," she said. "The argument is over. She was very condescending to you, and that was very rude. It's over," she said, trying to calm me.

"It's not like me to get angry," I said.

"I know," she said. "Try to forget it."

But I could not. In fact, I've thought about this incident a great deal since.

It was wrong of my classmate to insult my home state and wrong to be so condescending toward me. That is not how friends behave, nor is it the way colleagues should behave. It was the antithesis of graciousness. That clearly was her problem, not mine. I have since learned to use the phrase "That makes me very angry," in a calm, modulated voice instead of exploding. It is a definite change from the child who was brought up to just accept whatever was dished out to her.

THAT NIGHT, July 13, I was looking forward to the planned fireworks over the harbor. The next day was Bastille Day, and there would be a local celebration on this evening with an illuminated boat parade, followed by fireworks. The larger celebration would be the next night, in neighboring Nice.

"Are you going down to the village to see it closer?" texted Susi.

"No, I *van* see it *fromage* here," I texted back, before realizing that my cell phone's autocorrect was set to French. "Oops!"

"Hahaha," Susi replied. "Then I will watch it from here."

"I'm looking at the people up above me, near you," I said, "and they all have friends over, with cookouts and music. I guess no one but us is working tomorrow. Isn't Bastille Day a national holiday?"

"Yes," Susi said, "but I'm going to do my homework anyway."

"Me too."

I glanced down at my homework. I had purchased some pens with erasers from the grocery store the evening before, but I was quickly realizing that the erasers didn't actually work. When I erased, it just made holes in the paper. I took a photo of my destroyed homework and texted it to her, commenting on the quality of the eraser.

"Oops!" replied Susi. "Yes, that really doesn't work."

"The sheet without holes is really difficult," I said, referring to our homework on the dreaded subjunctive tense. "Maybe I should add a few holes to it."

"No! No more!" Susi texted back.

"I need to reread that pen packaging. It probably says, 'If you get something wrong, make a hole,'" I quipped.

As the evening wore on, absolutely nothing happened down on the harbor. At 9:30 Susi and I agreed that neither the boat parade nor the fireworks were going to happen. We found out the next day that they had been cancelled due to high winds.

On the next evening, Bastille Day, the national holiday of France, we had a school-sponsored dinner at La Belle Étoile down in the village. It was a convivial evening, in an elegant restaurant decorated in all-white. If I leaned forward across the table and looked out the door and down the cascading street, I could see almost all the way to the harbor. Shortly after dark, I heard the initial *thud* of the *feu d'artifice* [fireworks]. I looked toward the harbor, hoping to see them since they had been cancelled the night before. Nothing. "Those are the fireworks in Nice," my classmate Katherine said.

After dinner, safely ensconced in my apartment for the night, I turned on my phone's Wi-Fi and received a text from Stephanie in New York: "Are you at home?"

"Yes," I replied. "Why?"

"I just wanted to be sure," she said. "I just saw a CNN alert that there was some kind of truck accident in Nice."

"I'm fine," I texted back, "and I'm in for the night, don't worry."

"Okay, 'night. Love you," she said as she signed off.

That's odd, I thought. *Why would someone report on an ordinary truck accident in Nice, halfway around the world?* I turned on the television, and was confronted with the horrific images from the live local coverage: "*Attentat à Nice*," the chyron proclaimed. "Attack in Nice." *Oh, no*, I thought. *No, no, no, no, no.*

A terrorist had plowed his truck through the holiday spectators who had been watching fireworks on the Promenade des Anglais, the beautiful miles-long seaside boardwalk, shooting a gun out the window as he ran over individuals. There were reports that he had actively targeted women and children. There were images of the body-strewn Promenade, and the truck's bullet-ridden windshield. It was obvious from the security personnel guarding the halted truck that the attacker was most likely dead. The mayor of Nice was telling everyone to go home, lock the doors, stay inside, shelter in place. No one knew whether this was an isolated incident, or whether there were more terror attacks to come, like the multiple coordinated attacks in Paris the previous November. Confusion reigned.

I texted my daughter again. "Steph, it was an attack. It seems to be over. Many people are dead and wounded. They are using the word *douzaines*—dozens. That's all I know."

Within minutes, my phone rang; it was my husband. He was horrified by the news, by the proximity, yet also relieved that I was several miles away. "Do you want me to come get you?" he asked.

"No, I'm fine," I assured him, "and you've seen my school. It's just across the street. I'll be safe here."

Next, I texted my son, the most practical member of my family. "Hey, Ben, it looks like there has been an attack over the mountain at Nice. Not much information yet. Just wanted you to know I'm fine and locked into my apartment for the night."

"Okay. How many miles away?" he asked.

"Only three or four. I'm over a mountain," I responded, "in the next bay over, a small town."

"What's the name of it?" he asked.

"Villefranche," I replied.

"I would definitely stay there until it calms down," he advised.

He called soon after, now watching the news online. He expressed his concern and wanted to make certain that I was secure for the night. "Stay safe," he said as he signed off.

I stayed up for another hour, watching the horror unfold from the safety of my living room. There were many first-person accounts from stunned witnesses and scenes of distressed survivors sitting next to deceased persons lying on the ground, now covered with blankets. There were also stories of incredible bravery, such as the heroic man who chased the truck on his motorcycle, pulled up alongside it, threw his bike under the wheels while climbing up onto the running board, and repeatedly punched the terrorist in the head before the driver hit him with the butt of his gun, knocking him from the truck and injuring him. Finally, I could take no more, and decided to try to get some sleep. Before I turned off the light, I wrote in my journal, "Attack over the mountain at Nice."

The next morning, I turned on the television to find that the reported death toll was forty-two. I sat on my balcony, and there was an eerie silence—no scooters, no sirens, no motorcycles, no traffic, no noise floating up from the village. The day dawned bright blue, with a sparkling bay and a brilliant sea beyond, as though nothing had happened. The sky was cloudless, with a cool fresh breeze belying the heaviness that had settled upon this beautiful land. I saw a woman walking down the hill, and I could clearly hear the slap-slap-slap of her flip-flops. Her tread was heavy.

Anna texted me from Germany: "Good morning, Cheryl. I heard about the terrible things that happened in Nice. Are you okay?"

"All is well," I assured her. "I'm on the other side of the mountain from Nice. Terrible, terrible. What is happening to this world? Terrible." I seemed to be at a loss for words other than *terrible*.

"Yes...terrible. But good to know that you are safe," she said.

At school, a teacher greeted me with a list in his hand. He asked my name, and marked me off his list. Apparently, the school had been receiving panicked calls from families. For those of us in Provence, the attack had occurred rather late at night, and many of my friends had silenced their cellphones and gone to bed, unaware. My European classmates had been receiving calls from their families early this morning as they woke up to the tragedy. But for those of us from North and South America, it occurred in the afternoon, so everyone there had heard almost immediately and had been trying to reach their loved ones for hours.

I ran into my classmate William, the young investment banker from London. He looked absolutely shell-shocked. "Are you all right?" I asked him in French. He nodded mutely. I went

The Girl on the Belvedere

to my classroom, but no one was there. A teacher passed by, said *"Bonjour,"* and promptly burst into tears. Isabelle, a student in the class next to mine, waved as she walked by, a stunned look on her face, crying. My classmate Katherine showed up at five after nine. She was the only other student to appear in the classroom. This was highly unusual, as class began at nine on the dot, and most of us were usually in our seats by 8:55.

"Is school cancelled?" I asked.

"I don't know," she said.

We decided to go to the main building, and ran into Luc on the way. "Is anyone up in the classroom?" he asked.

"No, I said, "no one."

"Let's go down to the Grand Salon," he said. As we headed in that direction, Luc said to me, "By the way, Susi is sick. A doctor has been here to see her."

We entered the Grand Salon and found everyone watching the televised address by the president of the French Republic, François Hollande. I'd already seen part of it earlier in my apartment. I couldn't bear to watch more and left the room to sit in the garden outside my classroom. The tragedy was unspeakable.

Gradually the class assembled. Surprisingly, all were present. Susi arrived, even though she was walking gingerly.

"Susi, what happened?" I asked. "You're ill?"

"I've developed vertigo," she explained. "My family called in the middle of the night to make sure I was okay, and they told me about the attack. I couldn't go back to sleep, and an hour later, it hit." She could barely walk, couldn't lean over, couldn't turn her head.

"How were you able to walk down to school?" I asked. "Why didn't you call me? I would have walked up to get you."

"I'm not sure how I made it," she confessed. "I think it's an emotional reaction to the attack. The school doctor stopped by, and he's sending medication from the pharmacy." As she sat at her desk, she tried to lean over to retrieve her notebook from her purse, but could not. Professor Luc knelt and retrieved it for her. She sat with her head leaning back against the wall, pale and spent.

I looked around the room. Everyone was clearly in shock, the women teary-eyed, the men wild-eyed. Luc and his family had not attended the fireworks in Nice, even though his children had begged to go. What a blessing.

He started the school day, although he dispensed with our customary study of a song. We discussed the tragedy instead, telling each other what we had heard. I mentioned that a young Muslim mother was the first person run down. "I heard that too," Luc said, "I also heard that thirty percent of the victims were Muslim."

After a few more comments, Luc started our study in earnest. He handed out a light-hearted worksheet on clichés about the French.

How does he do it? I wondered. *He lives in Nice. He undoubtedly has not yet been able to make sure all of his family and friends are safe. He certainly hasn't had time to process the tragedy.* Yet not once in the coming days would he deviate from his professional demeanor.

The director of the school stopped by our classroom and asked if we had spoken to our families. "It's the most important thing," he said. "If you need some time, if you feel you need to go to your apartment, please do so." He let us know that the Wi-Fi was available—normally, cellphone use was highly discouraged as it made us revert to our native languages—and that our usual twenty-minute break would be extended to thirty minutes.

Somehow, we got through the morning. Luc had us laughing within an hour as we tackled some difficult grammar. I marveled at his ability to disassociate from the horror that had taken place in his hometown, just a few miles away and a few hours ago.

Later, in the language lab, Susi broke down sobbing. Therese whispered to me that the death toll was now at sixty, including many children. People were still missing, some were in comas, and hundreds were injured.

The lunchroom was very subdued, very teary. On this sad day I sat next to Chloé, the young professor. She had been at the fireworks the night before, and had to run from the attacker. She had been with her best friend, and they were both uninjured, but her friend's brother had not yet been located. I was sure that conversations like ours were being repeated all throughout Nice and its suburbs.

I found that all the emotions I had experienced after the Oklahoma City bombing in 1995—helplessness, sorrow, anger, and incredulity, all accompanied by tears, so many tears—came rushing back, as they did after 9/11.

The morning of the Oklahoma City bombing, my husband had called to tell me that he could not locate his brothers, both of whom worked near the Federal Building that had been destroyed. Later, I learned that one brother had taken a different route to work for the first time in a year, and had been south of the Murrah Building when the bomb detonated. The blast went north, sparing him. He spent the next several hours with his first-aid kit, helping to treat his wounded co-workers. My husband's other brother, who worked in that same Oklahoma City office, had lingered at home that morning to enjoy an extra cup of coffee with his wife. My own brother had considered attending a seminar in the Murrah Building that morning, but did not go in the end, possibly saving his life.

Not every family was so lucky. 168 people, including nineteen children, lost their lives that day. I took flowers to the bombing site and wept for those mothers and those slaughtered children. I saw the building before it was fully demolished; I saw where people died. At one point I turned around, and wondered about the heaps of twisted metal behind me. It had been playground equipment.

That pain is still close to the surface for many. Emotions still run high about that bombing, and to this day Oklahomans mark April 19 as a day when our perception of a "normal" life exploded. The names of the deceased are read out at the memorial every year on this difficult day. Nine months after this French course in Villefranche, I would unexpectedly weep in Spain, when a photo of an Oklahoma City firefighter holding the tiny body of a baby was flashed around the world once again, this time in honor of that brave man's retirement. Now, being so close to the horror of the truck rampage affected me deeply. How sad for the people of Nice that their national holiday, Bastille Day, would be forever marred by the terror of this attack.

Somehow, we made it through this most difficult day amidst many tears and rumors of some students being unaccounted for.

I went home to my apartment and immediately retreated to the balcony, where I sat, stupefied, thinking about the horror that was still unfolding in Nice. It was a gorgeous evening. The Mediterranean was calm, and ended in a bright-blue line at the horizon of a lavender sky. *How can that be,* I thought, *when there is so much anguish within sight of this beautiful sea?*

TERROR WAS CONSTANTLY in the news here, even before the truck attack. Since my arrival at the school, eight had been killed in Lebanon, fifty in Yemen, forty-four in Turkey, fourteen in Syria, twenty-nine in Bangladesh, and 242 in Baghdad. After that, there were *another* thirty-two people killed in Yemen, thirty-six more

The Girl on the Belvedere

in Baghdad, and fifty-six in another part of Iraq. Then eighty-one in Nigeria, twelve more in Iraq, and now eighty-four in Nice. We occasionally hear these numbers in the United States, but they are simply mentioned in passing, ignoring the real agony of those injured and those left behind to grieve. I had already noted the hundreds of lives lost and had remarked upon it in class during our "current events" discussion in our first week. And now, it had occurred again, just a few miles away.

I thought of my Muslim friend Ibrahim, who by his birth, his heritage, his nationality, was unavoidably caught up in this maelstrom. Dear, gentlemanly Ibrahim, one of the kindest people I know, was labeled by some as "the enemy." I once asked him about his feelings on Islamic terrorism. "These people are crazy," he had said. "All anybody wants to do is to live and raise their family in peace and dignity."

That night, a group of us met at the harbor for drinks at the Hotel Welcome. I went down the hill by myself, as Susi had gone home from school early. She was still suffering from extreme vertigo, and her husband had arrived from Switzerland. They were planning a quiet weekend in her apartment.

We sat in this beautiful location, watching the sea, watching the harbor, watching the glamorous boat people stepping onto the quay, the women wearing sundresses with beautiful jewelry, the men wearing pastel jackets and pale slacks. Their attendants, left behind on the yachts, were dressed smartly in white uniforms as they performed their duties onboard. After drinks on the harbor, my friends and I walked up toward the restaurants in the village for dinner at a tapas bar.

After dinner, I chatted briefly with William. He explained that he had been unable to speak when he ran into me this morning at school. He had a friend visiting from London who had gone to the fireworks in Nice while William attended the school dinner at La Belle Étoile. His friend had been in the path of the rampage, had been forced to run, and had witnessed the horror unfolding: bodies flying, people caught underneath the truck being dragged to their deaths, body parts left behind, children run down, mothers with strollers targeted. He told William over and over again that, had they been there together, they might both have been killed. "I was in shock when I saw you this morning," William said. "I had just gotten off the phone with him."

"Where is he?" I asked.

"He's staying in Monte Carlo," he said. "I'm going over to go see him now."

"William," I said, "you don't know this about me, but I have had some training in counseling. Your friend is going to recount everything he saw over and over. He will repeat himself. He will relive it, over and over. You need to be prepared for that," I warned.

"Okay," William said. "I know he's still in shock."

"Encourage him to get help when he gets home," I added. "He's going to need it."

I walked home with Emily, and we marveled that we had not heard anything the night before in the moments just after the attack—no sirens, no helicopters, just the silence of a beautiful coastal evening. An unusual silence, now that we thought about it.

I spoke with my loved ones at home. My daughter and my husband encouraged me to return to the United States, most likely knowing even as they suggested it that I would not. They were concerned for me and felt helpless, and I understood. They feared that because I had been just a few miles from a major attack, I was now a target. But I had no intention of leaving the program; I was perfectly calm and felt very safe. My son was more circumspect, saying, "It's best that you stay put for a while. Let things settle down."

"The program only lasts another week, and then, I'm off to Germany," I reminded him.

"Okay, stay safe," he said as he signed off.

Yet, if truth be told, a part of me was a little nervous. I read online in a French publication that Daesh—better known in the West as ISIS—was calling for the death of all French and all Americans.

I watched the local television coverage until I could take no more. Then I moved out onto the balcony and stared at the beautiful lights along Cap Ferrat until it was well past time for bed. When I turned in, the death toll stood at eighty-four. It would eventually climb to eighty-six. I wrote in my journal "Sad sad day at school. Rumors of friends and staff being unaccounted for. Some witnessed the tragedy."

ON SATURDAY, I decided to follow my previously set plan: I was going to visit the Villa Ephrussi de Rothschild and its gardens in Saint-Jean-Cap-Ferrat. I could see it from my apartment; it was pink by day and a beautifully lit, rich apricot color at night. It sat high upon the ridge of Cap Ferrat and promised to have amazing views from both sides.

While dressing, I turned on the television and saw that they were just replaying the same reports. I decided to see if there was anything new online. "At least 84 deaths, of which 10 are children and adolescents, in the attack of 14 July in Nice. 202 injured, the attacker identified," screamed the French headline. I decided then and there to take a news holiday. I turned off my phone and set out.

On the way, I stopped at the tourist bureau to inquire where I might buy mailing supplies. I needed some packing tape; I was planning on visiting my friends in Germany once the course was over, but I would not need all the clothes I had with me, so I was going to mail some of them home. In the office, they told me that I would have to go into Nice or into Beaulieu-sur-Mer, in the other direction, to buy the tape.

"Really?" I asked, surprised. "No one sells packing tape anywhere here in Villefranche?"

"No," was the reply. "Nice or Beaulieu."

I decided on Beaulieu, as it was the coastal town on the other side of Cap Ferrat, and I was headed that way anyhow to see the villa.

The Rothschild Villa did not disappoint; it was everything I thought it would be and more. One stunning room followed another, and most windows had spectacular views of either Villefranche or Beaulieu-sur-Mer. I happily wandered the gardens for an hour or more, looking west at Villefranche, trying to locate my apartment on the hillside, and then crossing the gardens to look east at Beaulieu. All of these views—from my apartment, from the school, from the harbor, from Cap Ferrat—were so beautiful that I sometimes shook my head in disbelief.

After my tour, I had no idea how to get down into Beaulieu-sur-Mer, so I asked that great font of information, Google Maps. It directed me down to the road in front of the villa, up another smaller road, and then up a very steep turning stone staircase. I soon found myself on a footpath, the *Chemin des Moulins* [Windmill Lane], with small entrance gates to the villas on my right and left. The villas themselves were obscured by tall walls and vegetation. I did not see a single person on my descent into Beaulieu.

I found my way to "Super U," my destination, and located the packing supplies. I spent some time looking around this high-dollar town and stopped in an ice cream parlor when I realized that I was about to pass out from the heat and from exhaustion. I chatted with the young French girl behind the

The Girl on the Belvedere

counter until I felt rested enough to again face the unrelenting sun. I made my way back up to Cap Ferrat, then down past more villas, and finally descended onto the beach of Villefranche-sur-Mer. I walked along the seaside, visited some shops, and purchased a pair of the famous *Tropeziennes* sandals on sale. I struggled up to my apartment and immediately lay down on the sofa and fell asleep.

My best friend, Marjorie, called from Tulsa, waking me from my nap. She was flying to France to join me for my last two weeks in Europe. "I've heard about the attack," she said. "Are you all right?"

"I'm fine," I responded.

"Are you staying?"

"Yes, of course," I said. "Are you still joining me?"

"Absolutely." That settled it.

The sea was calm that night. It ended in a sharp, bright-blue line against the darkening lavender sky that heralded the end of another day. The apparent tranquility belied the terror and confusion resulting from Bastille Day in Nice.

On my last Sunday in Villefranche-sur-Mer, I tried to copy some notes and do my homework, but I was constantly drawn back to the view of the sea below me, silver in the morning sun. The view from my balcony never failed to mesmerize me, and I would miss it terribly. *Quel bel été*—what a beautiful summer. The church bells down below played their Sunday concert as I sat with my coffee and reflected on all that had happened since my arrival: a wedding celebration in Versailles, a tour of the Loire Valley, weeks of an intense French class, a major terror attack nearby, and now, my best friend arriving tomorrow. Contentment, excitement, exhaustion; exhilaration, sadness, anticipation. This day of reflection passed quietly.

Both the sky and sea were pale that Sunday evening, the horizon a gentle blur in shades of blue and lavender. A full moon hung low over the bay and cast a bit of a white glow upon the pale-blue water along Cap Ferrat. There was a fresh, cool breeze, so welcome after the hot days of the past week. The weekend pleasure boats were gone, and the village was tranquil. Lights were just beginning to twinkle on the remaining boats, and some of the salmon-colored houses were already shuttered for the night. Soon, I would lower my own shutters, marking another day that had passed, a day spent on laundry, homework, and short naps.

My friend Marjorie was in Chicago now, awaiting her flight to Paris. She would arrive in Nice tomorrow and take a bus to Villefranche. It had been many, many years since we traveled together, on tour with the young company that is now Tulsa Ballet. Marjorie had four grown children, one grandchild, and taught ballet at the University of Tulsa. This trip was a much-needed respite from the demands of family and the looming academic year.

An hour passed in quiet reflection, and I realized that I was still transfixed by the scene below and had not moved from the balcony. But I simply had to go to bed. Before I went inside, I took one last look at the Mediterranean on this, my final evening alone on my balcony. The sea and sky were banded now, with pale blue stretching toward the horizon, deep blue where the sea met the baby-blue sky, and above that, lavender fading to pink, crowned with the full moon. The lighthouse with its rotating beacon was visible, signaling the night ahead. There was a silver moonlit path from the village to the horizon. *What magic this is!* I thought. The yellow lights of Cap Ferrat were reflected in the blue water along the shore, those perfect Provençal colors of blue and yellow. A cruise ship, lit with twinkly white lights, slipped by silently far out to sea. The palms were silhouetted against the deep azure sky. Slowly the stars appeared, along with the sounds of the neighbors lowering their shutters for the night. The beauty of the moonlit Mediterranean made me want to weep. My best friend would soon be winging her way toward me through this vast blue night, over this same silent sea. After a last look on this final Sunday, I stepped inside and lowered the shutters.

16

BEST FRIENDS

France fell silent on Monday, in honor of the victims of the rampage. We gathered at noon in the lunchroom, eyes downcast, while church bells rang out the time. In Villefranche-sur-Mer, at least, life seemed to be slowly returning to normal, although the attack was never far from our minds.

My friend Marjorie had landed in Paris around ten and was now on a plane to Nice. I would see her in a few hours and could hardly wait. We'd known each other since I was fourteen and she was twelve.

One Saturday in ballet class, I'd noticed a new girl with impossibly long legs as straight as scissors, and thought, *Who is this?* It was Marjorie, who had such prodigious talent that her parents put her on a Greyhound bus from her small hometown every Friday afternoon. After arriving in Tulsa, Marjorie would take a taxi by herself to the ballet studio in order to take the professional classes offered by the Jasinskis, then spend the night with her aunt. She would reverse the trip after Saturday classes, arriving back in her hometown late in the evening. Eventually, her parents sold their business and moved their family to Tulsa so that she could study every day with the Jasinskis. Not long after, we ended up in the company together.

Weight was a constant topic in the dressing room at the studio. We regularly engaged in a classic binge/starve pattern to remain thin for the stage. Examples: Marjorie and I attended an ice-skating exhibition of Olympic stars, including the sublime gold medalist Peggy Fleming, who performed her famous "Ave Maria." We each bought and consumed four ice-cream cones that night. So much for worrying about our waistlines.

One Saturday afternoon my mother served my family Fritos and dip—a rare treat—while my father grilled hamburgers. I had some of those Fritos. Then I had more, and more after that, and more, more, more. When I returned to class the next Monday, Miss Larkin looked me up and down with a critical eye, and I thought, *She knows about the Fritos.* That was a crazy thought, and I knew it, but it was enough to send me into a week of eating very little.

Many of us in the company engaged in such behavior. Miss Larkin once told us that no one needed more than 1200 calories per day, so that was always my goal. After a full day of school, I would take two or three ballet classes, then rehearse, yet would still fret if I consumed "too many" calories, meaning more than 1200. That small amount did not sustain me for such exertion, though, which then led to bingeing. During those times, I always felt "fat" in my leotard and tights. I was five-foot-eight, and my "high" weight was 118. For performance, I always dropped to 115.

This thinking led to the cessation of my monthly periods and a trip to the doctor. He yelled at me upon finding out that I eschewed protein as it contained "too many calories." My bloodwork was deficient in several areas; he handed me a booklet on nutrition guidelines. I altered my diet accordingly but feel the effects to this day. I have severe osteoporosis for which I gave myself daily injections for over a year and now receive twice-yearly shots. I had starved my bones of critical nutrients for too many years.

Eating disorders were not yet well understood, so we didn't know that we were flirting with danger. Luckily, the saving grace for dancers then—and now—is that dancers simply love to eat. They need the fuel. Not even the fact that Miss Larkin publicly weighed us could not deter us from eating for long, even though we always tried to "make up for it later." Conversely, not even her comment about me to the rest of the company, "It's always the ones who don't need to lose weight, that do," could convince me that I was thin enough. Leotards, tights, and mirrors are tough critics.

Fifty years later, my daughter and Marjorie's are good friends and were raised to be healthy, not bone-thin. My daughter is very trim, watches the quality of what she eats, and measures its impact on her health—one of my minor victories in childrearing. I'm sure Marjorie's daughter, a physician, does the same.

And now Marjorie was wending her way toward me. She had not been to France since she studied ballet on the Riviera forty years ago with Rosella Hightower, the Oklahoma Indian Ballerina who had been a huge star both in the United States and France, and later opened her own school in Cannes. Marjorie was a lifetime away from the young dancer she had been and was wise in the ways that only age can bring. Now, to be here in France with my best friend was a dream come true.

On this Monday, I watched the clock all day. Marjorie had texted me from Paris that she had arrived and was awaiting her flight to Nice, but that was the last I heard all day. By the time class ended, I was growing concerned. Her flight had landed in Nice hours ago, and she should have been in Villefranche by now. I walked toward my apartment, and as soon as I passed through the large traffic gate, my phone rang.

"Where are you?" I practically shouted into the phone.

"I'm by some apartment buildings with blue awnings," Marjorie said. "They told me at the tourist bureau how to get there, but I've been walking up the side of this mountain forever."

"Stay put," I told her. "I know exactly where you are." I walked down the hill to "Scooter Corner," and there she was, my friend of fifty years. I took her bag and pulled it behind me as we ascended the hill the rest of the way to my apartment.

She had to be exhausted after flying from Tulsa to Chicago to Paris to Nice and then taking a bus to Villefranche. I showed her how to work the elevator with its two doors, then opened the door for her to my apartment. When I raised the hurricane shutters, she gasped.

I pulled out two frozen chicken Kiev portions from the freezer and popped them into the oven while she unpacked. After dinner on the *terrasse*, we walked down into the village so that she could find her way around in the morning. My rental agreement stipulated that no one could be in the apartment without me, so Marjorie would have to leave and arrive with me each day.

IN THE MORNING, after breakfast on the balcony, we said goodbye on the street. I watched her walk down the hill and prayed that she would find her way around town and back up to the apartment gate in the evening.

That afternoon, I sat in one of the gardens, ditching class and writing, when the pretty young professor, Chloé, sat down next to me. We talked about the attack. I was afraid to ask about the fate of her friend's brother, and we just spoke in general terms. I told her about the Oklahoma City bombing, with its loss of one hundred and sixty-eight lives, and said, "While one adjusts intellectually, one never forgets an attack so close, so personal. It gets easier over time and becomes less emotional to mark those anniversaries, but I'm sure the pain never leaves those who lost family and friends."

She nodded and asked, "How long does it take?"

"The first year is marked in days, weeks, and months," I said. "The nation's eyes will turn away, while your eyes will stay glued. After that, the years fly by for those not personally affected, and suddenly, it's been two years, five years, ten years. While one never forgets, it becomes the new reality. On April 19, the Murrah Building in Oklahoma City exploded. On July 14, Bastille Day, a madman with a truck and a gun attacked people at the fireworks in Nice. These things are now, and will forever be, true."

I thought about what it would mean to me if such a thing had happened in Tulsa on the Fourth of July. What would my reaction be the next year and the one after that? How would the city mourn? The rest of the state? I was so terribly, terribly sad for the people of Nice.

I said goodbye to the young professor and pulled myself up to attend my last class of the day. We were now trying to connect all we had learned in a meaningful way, and for me, it was a steep uphill climb. I was still amazed that I had ended up in *Avancé II* with our "super prof," Luc. My mind did not work as quickly as it once had, and this class had been a major challenge.

The week before, we had all agreed that we wished we could stay for another session. This week, we realized the impossibility of facing another month at this level. We were all hanging on by a thread, counting the hours, exhausted.

After class, Marjorie was waiting for me on the apartment grounds, and I was relieved to see her. It cannot be easy, after thirty years at home with children, to travel halfway around the world and set off by oneself in a strange place. I remembered well those first few daunting hours in Quebec, before Stephanie arrived.

Marjorie told me that she had started her day at the Hotel Welcome with another cup of coffee, watching the early morning passersby. She spent the rest of the day wandering the ancient village.

AFTER A SHORT STOP in the apartment, Marjorie and I went up the hill to meet Susi and her husband on the switchback street. We were going to get pizza up on the "*Col*," the mountain pass between Nice and Villefranche-sur-Mer. While we awaited our order, Susi and I discussed our day at school; her husband and Marjorie were quiet and attentive to our discussion, as we were speaking English for their benefit.

"Did you hear about Isabelle?" Susi asked, naming a friend in the classroom adjacent to ours. "She was just twelve meters from the truck. She and her family had to run. They huddled in a doorway because the driver was shooting, too. The owner of the building opened the door and pulled them in."

"I didn't hear that," I said, "but I saw Isabelle on Friday morning after the attack. She went into her classroom and waved at me, but said nothing. She was crying. I didn't see her again until today."

"I think she went into Nice to stay with her family," Susi said.

"I don't blame her," I said. "How horrible."

We changed the subject after that—it was still so painful—and spoke of happier things. We asked Susi's husband about his drive from Switzerland and where he had learned his very good English. We relaxed and laughed, a much-needed respite from the seriousness at school.

That evening, the moon beat a golden path across the bay, shimmering and brilliant against the inky blackness of Cap Ferrat. The sky was azure fading to indigo; the moon, yellow. Never in all my days had I seen a sky so splendid or water so enchanting. The moonlit path stretched beyond the cape to the horizon. Marjorie shook her head in silent wonder and snapped my photo on the balcony against this view. While the shot didn't really capture the magnificence of the evening, it does serve as a reminder of that moment.

THE NEXT MORNING dawned gloriously clear. A gull, illuminated by the sun on one side, its golden wings flapping, flew toward me, intent on its perch on the roof. Boats in the Beaulieu harbor were pinpoints of light. The villa on the hill above shone pale peach in the early morning radiance.

On this third-to-last morning in my apartment, I wandered outside to the balcony several times, hoping to memorize the sight of the ascending sun reflecting on the waters of the harbor, the stucco houses golden in the sunshine, and the dark stone of Fort du Mont Alban illuminated far above me. Marjorie joined me outside at the small iron and glass table, and we sat silently sipping our rich coffee, enjoying our yogurt, and marveling at what we saw below us.

At lunch, I again spoke with Chloé. She and her friend had run from the carnage, but her friend's brother, now located, had witnessed the entire event. "He needs help, but refuses to get it," she confided to me.

"I hope he will reconsider," I said.

I heard that there had been another attack, this one with a hatchet on a train in Germany. Terrorism seemed to be everywhere in Europe these days; there was no escaping it. And aside from the more obvious precautions—"If you see something, say something," as we say in the United States—it was random and unpredictable.

This last week of class was just as difficult as the first. Luc was intent on opening our heads and pouring in as much information as he could. I did notice some improvement in myself, which was welcome. I had started taking notes this last week and wished I had been doing so all along; it made a huge difference. Luc gently chided me for writing while the class was engaged in an oral exercise, but this time, I kept writing instead of putting my pen down. When he asked me a grammar question, I answered correctly while still writing, barely glancing up. I'd had no idea that I could write and speak French simultaneously—and on two different topics! It was a small victory. Unhappily, on this day, the second-to-last day of class, I was stuck yet again with a migraine. *Malchance*. Bad luck.

I was going to miss my class with its unique chemistry, but all good things must come to an end, and the end was now palpable. This immersion course had been so difficult, as I had expected it would be. The program was less academic than the one I attended in Quebec, but it was more intense; arriving at 8:30 a.m., departing at 4:45 p.m. and speaking nothing but French all day long was exhausting.

I did regret that, at sixty-three, I was no longer the quick study I had once been. It's a natural progression, but one that can be hard to stomach. On the other hand, *I was here*. I was somehow able to screw my "courage to the sticking-place," as

Shakespeare famously wrote, and take this class, a very difficult course, alone, in a foreign country, far from home. That must be worth something. As the French composer Daniel Auber said, "Aging seems to be the only available way to live a long life." Well said, Monsieur Auber. Well said.

I sat in one of the gardens for the last time, looking at the hills. The cicadas were singing, *comme d'habitude,* as usual; the skies were empty, save for a gentle breeze pushing a lone cloud behind the mountains. Ten days from now, I would be at home. Would I remember this tranquility, this *mélange* of color, this ancient beauty?

At this very moment, my friend Marjorie texted me to say that she was visiting the hilltop town of Èze. It was a mere eleven-minute bus ride away, costing only two euros, but I had not made the trip. A small regret.

On this final Thursday night, our class had a delicious dinner at Les Garçons, an al fresco restaurant down in the village. We had the best seats in the house: a long table at the back, against a stone wall, with a fountain gurgling nearby. I sat next to William and asked him about his friend who had witnessed the truck attack the week before.

"He's gone back to London," he said. "It was just as you predicted. He's been recounting the horror he saw over and over again. He can't stop."

"Is he going to get professional help?" I asked.

"He says he is," William said.

I sincerely hoped that this young man would be able to find the help he needed in the aftermath of this terror.

Finally, it was my last day in the South of France. Marjorie and I said goodbye on the street that morning. She was off to tour the Rothschild Villa, then a church in town that had been redesigned and refurbished by the artist Jean Cocteau. I watched her set out, then walked through the school gate. I

The Girl on the Belvedere

glanced at the building's beautiful front door and walked onto the garden pathway that led to my classroom. We kept our noses to the grindstone for most of the morning, with Luc cramming in more verbs, more vocabulary, more, more, more. We took our final exam and then went into the lab for one last torture session.

At my last lunch, I sat with my professor, Luc. "Where are you going after the course? Are you going home?" he asked.

"I'm going to Germany," I said, "to see some friends."

"Oh, to Germany!" Luc exclaimed, seeming pleased.

"What are you doing next week on your vacation?" I inquired.

"I'm going hiking in the mountains," he said.

"Wow," I responded. To me, that was truly formidable. These were, after all, the Alps.

"I'm looking forward to it," Luc said.

Silence descended at our end of the table. I looked around, and when no one else seemed willing to speak, I said, "Everyone in Oklahoma speaks Spanish, but hardly anyone speaks French."

"Oh, do you speak Spanish?" he asked.

"No," I said, "but my husband speaks it very well." I changed the subject and asked Luc what he had done in the United States, since I knew that he had lived there for several years.

"I taught French at a college," he said. "It's all I know how to do." He was such a talented teacher that I was amazed that he didn't seem to realize what a rare gift he had—and what that gift meant to others. He was serious, sometimes even stern, but when someone or something made him laugh—as happened about a thousand times a day in our class—his face would break open in a grin before he could wrestle it back under control.

After lunch, as we were reassembling and settling back down in the classroom, William and Henry were engaged in a conversation about Bluetooth technology. In French, I asked, "What is the French word for 'Bluetooth'?"

"Bluetooth," Luc said.

I thought about the word Bluetooth, about how nonsensical the idea of blue teeth was. I found myself wondering about its origin. "What does Bluetooth even mean?"

"They're these things you put in your ears," said nineteen-year-old Henry, placing his hands over his ears as though he had earbuds, taking me literally.

There was a moment of silence in the classroom, followed by an explosion of laughter. Oh, the naiveté of the young. I must have seemed ancient to this young man.

"What will you miss most?" Luc asked the class as we settled into our seats.

"I will miss my view of the sea," I said. Luc gave me a quizzical look, but indeed, those views—which I see now, in photo after photo—would calm me in the years to come, as I recalled that beautiful blue sea and sky.

We had individual exit interviews with Luc. He told me that I had done very well overall, but on my final exam, he noticed that I had not improved the listening portion at all. He suggested that I spend some time listening to music in order to improve my listening skills. I was too embarrassed to tell him that the problem was my actual *hearing*. I had grown up listening to music, dancing to it, counting it, dividing my steps among its measures. But now, I was simply unable to hear some sounds. I was clearly just a touch too old for the course.

I stood outside one last time, regarding the sea, chatting, taking final photos with my classmates, and waiting for the graduation ceremony where we would receive our certificates, proving to the world that we really had been here. While we waited, several of my classmates—Emily from Seattle, young Henry from Los Angeles, Neill from Scotland—slipped away, having early flights to their various destinations. I said goodbye to Susi who was driving back to Switzerland with her husband, having been through the graduation exercise once before on an earlier sojourn at the school. I found myself becoming a little teary-eyed; I had shared so much with these individuals, and most of them I would never see again. After their departures, the rest of us chatted, watched a film on Provence, and strolled through the gardens, waiting for the festivities.

The graduation ceremony was a formal affair in the beautiful Grand Salon overlooking the Mediterranean. One by one, we were called up to the front of the room, to the polite applause of our classmates. There was a routine to the presentation. The professor would hold out the diploma, there would be *la bise*—the kiss-kiss on each cheek—and then the professor would hand over the diploma, to which one said, *"Merci."*

My name was called. I heard the applause as I walked to the front of the room. I approached the professor, and then, it happened. I accepted the diploma before I kiss-kissed. This would not have been a big deal in the United States, but this was France, that arbiter of beautiful manners, of formality, of correctness of behavior. I knew what I had done the moment I saw the look of surprise on the professor's face. I finished with the kiss-kiss, but I knew—and she certainly knew—that it had not been done according to protocol. *I'll get it right next time*, I thought, knowing full well there would be no "next time." I reminded myself, however, that I had finished the course, learned a tremendous amount, and made friends from around the globe. And, I did have that certificate.

I bid Katherine goodbye and wished her a happy vacation in Antibes. I hugged Fiona, my Irish friend. I waved goodbye to Therese, who was sitting and chatting with a girlfriend. The last person I hugged was William. "If you're ever in London..." he said.

"Yes," I said, "if I'm ever in London…"

I slipped out while the reception was still in full swing, without a backward glance at the gathered crowd. It would bring me little comfort to stay any longer.

Once outside, I turned and looked again at the beautiful front door of the villa, framed by the *jardinières* filled with ficus and at the flower-lined garden path that led to my now-former classroom. I walked through the green metal gate, turned right, and looked straight ahead at the road that led down into the village. The gate clanged shut behind me. I started down the hill, giving my shuttered apartment with its magnificent view a fleeting glance as I passed it. Around the curve I went, trotting kitty-cornered across the busy little intersection where I was almost run down by a scooter. I went around the safety bars and stepped down, down, down into the long, steep pedestrian street. I paused to look up at the houses, the apartments, the hill, the stone cliff. I turned left onto the main street and glanced at the gorgeous fruit displayed on the stands outside the Casino grocery store. I crossed the street and walked along the park. I regarded the palm trees above me and the boutiques across the street. Down below to the right, I could see a bit of the Citadelle and the blue bay beyond. I was teary-eyed. It was over.

I finally arrived at the hotel where Marjorie and I would be spending the night, but she wasn't in the lobby. The *hotelière* told me that "*votre amie*" ["your friend"] was in the room. I struggled upstairs after identifying my large bag, which had been delivered by the school earlier in the day, but Marjorie wasn't there. I returned to the lobby to wait for her, only to find out from a school friend that there had been *another* attack in Germany, this one at a shopping mall in Munich. A madman had targeted people at a McDonald's, then proceeded into the nearby mall. He had shot nine people dead, and injured several others. Again, it was beyond description, too horrible for words.

Marjorie soon arrived and found me speaking to Marianne, my school friend from Australia, about the latest attack. After hearing what had happened, Marjorie asked, "Are we still going to Germany tomorrow?"

"Yes, of course," I said, but I was a little unnerved. It seemed like the last few weeks had been nothing but attack after attack after attack. Truck attacks, axe attacks, and now this shooting attack. I wondered if it were possible to adjust to these attacks, if such horror would eventually seem normal.

We rested a bit in the room and then set out for our last evening in Villefranche-sur-Mer. We had dinner on the waterfront, and then Marjorie showed me some sights that I had not seen during my long month in this town. We strolled beside the sea on a narrow path below the fortified walls of the Citadelle to the other port. I'd seen it from the road above on trips into Nice, but had never made the short trek. There were more restaurants and shops here, and Marjorie showed me the open-air seafood restaurant where she had lunch while exploring the area on a rental bike. *Next time,* I thought. *Next time.* We made our way back into town, and I snapped a few last photos of fountains, of colorful doorways, of street scenes. We climbed the few short blocks to our hotel, and back in our room, I immediately opened the full-length windows to experience those glorious sea breezes one last time.

I turned on my Wi-Fi, and read a text message from Susi, who told me of her safe arrival in Switzerland, and wished me well for the remainder of my trip. I told her that I would text her soon, and as I shut off my phone, I wondered when I would see her again.

I glanced at Marjorie. She was already asleep.

The next morning, while waiting for our taxi, I looked at the local paper, *Nice-Matin*. The headlined screamed, *"Terreur à Munich"* above the gory, now-familiar photos. It was reminiscent of coverage after the truck rampage. It felt like the news headlines had taken on a different tone after the truck attack, and the images they chose to run were violent and gruesome. And why wouldn't they be? We turn away from evil as a society only when we can see its true effect. Talk is cheap.

WE GOT INTO OUR TAXI, and I started a conversation with the cabbie. As we passed through the flower-laden attack site in Nice, the cabbie became visibly distraught and very vocal. "My wife and seven-year-old boy were there," he said. "They were two hundred meters behind the truck and saw the whole thing. They could have been killed! We need to find these people and do to them exactly what they have done to us!"

Marjorie shot me an alarmed look. She couldn't understand his words, but she clearly understood the emotion of extreme anger.

"His wife and son were at the fireworks," I said in English for her benefit, "and witnessed the attack."

"This is not about religion," the cabbie continued. "These people are murderers, and we need to get rid of them." I studied him from the backseat. He appeared to be partially of North African descent, like so many people in southern France. He was as French as they come, and his hometown had just been attacked, with three hundred of his townspeople run down.

"I understand," I said. "We are from Oklahoma and had a bombing about twenty years ago that killed 168 people and injured more."

He looked at me in the rearview mirror. "I remember that," he said, shaking his head. "I don't understand it."

"Neither do I. It's inconceivable."

He ended this conversation by muttering, *"incroyable, inhumain, barbare."* Unbelievable, inhuman, barbaric.

We turned our attention—and our conversation—to the beauty of Nice: the pastel-colored buildings, the palm trees, the flowers. "Do the flowers bloom all year?" Marjorie asked.

"Yes, they do," he said in answer to my translation. "Nice is always beautiful." He went on to tell us that he had visited family living in Boston and liked the United States very much, calling Boston *"Une jolie ville"*—a pretty town.

We shook hands at the airport, and he wished us a heartfelt *"Bon voyage."* He said he had enjoyed our conversation and hoped that we would visit Nice again soon.

"Me too," I said. *"Au revoir, merci."*

"Bonne journée, Madame," he said with a genuine smile as he got back into his taxi.

MARJORIE and I walked into the terminal and found that the Lufthansa line was non-existent. *Great!* I thought. *We'll breeze through check-in.* However, we were stopped by an attendant who informed us that the line would not open for another half-hour and asked us to please come back at that time.

We got a quick cup of coffee, then headed back to the Lufthansa counter at the appointed time. Now the line snaked completely through the cordoned-off area and halfway down the terminal. It was so congested that people making their way to a different counter had to excuse themselves and push through the queue.

We dutifully got in line, and I immediately felt like a sitting duck, remembering the recent attack at the Brussels airport. I could tell that I wasn't the only one. The crowd around us was agitated, with people glancing about, chatting quietly looking behind themselves, glancing at the doors. Marjorie was visibly nervous. I was, too, but was the tiniest bit more circumspect. While I felt that we definitely needed to pay attention in this wild, congested area, I also realized that if our number was up, it was up. We were going to Germany. We had our tickets, our hotel, my Quebec friends. We were committed.

I soon fell into conversation with a Frenchman who was standing in line with his son and grandson. He was traveling with them to their home in New Zealand. "I've lived in Villefranche," he told me, "and I've lived in Oklahoma, in Midwest City. I used to drive to Tulsa to buy accessories for my motorcycle. I liked Oklahoma very much. I live in Nice now."

We talked briefly about the Institut de Français, about the weather, about this and that, but we did not discuss the recent attack.

A little later, our luggage checked, we passed through a disorganized security line and arrived at our gate with just ten minutes to spare before boarding, despite having arrived at the airport three hours before departure. After showing our boarding passes and passports again and again, we were tightly packed onto an airport shuttle bus, along with the pilots, for the short trip out to the plane.

After the chaotic airport, the plane felt like an oasis of calm. Over the intercom, we were addressed in German and in English, but not in French—that announcement was prerecorded. As we taxied and ascended, I wondered how long it would be before I returned to Nice, with its beautiful flowers and friendly people.

During this hour on the plane, without the pressure of studying, navigating or translating, I was the calmest I had been since my arrival in France. I was looking forward to Germany and to a hotel, where everything would be done for me. I was utterly exhausted, and yet, I would not have traded my experiences for the world. I was suddenly full of wonder at the path my life had taken. I was an international student and traveler sitting on a plane somewhere between France and Germany. Without my parents' vision of travel-as-education, I would not have been sitting here now, leaving new friends in France, on my way to Germany to see old friends from Canada.

17

REUNION

We arrived at a very calm Frankfurt airport and collected our bags.

"Do you see your friends?" Marjorie asked.

I looked around, but saw no one except other travelers from our flight. I realized that even though the European borders were open, this area was sequestered, and we needed to exit into the greeting area to meet up with the members of the non-flying public. We walked through the doors. At first, I didn't see any familiar faces, but then Anna came into view. As I hurried toward her, both of us all smiles, someone grabbed me from behind in a bear hug. It was my other friend Lucía from Mexico, who had told me that she would not be able to see me until the next day. I hugged Lucía, then Anna, and then both of them at the same time. Then I looked around for Ibrahim.

"He's not here," Anna said. "He's in Israel, helping his family prepare for his sister's wedding next weekend. He's flying back tomorrow night."

We took the high-speed train from the Frankfurt airport to Mannheim and then set off to find our hotel. After checking in, we took the tram across the Rhine into Ludwigshafen and walked to a nearby restaurant on the river. Over pizza, I told them I that was writing a book about our adventures in Quebec. Excited shrieking followed the initial open-mouthed silence.

As we finished dinner, Anna said, "I read that there is a *Québécois* band playing tonight at the festival here."

My mind flew to that band from Quebec, Fanfarniente della Strada, and their marvelous song, "Zaza." "You're kidding," I said, hopeful, but not actually expecting it to be them.

She looked it up on her phone; it was indeed Fanfarniente della Strada. "I don't believe this," I said. "They were my favorite at the summer festival in Quebec, and now they're here? I play their CD all the time."

We picked up a schedule from the festival information booth and watched a few other acts while waiting. I marveled at the tall giraffe puppets walking down the street amongst the children, dipping their heads to be petted. Anna bought us bottles of a cold carbonated apple juice drink, *Apfelschorle*, and we enjoyed it while watching the crowds.

At last, we located the band, and I could tell immediately that they were indeed the same performers. They were even wearing the same Bavarian/Bohemian costumes. Lucía was mesmerized by the music, and there was a dreamy look on her face.

After this long day, Lucía and Anna escorted us back to our hotel, where Marjorie and I promptly collapsed. The stress of travel and terrorism had taken its toll.

THE NEXT MORNING, Anna and Lucía walked us to a nearby bakery-café. It was very similar to its counterparts in the United

States, except that here in Germany there was one on almost every corner. After breakfast, we caught a tram to the train station. We were going to board the train to Heidelberg, where Lucía was attending school. Heidelberg is a romantic university town on the Neckar River, and it is where Anna and Ibrahim met during their university days.

While waiting on the train platform, we were all laughing about something when an elderly German man nearby started muttering under his breath and shaking his head. "He thinks we are too loud," Anna said. "German people are grumpy."

I believed her, of course, but Anna was one of the least grumpy people I knew, and *she* was German.

On the train, my illogical fears reared their ugly head. We found a perfect set of four seats, facing each other, up high, with a good vantage point for viewing the countryside. On the other side of the aisle, however, there was an unattended bag. Without a word, I passed the empty seats and chose less desirable ones down a level, at the back of the car. My two Quebec friends looked at me quizzically, but said nothing.

A few seconds later, a young man rushed through the car with a cup of coffee, a worried look on his face. He sat down next to the unattended luggage. The mystery of the bag was solved, but it was a few heartbeats too late to alter my choice of seats; another group had already claimed them. I said nothing to my companions, but Marjorie looked at me in silent agreement.

When we arrived in Heidelberg, we immediately set out to walk through the magnificent Old Town. While standing on the Old Bridge, with its town gate centered between two towers, we stared up at the castle, high on the mountain overlooking the city. "I thought we might walk up there," Anna said.

"Sure," I agreed.

"Are you certain you can make the climb?" Lucía asked.

"Absolutely. I've been living in the Alps," I assured them. I successfully reached the top without stopping to rest. Once on the summit, I was not a bit out of breath.

Afterward, we had cake and coffee on the square in Heidelberg. This was evidently a daily ritual in Germany. We said goodbye to Lucía, who had a dorm room in Heidelberg, and made our way to the train station for our return trip to Mannheim.

Once back in town, Marjorie, Anna, and I took the tram to the town center. At the large *Marktplatz*, we saw a huge police presence. Anna was perplexed and could see no obvious reason for the many police cars congregated in the center of the plaza.

Uncertain as to whether Ibrahim would get back in time for dinner, we decided to stroll for a bit. We passed many shops selling drop-dead gorgeous Turkish wedding gowns, jewelry stores, pastry shops, and mosques. As we walked, we were passed six, seven, eight times by police vans. We noticed that the neighborhood was buzzing with concern. People stood in small clumps with worried looks on their faces.

We arrived at the open-air restaurant Istanbul, which Anna said was the center of Mannheim's large Turkish population. It was one of her favorite restaurants, and she ate here often. We took a seat and ordered an appetizer. Anna had heard from Ibrahim; he would be at least another hour in arriving. Meanwhile, police van after police van assembled in the large plaza. Anna was becoming very nervous, as were we. She asked a waiter what was happening, and he explained that the police were worried about an outbreak of violence in the wake of the recent failed coup in Turkey.

I would remember this scene a year later in the aftermath of the riot in Charlottesville. My husband and I had lived in that town for six years and loved it. Our son was born in Charlottesville, and we were very sad to leave. On subsequent visits, it tugged at our heartstrings, this sublimely beautiful, historic city, full of our happy newlywed and new baby memories. What had happened there? How and why did two warring groups, both at the boiling point, get close enough to trade blows?

I deplore hate speech and detest any kind of avowed "supremacy," even as I recognize that protest marches and free speech are protected under the law. Yet that day it led to an act of terror every bit as awful as the attack in Nice, the attack in Oklahoma City, and the attacks in Germany, just smaller in scale. Terror is terror. A year after my trip to Germany, when a young woman was so cruelly run down by a car in Charlottesville, I gained a better understanding of the political violence the German police were trying to prevent among their Turkish residents that night.

Anna was relieved that it was not related to religious terrorism and relaxed. Later, as we walked down the high-end shopping street, she said, "No one on this street seems worried." We looked in the shop windows and decided to wait for Ibrahim's arrival in the city square beneath its 1889 water tower, one of the few things left standing in Mannheim after World War II.

We sat and gazed at the stately central fountain. There were beautiful tall *torchères,* and an abundance of pink and red flowers in the square. The water tower itself was a marvel of brown brick with a large copper dormer roof. We sat quietly, watching the crowd, watching the play of the water in the fountains, watching for Ibrahim.

Anna finally broke our silence by excitedly announcing, "My *Schatzi* is coming back to me!"

"*Schatzi?*" I echoed.

"It's the nickname my family gave him, and now, everyone

calls him that. It means 'darling.' When I'm with him, I call him *Schatz*."

Anna suddenly smiled at someone behind me. I turned and recognized Ibrahim immediately: The shock of black hair, the glasses, the backpack, and the wide smile were all so familiar. I was so happy to see my friends again and marveled that it had been two years. We chatted as if it had been only two weeks.

THE NEXT MORNING, we woke to the news of a suicide bomber near the music festival in Ansbach. The terrorist had killed no one except himself, but he had severely injured several others. There was also a machete attack in Reutlingen, killing one and injuring two. These attacks so soon after the shooting deaths of nine in that shopping district in Munich, plus the axe attack on a German train —not to mention the truck rampage in Nice—rocked Europe.

Marjorie and I sat in the lobby of our German hotel with cups of coffee, reading the English-language newspaper, and relaxing. The trams glided by silently, and we marveled at the abundance of mass transit available here. Only a bus system existed at home in Tulsa, but even in New York there was not this ease of accessibility.

We had breakfast high above the city at a rotating restaurant atop a tower. Ibrahim presented Marjorie with a brightly painted ceramic cow that she had admired while window shopping earlier. It was the first of many gifts this couple would bestow upon us.

Anna and Ibrahim drove us to Ladenburg. It is an ancient village, once Celtic, then Roman, now full of pastel, half-timbered German houses, most of them adorned with flowers. We stopped for ice cream, and I snapped photos of Anna and

Ibrahim sitting at the outdoor café-style table, chatting in German and laughing. We walked to the Neckar River and sat, watching the geese and admiring the sun sparkling on the water against a distant grey rainy sky.

"Someday, we'd like to live in a town like this," Anna said. I could understand why. It was small, charming, picturesque, and friendly. I'd like to live there, too.

A DAY LATER, we set out by car for the nearby town of Schwetzingen, famous for its pink palace and extensive grounds. Lucía was waiting for us there, and together, we strolled the *allées* of cool green trees, laughing, telling stories, and chatting easily. I still could not believe that the four of us were together again, this time in Germany. Marjorie was a nice addition, and she fit in well, laughing with us as we toured the palace.

I took some pictures inside the classical eighteenth-century bathhouse and was admonished by the German employee at the desk. "I don't understand," I said. "English? Français?"

To my delight, she spoke French, and we chatted for a few minutes once she had explained that no photos were allowed. I was amazed at how easily I conversed with her. What joy.

We discovered the palace's beautiful mosque, complete with a Moorish courtyard and a reflecting pool in the middle of the palace grounds. Momentarily gone were the constant thoughts of terrorism that plagued me, disrupting my sleep and shattering my peace of mind. The cool green expanse outside the windows erased all thought of those taken hostage earlier in the day in a church in Normandy. The priest had been murdered. It was the fourth European terrorist attack in five days. I breathed in the scent of the nearby woods, fresh and green, and cleared my mind of distressing thoughts.

The Girl on the Belvedere

On our way back to the car, we traversed those woods. Tall trees arched their leafy limbs overhead. I walked with Anna and watched Marjorie chatting easily with Ibrahim and Lucía up ahead. *How lucky I am to have friends like these.*

Later, while resting in the car while the others were in the grocery, I received a text from my husband asking me to be very, very careful in the wake of the latest attacks. I was being careful, but these attacks all seemed so random and unpredictable. What could one reasonably do?

That night, we had dinner at Anna and Ibrahim's apartment. Ibrahim presented me with a cookbook from Israel. While I perused its glossy pages, he set fresh green grapes on the coffee table as our appetizer. The main course was salmon and red onion pizza on impossibly thin crust with a crème fraîche sauce and a colorful salad with balsamic and olive oil. We had watermelon for dessert, plus coffee with cardamom. So healthy, so simple, so delicious.

Afterward, I bid Lucía goodbye at the train station. I would not see her again this trip; she had classes all day and needed to study at night for her final exams. I gave her several hugs and promised to keep in touch.

WE WERE UP EARLY the next morning, though Anna and Ibrahim could not join us for an early breakfast. They were leaving for Israel in two days, the day after our departure, and they were starting their packing this morning. Marjorie and I decided to get coffee at an outdoor café we had spied while waiting for Ibrahim's return from Jerusalem several evenings before. It was an Italian café, with excellent cappuccino and croissants. The day was clear and sunny. I should have been perfectly content.

And yet, after Nice, after all the attacks here in Germany, I felt my fear rising. I looked at every car, every motorcycle, constantly expecting to see guns protruding. I looked at every truck, expecting to be run down. I sat in fear. Logically, I knew that this was completely ridiculous, yet, still, I sat in fear. At my request we moved back from our street-side table to one partially hidden by concrete pillars. Gail, too, seemed more relaxed sitting away from the street.

We soon saw Ibrahim waving to us, and we joined him and Anna in their car. They were taking us to a second breakfast—at a shopping mall. Marjorie and I traded alarmed looks in the back seat. Marjorie was counting on my supposed knowledge of Europe to keep her safe, and I had promised my family that I would stay away from crowds. I asked Anna if she was afraid of the mall in light of the recent Munich attack.

"No," she said. "It can happen anywhere. Next time it might be a train station."

"Or a church," I said, remembering the attack on the priest in France the day before.

The mall was almost deserted when we arrived, even though it was the middle of the day. The weather was beautiful, and I could see the sun sparkling on the Rhine River. I made myself relax and enjoy my peaceful surroundings.

Afterward, we drove along the Rhine, took a ferry across the river, walked to a park on an island, and stopped to sit on the rocky shoreline. As we sat, longboat after longboat glided by. I'd seen narrow river cruisers like these advertised on *Masterpiece* on PBS on Sunday evenings, and here they were, of every color, size, and nationality. The tourists were standing out on the deck or on their individual stateroom balconies. *Someday,* I thought, *someday, I will take one of these small, glamorous river cruises and see the castles on the hills and those small villages with red rooftops clinging to the mountainsides.*

We moved into the shade and settled on a park bench.

Ibrahim told Marjorie and me the romantic story of his sister's engagement, and we peppered him with questions about her upcoming nuptials in Israel. What will she wear? What will the groom wear? What will the ceremony be like? Would there be a dinner afterward?

When we realized we were hungry, we walked back across the bridge to the car and returned to Mannheim, where we enjoyed a Turkish dinner of *kofta* [spiced ground beef], rice, and chicken with *tzatziki* sauce, followed by ice cream and espresso. After dinner, I was so exhausted that I was falling asleep, even though it was only six o'clock. At the car, Ibrahim presented me with the Middle Eastern spice *za'atar*, which I would need for many of the recipes in the cookbook he had given me, plus packing material for Marjorie's ceramic cow. Thus ended our last full day with my good friends.

ON OUR FINAL morning in Germany, Marjorie and I went down to the counter to check out of our hotel. Since I didn't speak a word of German, I asked the hotel representative, "English or Français?"

"English," she replied. Only the museum guardian at the Schwetzingen Palace had responded *"Français"* to this question here in Germany, even though the two countries share a common border.

We dragged our suitcases toward the station and bought one last pastry and coffee. Then we sat down to await the arrival of Anna and Ibrahim, who would see us onto our train. I was deeply exhausted after almost two months in Europe, but I was sad to leave; I truly loved this young couple and had no idea when I would see them again.

As our departure time neared, they appeared, and the four

of us walked across the tram tracks into the train station. There we discovered that our train to Paris had been delayed. We sat, we stood, we watched the soldiers with machine guns on high alert passing through the crowds, making their rounds. I continually watched the electronic schedule board for updates. "It's okay," Anna said. "This is your track, right in front of us. We'll make sure you get on the right train in plenty of time."

I must admit that I fall apart in foreign train stations. The timetables, the changing track assignments, and my inability to speak multiple foreign languages all confuse me and leave me almost unable to function. Now, in this Mannheim station, I was as nervous as I'd been the first time I ever boarded a European train.

Our train was ninety minutes late, and at the last minute there was indeed a track change. We had to run to catch the train. Down the escalator we went and through a tunnel under the tracks, emerging on the other side just as the high-speed train approached. I took one last look at my friends as the train glided to a stop. I still couldn't quite believe my good fortune: in these whirlwind five days in Germany, I had reconnected with them and reaffirmed those bonds that had held us together in the two years since Quebec.

I took my leave of Anna and Ibrahim. There were no tears; those would fall later. I hugged Anna and tried to hug Ibrahim, but his arms were already full; he had insisted on loading my heavy bags onto the train for me. Once he deposited them, we shared a quick hug, and then he hopped off. By the time I got to my seat, they were outside our window, my dear international friends, waving goodbye. I flapped my arms like wings and gave them a thumbs-up, wishing them well on their own journey to Israel the next day for Ibrahim's sister's wedding. They did the same, pointing to me. How I would miss them! But now I knew that I would see them again, which sweetened the sad parting.

In my suitcase were the Middle Eastern spices and cookbook from Jerusalem, gifts from afar brought back for me by Ibrahim. I only hoped that if they visited me in Tulsa I could make them feel as welcome as I had felt on this most personal look at Germany.

As we glided through the mountains of southern Germany on this silent high-speed train, I saw one beautiful town after another, all connected by peaceful two-lane roads. I imagined my husband and myself driving these same roads, carefree, stopping along the way to admire a house, a hill, a forest.

WE ARRIVED IN PARIS, exited the train station, and hailed a taxi. As we pulled away I was surprised to realize that I knew exactly where we were, that the streets were familiar. I chatted easily with the driver and gave him the location of our hotel. It was my favorite hotel in Paris: small, inexpensive, with charming rooms and a wonderful breakfast in a private garden. We stashed our bags there, set out for a bit of sightseeing, and had an early dinner near the church Saint-Sulpice.

At dinner, we met an American woman, a professor on sabbatical from Boston, with a yappy dog in her lap. I was surprised that I spoke much better French than she, even though she was living in Paris.

The next morning, over strong, fragrant coffee, yogurt in little glass bottles, excellent jam, and croissants, we plotted our day of shopping. It was my last day in Europe, and while bone-tired, I was determined to enjoy this most beautiful city.

My baby granddaughter had a birthday coming up, her first, and I was determined to buy her a French baby outfit, like the many I had drooled over in various Paris windows. We browsed several shops, and then suddenly, on Boulevard Raspail, I saw it:

the perfect striped little-girl dress. Forgotten was anything for myself, so wrapped up was I in the idea of my baby girl dressed in the latest from Paris. I spent many happy minutes choosing the size and deciding whether to buy the matching fabric rose brooch or the hat. Marjorie, in the meantime, found a striped sweater of her own.

That happy errand done, Marjorie and I walked to the area around Le Bon Marché, the elegant department store in the 7th *arrondissement* [district]. I knew that there was a Guerlain store nearby, and we had decided to choose new fragrances from the famous *parfumerie*.

I had worn Guerlain's *Shalimar* since the sixth grade. Beatlemania had just begun, and as a young teenager, I read an interview with the model Pattie Boyd, George Harrison's girlfriend, in which she confided that her favorite perfume was *Shalimar*. That was good enough for me. I requested and received the fragrance for Christmas, and a fifty-year love affair began. Although I have tried many perfumes during my now-long life, I always return to *Shalimar*. Happily, Pattie Boyd had excellent taste.

My other scent obsession is lavender, so reminiscent of the scents of Provence. While in Villefranche, I had searched the internet for the "best French lavender perfume." I was delighted to find that one of the contenders was *Jicky* by Guerlain, which had been made since 1889. At least it would be a start on the search for a new scent.

We located the elegant Guerlain boutique after wandering around a bit and were soon waving paper perfume-scented wands in front of our noses. Although I sampled many, *Jicky* won the day, as I suspected it might. Marjorie chose *Souffle de Parfum de Shalimar*, but wanted to think about it a bit. I purchased mine, and after walking a half block from the store, Marjorie said, "Let's go back. I want that perfume."

"Of course!" I said. "Where else would you choose a new perfume? We're in *Paris*!"

Fancy packages in hand, we entered Le Bon Marché, submitting bags and purses to the jittery security guards at the door. It was founded in 1838, and is one of the first modern department stores. It occupies a whole city block and has three levels, boasting every manner of clothing, shoes, cosmetics, and housewares one could desire. We wandered through several departments and finally crossed the air bridge into an adjacent building, containing several restaurants and a very modern food hall. "Wow," said Marjorie, surveying the options. "This is incredible."

We realized that we were starving, and even though we were amid two floors of food from all across France—cheese, olives, meats, chocolates, salts, vegetables, and cakes—we couldn't decide what we wanted. We exited the store and started down a promising street, in search of a café.

Halfway down the block, for no reason at all, a feeling of dread overtook me, and I stopped. Marjorie stopped, too, and looked at me quizzically. "What is it?" she asked.

"I don't know," I said. "Probably nothing."

I looked at the street around us. It was a normal Parisian street in a commercial area, with restaurants, shops, and lots of foot traffic. We took three more steps, and I stopped again. "There's something wrong," I said. "We can't go down this street."

"Why not?" Marjorie asked, concerned, peering down the block.

"I don't know," I said. "I'm afraid. There's something wrong."

"All right," Marjorie said. "Let's turn around."

We turned and walked quickly in the other direction.

There were no terror attacks that day, but the hair on my neck had been standing up. To the end of my days, I will believe that we were facing danger, although I'll never know what it was. And that, too, is the nature of terror.

We settled on a corner café, and I ordered a Coca-Cola, my energy flagging. Marjorie ordered a coffee. We sat at a table on the narrow sidewalk, both facing the street, wedged in between a gentleman reading a newspaper and two fashionable women delicately eating their salads while smoking cigarettes. So very French.

We relaxed and chatted, only occasionally glancing at the passing traffic. I barely had any morbid thoughts of bullets flying from passing cars. We did not discuss my bizarre and irrational episode of fear, but it hung unspoken between us. On this, my last day in Paris, my last day abroad after almost two months away, I was content to go home and resume my normal life.

We wandered through the charming *quartier* [neighborhood], went into some boutiques, and passed by others. I had only two more items on my shopping list: gifts for my daughter, Stephanie, and my daughter-in-law, Sarah. We found a boutique on Boulevard Saint-Germain, and I picked out two scarves designed in France.

We strolled further along the Boulevard, then turned north and walked to the Luxembourg Gardens. We watched a group of old men play *pétanque* and stopped at the famous basin to watch children pushing their sailboats along with sticks. I had so many memories here—with John and the children, with my co-author Georgia, with my friends Claire and Michael, and now, with Marjorie. I was so sad to leave even though I was exhausted and had been away from home for a long, long time.

We took a long last walk along the Seine on the Right Bank to the Louvre, had dinner at an Italian restaurant on the Left Bank, and returned to our hotel, exhausted by our day and ready to pack our suitcases.

In our hotel room, I texted with Lucía. I told her a bit about our day, and that we would leave in the morning. I said my goodbye, signed off and looked at Marjorie, who could tell at a glance that I was sad to close this latest chapter with my Quebec friends.

We read for a bit, then turned off the lights.

18

AU REVOIR ALL OVER AGAIN

The next morning, we had a wild ride to the airport, punctuated by a verbal altercation between our taxi driver and a limo driver. It was in such rapid, angry French that I had no hope of comprehending. I looked at Marjorie, and she seemed alarmed. I glanced out the window and realized that getting out of the taxi in this neighborhood was not an option; it was very run-down and poor-looking, with groups of men simply standing around, staring at us. I took a deep breath and said a prayer. The light changed from red to green, and the argument ended as we sped away.

In the airport, we glanced through the outposts of famous Parisian shops, then settled down with some coffee to await our boarding call. As we took off, I could see the Eiffel Tower and the Montparnasse skyscraper. I took one long, last look at the Seine and all of Paris before we turned away and headed toward the Channel.

As we flew over Scotland, then Ireland, I thought of Neill and Fiona from those isles, and the others from points afar. It still felt strange to not see my classmates daily. We had been

The Girl on the Belvedere

thrown together by virtue of ability and had been separated just as quickly. I was privileged to know them.

I thought back two years to my sadness at departing Quebec, the site of so many adventures with my friends. Now, I had seen them again and knew that it would not be long before we were once again laughing about our adventures in Germany, in Israel, in Mexico, in Oklahoma, or in some other location. I smiled as I thought about my old friends from Quebec and my new friend, Susi, from Switzerland. What a surprising turn my life had taken. Who would have thunk it?

A FEW DAYS LATER, I sat in my son's family room, with its wide windows overlooking a slope of the Ouachita Mountains painted in glorious shades of green under the strong August sun. My granddaughter sat on the rug in front of me, eating Cheerios, while the Cavalier King Charles Spaniel sat nearby, hoping for a crumb. My grandson was in the tub, content after a morning of fishing with his father and grandfather. We had just enjoyed a huge breakfast, compliments of my *belle-fille*, beautiful Sarah, my son's wife. My daughter in New York was most likely having her customary weekend brunch with friends.

The fear that had felt so all-consuming while in Europe was just a memory now, even though common sense told me that rough seas lay ahead. I thought about that truck in Nice, that shooter in Munich, those knife attacks, those axe attacks, the murder of the priest in Normandy, and further afield, the constant suicide bombs and car bombs in the Middle East. I thought about Anna's fear while sitting in the open-air Turkish restaurant, my fear while sitting in the pretty café near the water tower, Marjorie's fear while standing in that interminable line in the Nice airport. I thought about all the times I had been uncomfortable in large crowds: standing near a tourist site, getting on a plane, waiting in a train station. I thought about reversing course on that Paris side street. I thought about my European friends and the dangers they faced. I did not know that within a few short days, there would be an attack in Switzerland, not terribly far from Susi's city.

I turned my attention to the present. My granddaughter played peek-a-boo with my husband on the floor in front of me. The spaniel hoovered the rug for crumbs. My daughter-in-law straightened the kitchen. My son assisted my grandson with his bath. The new pet rabbit was happy in his hutch, the big chocolate lab was content on the tile floor, and our dog, Nutmeg, rested in her travel crate, paws crossed, door open, queen of her one-room kingdom.

My husband, my children, my grandchildren. Everything I need is right here. I am safe, I am loved, and that is enough.

I am home.

IMMERSED IN OKLAHOMA

19

ANTICIPATION

One year later, my husband and I headed to the airport late one Saturday night. I'd been receiving text updates from my friends Anna and Ibrahim all day as they made their way to Tulsa. They had sent me a photo from Frankfurt: a selfie taken on their departing flight, sitting in their seats, ready to go. And now, they were almost here, arriving from Atlanta.

"Will you recognize them?" John asked.

"Of course," I said, peering into the multitude of people streaming through the one-way security door.

And suddenly, there they were: Ibrahim with his customary backpack and checkered hat, and Anna, her hair pulled back, dressed in black with minimal makeup for the twenty-four-hour trip. We exchanged the usual post-flight pleasantries before hoisting their bags from the carousel and heading to the car.

They were surprised by the size of John's car, a full-size SUV. "Do you carry your saddles in the back when you're going out to ride your horse?" Anna asked, laughing.

"Yes," he said. The new arrivals giggled in the back seat.

"We'll take you out to the barn," I added, completely serious.

"Oh, good!" Anna said after a heartbeat of silence. "I would like to see some horses."

When we arrived home and walked through the front door, my two friends gasped. "Oh, wow," Anna said. "It's so big!"

We do have a large home, and to these two young Europeans, who lived in a small city apartment, it must have seemed like a castle. I knew how they felt; our New York City apartment had been so small that I had to back out of the kitchen to open the oven door. I showed them the kitchen and where to find coffee the next morning. Then I took them to their room, brought them some water, and told them to make themselves at home.

"We are very casual here," I said, "and if you need or want something and can't find it, just ask."

As I retired for the night, my mind flew back to the last time I had seen these two, in the Mannheim train station.

There had been soldiers with machine guns circulating through the station in the wake of the terror attacks in Nice, Normandy, Ansbach, and Munich. Over the past year, there had been more attacks here in the US, in Europe, and in the Middle East. That had not changed, but my response to them had. I was still wary, but more resigned to the danger and more determined to just live my life on my own terms.

How many of my fears, both large and small, were based in my childhood? Had I been predisposed to them due to my upbringing? Is there a difference between fear of your parents, and fear of terrorism? I'm not sure—when you are a child, your parents are your entire world. You are totally dependent upon them for food, for shelter, for affection, for direction. They hold the keys to understanding your life. As I child I never knew what was going to happen next, which holds its own terror.

Ideologic terrorism is sudden, explosive, and deadly. That much is true. But were my reactions to the terrorism in Nice and

Germany normal, or excessive? I think now that they were a bit of both. From staying at the Institut and not responding to my family's pleas to return home, to my determination to travel to Germany in the midst of continuing attacks, I just decided I would continue on, fear or no fear. *This* is what I had learned in Europe in addition to French. It is a very different frame of mind from the infrequent but real panic attacks of the past when I feared I had said or done the wrong thing.

I will never know whether my childhood fears and my fear of terrorism were linked, but now, I found that their origins didn't really matter. Life has always been fraught; that would never change. I think now that my childhood suffering taught me a certain stoicism, a certain resolve to keep going, which aided me in Europe in the midst of its misfortunes.

However, at this moment, there was no danger. I was hosting my friends from Europe and wanted to show them the best time possible and to repay the courtesy that they had shown me in Germany.

What would we do tomorrow? Where would we go? The day ahead lay open to all possibilities, which left me full of joyful anticipation. With that thought, I dimmed the lights in the house and turned my attention to the adventures that would begin in the morning.

20

DISCOVERIES

I had made a list of things to do while Anna and Ibrahim were here for their three-week visit, unaware that they had done their research and had a list of their own as well.

Over coffee on the patio, Anna asked, "Can we go to Stillwater?"

"Stillwater?" I asked, confused. I must have misheard her. Oklahoma State University is located there, but I couldn't imagine that she was interested in seeing the beautiful campus.

"Yes, Stillwater. I was looking at a map of Oklahoma, and I saw that there is a town called by that name. We just finished a project called Stillwater, and it would be so funny to send the office a picture from there. I'd like to stand at the city limits if there's a sign that says, 'Welcome to Stillwater.' Do they have signs like that in the United States?"

"I'm sure there will be a welcome sign at the city limits," I said, smiling. "I'd be happy to drive you there."

Anna was now a consultant for a multinational firm and had colleagues here in the United States. "My colleague in Virginia told me that he knows nothing about Oklahoma except that there was a bombing," she said.

"I've lived in Virginia," I said, "and I'm surprised that he knew that much. It's a huge country, very diverse, with a very diverse landscape. It takes two long days to drive to Virginia from Tulsa."

"How far is Santa Fe from here?" Anna asked.

"It's one very long day from here," I said, "in the opposite direction."

"I'd like to see it sometime," she said.

"New Mexico is incredibly beautiful," I assured her. "Sometimes the clouds are so white and puffy against the turquoise-blue sky that they look as if they're being held up by wires. The next time you come to the US, fly into Albuquerque and we'll pick you up there."

"I'd like that," Anna said with a grin.

She and Ibrahim were understandably exhausted after their long trip, and we decided to simply take a walk along the Arkansas River this first day. I snapped a photo of them posing in front of one of the bridges over the Arkansas River and sent it to Lucía in Mexico City.

"Wishing you were here!" I texted.

We went to Whole Foods to do a bit of grocery shopping. I encouraged them to pick up their favorite breakfast foods, and Anna said, "We are very slow. It's going to take us awhile to decide on what we want. It's best if you finish your own shopping, and we'll try to hurry. We're very slow at home, too."

As we shopped, we talked about dinner menus for the coming week. "Ibrahim and I are going to cook for you," Anna announced.

"That's terrific!" I said. "How long can you stay?" We all laughed.

~

The Girl on the Belvedere

THE NEXT MORNING, Anna and Ibrahim joined me for an early-morning walk. "You say hello to everyone," Anna observed, "or they say hello to you. And you give them eye contact."

"Yes, of course," I said. "It would seem rude to pass someone on a neighborhood street and not say hello."

"That's very different from Europe," Ibrahim said.

As we walked along and I said hello to both neighbors and strangers, I thought about this practice. Oklahomans are famously friendly, but did I really maintain eye contact and say hello to *everyone*?

In the coming days, we would take several of these walks, and by the third morning, my two guests were saying "Good morning!" to everyone we passed, usually beating me by several seconds. There were huge smiles on their faces as they did so, and I realized that this—*this*—was the United States to them. They had enjoyed their short tour of the Northeast after their time in Quebec, but they were on vacation, and while they found Americans very friendly and helpful, they had not been immersed in a neighborhood as they were here. It was the first revelation about my own life that I would have while they were my guests. After that first early morning stroll, I asked them what they would like to do that day. "A museum? Some shopping? Route 66?"

"I'd like to see a small town," said Anna, taking me by surprise.

"A small town. Hmmm. Okay," I said. "We'll go to Broken Arrow."

"Broken Arrow?" Ibrahim echoed. "As in, an arrow that you shoot?"

"Yes," I said. "That kind."

By the time we got out the door, it was almost lunchtime. "Okay," I said on the expressway, "I'm taking you to a typically Southern lunch place: Chick-fil-A."

"Oh, we saw that in the Atlanta airport," Anna said.

"What is it?" Ibrahim asked.

"Chicken," I said. "You'll love it."

When we arrived, I ordered for them. "How about chicken nuggets and waffle fries?" I asked.

"Sounds good," Anna said, even though she gave me an odd look.

They took pictures of the cow photos on the wall while we waited for our food. One was a close-up of a cow in front of the Tulsa skyline with the tagline, "Tulsah—thankz 4 eatin chikin. Xoxo, tha cowz." It made my friends giggle.

Our food arrived, and after a moment, Anna said, "These fries really *are* good. Why are they called 'awful fries'?"

"No, they're *waffle* fries!" I explained, laughing. "They look like waffles!"

Later, on Main Street in Broken Arrow, Anna said, "These are really cute shops."

"There are tons of fun restaurants, too. John and I really like coming out here for dinner," I said. "A few years ago, Broken Arrow decided to reinvent its Main Street, and it's become very popular."

"I really like that easy-listening music playing outside on all the loudspeakers," Anna said.

We passed a Belgian chocolatier and stopped to look in the window. "Okay," I said, "we can get some chocolate, or we can drive to Krispy Kreme. Or both."

"What's Krispy Kreme?" asked Anna.

"Hot doughnuts," I said.

"Oh, let's get doughnuts!" she exclaimed.

Unhappily, while the "hot now" red light was on outside the Krispy Kreme, signaling that the mechanized line was churning out glazed doughnuts, it was at a standstill, so we purchased a dozen glazed, plus a few flavors from the case. We almost made ourselves sick from too much sugar, and agreed that the maple ones were our favorite. I promised them that we would come back one morning when the doughnuts were hot coming off the line.

THE NEXT MORNING, we relaxed on the patio. They were still exhausted from their twenty-four-hour trip and had asked for a quiet day. At one point, Anna said, "How long has the turtle been here?"

"What turtle?" I asked.

"The one here in your back yard." She pointed, and sure enough, there was a turtle making its way across the walk.

"No idea," I said.

"He's living in those bushes near the fountain," Anna said, pointing.

On this particular quiet, stay-at-home day, the new Apple products were announced via livestream, and Anna and Ibrahim watched it to see what was new. Anna decided that she wanted the latest Apple watch and asked to go to the Apple store on the day they were released.

"No problem," I said.

I had French class that evening and decided to attend by myself, as my best friend Marjorie had asked if she could take my friends out to dinner and introduce them to her extended family. I met up with them again at Starbucks after class, and everyone was smiling. I was so glad that Marjorie had joined me last summer and that my friends were now her friends.

The next day, we set out for Stillwater. At one point, we passed a highway sign that said, "Watch out! Don't hit our workers—$10,000 fine."

"That's really strange," Anna said. "You get fined if you kill someone? That's all? No other consequences?"

"I've never thought about it like that," I confessed. She was right, though: it was a bizarre sign.

As we drove through rolling grasslands and past ranches and farms, I looked left and right, enjoying the early morning view of livestock. As we passed one large ranch with a herd of cattle standing in a pond, I casually announced, "Cow."

"Cow," Anna and Ibrahim repeated. It was the first repetition of what would become a private joke as we travelled the rural roads of Oklahoma in the coming weeks.

We stopped on the way into Stillwater for the requisite photo of Anna at the city limits. Then we continued on to the beautiful campus. They both were fascinated by the bald cypress trees growing right out of the water in a large pond and declared the campus to be very pretty with its uniform brick buildings and orange flowerbeds.

As we walked around campus, I realized that I neither made eye contact with nor greeted any of the multitude of people we passed. I mentioned this fact to Anna and Ibrahim, and they nodded. This large campus with its thousands of students was very different from my small neighborhood, where we habitually greeted all neighbors as we passed, establishing eye contact. Here, some people walked in twos or threes, chatting, but most students walked quickly, by themselves, and kept their eyes on the ground or straight ahead, without once looking at us. These unwritten cultural rules are so difficult to decipher in a newly experienced country and can leave one feeling bewildered. I had never even thought about it until Anna and Ibrahim had pointed out my behavior in my neighborhood.

I noticed Ibrahim looking around at all the international students who were walking along, checking their phones, and chatting with people who did not look like themselves. Ibrahim had a quizzical look on his face. We had discussed European versus American attitudes toward different nationalities several times. Though he didn't say it here, his frequent saying about casual and immediate acceptance of others, as he had said about our neighborhood greetings, was, "That would never happen in Europe."

As we strolled along, passing students of every race and nationality, I wanted to turn to Ibrahim and say, "We live in a great, great nation of immigrants. We try not to judge people on their heritage, their religion, or their looks. We have been through the crucible of slavery and through the narrow tunnels of anti-Irish, anti-Asian, anti-Catholic, anti-everything sentiment. We have experienced a sea change in this country, and while there have been and still are rough seas ahead, as we grapple with bigotry, civil unrest, and brutality, the majority of people have found safe and gentle harbors."

What I actually said to Ibrahim was...nothing. Not one word. *Nada*. I couldn't be absolutely sure what he was thinking, and thought it best not to speak.

We decided to have lunch at Freddy's, a hamburger chain with delicious ice cream.

"What is relish?" Ibrahim asked, looking over the menu.

"It's usually made of pickles," I said, "and it goes on your hamburger."

"I have to try this!" he exclaimed, rising from his chair.

"What's a turtle sundae?" Anna asked, clearly perplexed by the name.

"I'll get us some," I offered. "Don't worry. There are no actual turtles involved." I made the mistake of getting three large sundaes. We finished them anyway, groaning at having eaten way too much.

We drove the backroads to the Pawnee Bill Ranch and Museum, which displays items from the famous showman's long career. He had lived among the Pawnee and then showcased them in his Wild West show, providing much-needed employment at a time when there was little for Native Americans. At least that's what the museum sign said. I had to wonder about the veracity of that statement, but it had a point: what else were the Indians going to do after being forcibly relocated to Oklahoma, with thirty-nine tribal nations crammed into the future state?

Anna stood before a glass case containing a dramatic, elegant, and beautiful six-foot-long feather headdress. "It really is real!" she exclaimed, pointing to the regalia. "I've seen cowboy movies, but I thought that cowboys and Indians were just a myth. Indians are real!"

"I'm sorry?" I said, surprised and confused.

"I thought that Indians dressed like this were just a story," Anna said. "I didn't know that they were real people."

I was very surprised. I had never considered the possibility that anyone would think that Native Americans, with their ancient, noble history, rich traditions, and beautiful manner of dress were pure fantasy. I had grown up in "Indian Country" (a federal designation). I was trained in classical ballet by a member of the Shawnee-Peoria tribe. I have a good friend who is a Cherokee princess. I know scores of people who are of Native descent.

"Yes," I said. "This is Oklahoma. 'Oklahoma' is a Choctaw word that means 'Red People.'" I told my friends about the shameful Indian Removal Act of 1830—an act of genocide, really —which robbed Native Americans of their homes, lands, and livelihoods and forced them to walk to the future state of Oklahoma from North Carolina, from Georgia, from Florida, and from other distant locations. Before the Removal, there had been only five or six indigenous tribes in our state.

"I live in Indian Territory," I added, "within the boundaries of the Creek Nation. Three Indian nations come together at Tulsa: the Cherokee Nation, the Creek Nation, and the Osage Nation.

"Oklahoma was originally home to the Caddo, an agricultural tribe with huge population centers, as well as the Comanche and other nomad tribes of the Southern Plains who followed the bison herds. We'll see bison at the Tallgrass Prairie Preserve near Pawhuska, up in the Osage. Today, there are sixty-seven Indian nations in our state, organized into thirty-nine federally recognized tribes. We have a very unique history, and we are very proud of our heritage—even people like me who have little or no Indian blood."

Anna and Ibrahim were fascinated by the artifacts in this small gem of a museum. When they were finished examining its treasures, they came to sit outside with me on a bench. For a long moment, we regarded the beautiful rolling hills of the ranch in front of us.

"I could sit here forever," I said, breaking the silence.

"So could I," Anna said. "It's so beautiful."

"Welcome to Oklahoma," I said, smiling.

I looked out over the land, not wanting to move. I couldn't help it. I had soaked up the spirit of the Southern Plains during my many years in Oklahoma. Away from the cities, out in the great expanse, I wanted to run across that field, ride to that distant horizon, cross those low prairie hills. I wanted to climb over the Quartz Mountains, walk over the Ouachitas, stride over the Great Salt Plains. I had grown up with the great sweep of icy-blue winter skies overhead, with the stormy black skies of spring, with the pure golden light of autumn, with the white-hot skies of summer. Oh, this land, this land.

My friends sat silently next to me, regarding the ranch and taking in this foreign place, this place where cowboys and Indians were real and where the wind really did come "sweepin' down the plain." Oklahoma.

THAT NIGHT, they cooked schnitzel for us, the famous German dish, and prepared a large salad. The schnitzel was the best I'd ever had, and I could see why Ibrahim was famous for it. "People say they only want one piece, but then they eat three or four," Anna said, bragging just a bit. Three pieces later, I understood completely. The next day, they teased me about eating the leftover schnitzel for breakfast.

We visited the Apple store in the mall even though the new products would not appear for another week. We had lunch at a Mexican restaurant nearby. It was not the best Mexican food I'd ever had, but it was far from the worst, and a decent introduction to this beloved cuisine for Anna and Ibrahim.

Together, we attended my French film class that night, and I introduced them, in French, by name, by nationality, and by number of languages spoken: five for her, six for him, which made my classmates' eyes go wide. My professor and fellow students were full of questions for my friends. Afterward, a professor of Spanish invited Anna to speak to her business class about her experiences working internationally. We made no promises, not knowing what the next week would bring. Indeed, our time together seemed to be disappearing at a breakneck pace.

On the first Saturday of their visit, we headed to the lake: John, me, Anna, Ibrahim, Stephanie—who had recently moved back from New York—and Nutmeg the dog. John rented a pontoon boat for fishing, swimming, and relaxing. We signed the papers and loaded everyone onboard, but just as we were pulling into the ship's store for ice, John realized that he could not keep the boat in gear. I zipped up my life vest and stood along the edge of the boat, shoving us away from other boats as we drifted. Somehow, we made it into an empty slip and called the owner.

After a quick inspection, the owner proclaimed, "It's still drivable in reverse," so he drove us backward into his marina. "I have another boat you could take," he said, pointing. We followed his gaze to a cigarette boat worthy of *Miami Vice*.

"This is not a good idea," said Stephanie. "Let's not do this. That boat is too powerful and too fast."

I said nothing, but followed my husband's lead. We had both grown up coming to Oklahoma's many lakes, where we had water-skied, driven boats, and swam. John was a responsible boat driver, and I trusted him.

So now, we stood in front of the new boat with its V-shaped hull. The dog decided to get in first…but she didn't make it. She slipped off the narrow hull and fell into the dark water below, our old Nutmeg, and John leaned over and quickly grabbed her collar. I realized, stupidly, that I was carrying her life preserver and had not put it on her. Did I think I was going to throw it to her, like in the movies?

Ibrahim leaned over and held her head above the water, but dear old Nutmeg was struggling and beginning to lose the battle, slipping farther and farther into the dark water. Stephanie and I held on to John, who was about to be pulled in by the flailing dog. The owner saw our difficulty, ran over, lay flat on the dock, and grabbed Nutmeg by her hind legs. The three men finally managed to hoist poor Nutmeg out of the water and place her on the dock. She was panting and shaking, with a wild look in her eyes.

"That's it," I said. "We're done. No boat today."

We opted to fish along the shore instead, which delighted Ibrahim. "I've never been fishing before," he said. "I've always wanted to." He was a natural, and caught several fish, which my husband, the former surgeon, expertly disentangled and returned to the lake. By now the life vest was securely on Nutmeg, but she still avoided the water.

Unhappily, this was not the first time we almost inadvertently drowned the dog. We had once purchased a little plastic wading pool for Nutmeg, our new Labrador puppy. She splashed in it happily for hours. One summer weekend early in her life, we rented a boat at the lake, and when we stopped to anchor and swim, Nutmeg decided that it was time to get in the great big baby pool. We caught one glimpse of her stretched out over the water, and then, suddenly, she was all the way underwater, receiving the surprise of her life. She popped right up again —luckily, she was wearing her life vest that time—but paddled wildly toward the boat, nearly removing my skin with her nails as she struggled to get back in. After that, nothing could ever coax Nutmeg back into the water. On subsequent trips, when John and I would jump into the lake to swim, she would pace the boat, crying, barking, and begging us to stop this foolishness. Did we not know that this baby pool was bottomless? And now, ten years later, we had neglected to protect her from that which she feared most.

Later, when we were alone, I said to John, "No more boats. We no longer have the judgment nor the agility to handle emergency situations. What if that had been a grandchild?"

"I agree," said John. "It's beyond us now."

We shook our heads sadly. Not only had we almost lost our dog, but we had absolutely lost something else: our youth, with its quickness of mind and body.

~

The Girl on the Belvedere

BACK IN TOWN, we continued our culinary tour of Tulsa and introduced our friends to chicken fried steak, invariably accompanied by mashed potatoes and cream gravy, green beans, and pecan pie.

"It's the official state meal!" I proclaimed.

"I've heard of it!" said Anna.

They both claimed to like it. After all, chicken-fried steak is not that different from schnitzel.

"We don't eat this very often," John assured them, "but as they say around here, 'I do like a good chicken-fry.'"

We were full after finishing the main course of the "official state meal," so we passed on dessert.

We talked briefly about our Mexican friend, Lucía, as this was her birthday. I was sad that she wasn't here with us, but she couldn't take much time away from her new job. She was hoping to join us the following weekend. I pulled out my phone and texted her a brief happy birthday message.

She texted back, "For my birthday, I had a chance to meet up with friends from university and enjoy traditional Mexican food and mariachi songs, and go out dancing to a nightclub."

"Wonderful!" I said, happy that she was enjoying herself.

"I'm on my way to my hometown where I'll continue celebrations with family and a couple of friends who are joining us. Will send pictures later. Hope y'all are enjoying the meet-up."

I chuckled to myself. I had taught them to say "y'all" while in Quebec, and now it was a regular feature of our social media threads.

"Fun!" I texted her. "Have the best day ever!"

THE NEXT MORNING, Ibrahim prepared a typical Palestinian breakfast. He made bread to go with the *labneh*—yogurt that had drained all night to create a delicious rich-yet-tart cream, which is scooped up with the bread. He also made a type of toast, *manakish*, using the bread, olive oil, and *za'atar*, the spice that he had given to me the previous summer. Breakfast disappeared as fast as he could make it.

As we ate, I asked, "What does 'halal' mean?" I had seen the word on food trucks in New York that featured Middle Eastern cuisine.

"It's the same as Kosher," Ibrahim said.

"Ah, that's why you look for Kosher foods in the grocery store," I said, connecting the dots.

The cookbook he had given me was written by two friends, one Jewish, one Muslim. There was a friendly "argument" running through it over which foods were authentic. The authors of this Arab-Israeli cookbook ultimately concluded, "Nobody 'owns' a dish, because it is very likely that someone else cooked it before them, and another person before that."

We were lazy this day after all the activities and calamities at the lake the day before, and we simply read, rested, and watched TV. I made a pecan pie, using cane syrup instead of corn syrup and arranged the pecans in a circular pattern on top. "Come look at this!" Anna called to Ibrahim, admiring my work.

While it cooled, I made a vegetarian dinner, and then it was time for the pie. At their first bite, they were completely silent, and I was afraid that they didn't like it. But then Anna said, "This is really, *really* good," as she continued to eat. Ibrahim said nothing, but just ate bite after bite. When he was done, he went back for another piece.

After dinner, we called Lucía in Mexico and put her on speakerphone. "I can't believe the three of you are together!" she said. "I wish I could be there right now."

"So do we!" Anna said.

"I'm going to try to come next weekend," Lucía assured us. "I think I can get one or two days off."

"See you then!" we all chimed in.

We signed off and cleared the dishes. Then these two light-hearted young friends of mine suggested that we watch *The Secret Life of Pets*.

21

BACKROADS

Monday was lazy. There was coffee on the patio; communing with Nutmeg the dog, Boris the cat, and Turtle; watching television, grocery shopping, and simple relaxing.

The next day, we got up early and headed to Afton via the Interstate so that we could travel the picturesque roads back to Tulsa. We would be driving along Route 66, the famous highway built in the 1920s that stretched across eight states, starting in Chicago, heading south to Tulsa and then west to Santa Monica, California.

We started at Miller's Pecans, where my guests stocked up on various small packages of pecans to hand out as gifts in Germany and Israel. I told them that Oklahoma was famous for its sweet pecans and that bakers prize them the world over. As we set off from the pecan store, we saw the rolling hills, cows ("Cow!"), horses, farms, ranches, and tiny towns of northeastern Oklahoma. In Germany, I had been amazed that small towns were so close together, sometimes within sight of each other. Here on the Southern Plains, the territory is vast and largely unpopulated.

I pointed out the occasional raised mound of an old tornado shelter and a preserved iron bridge on one of the original Route 66 "alignments," the authentic sections of the route that now parallel the modern highways. We eventually arrived at the Blue Whale of Catoosa, one of the most famous attractions on Route 66. While we were there, several busloads of tourists from the Czech Republic pulled up. As they unloaded, they chattered as excitedly as school children, most holding cameras and cell phones.

Route 66 was once known as the "Mainstreet of America" and connected the main streets of many rural towns. It was dubbed the "Mother Road" by John Steinbach and symbolized a road to opportunity for migrant workers in *The Grapes of Wrath*. There was also a popular television show called *Route 66* in the 1960s, although it must have been a bit racy because I was not allowed to watch it.

I have known about Route 66 all my life. I was born and raised in its epicenter, Tulsa. The route was conceived of and promoted by a Tulsa businessman, Cyrus Avery, and he succeeded beyond his wildest dreams—if only he could see the multitude of American and international tourists along its alignments now! The gas stations, cafes, motels, barns, and "giants," those kitschy outsized sculptures, like Tulsa's own Golden Driller, are world-famous and have been photographed and documented in scores of books about Route 66.

My husband and I have even driven half of Route 66, from Chicago to Tulsa. I have photos of John standing next to all of the giants along the route. My favorite photo from that trip is one of John standing next to the Gemini Giant, an old-fashioned astronaut wearing a green space suit and a white helmet on the property of a small drive-in restaurant in Illinois. We went inside to order two Coca-Colas to go, but were enticed to sit down and enjoy a piece of pumpkin pie that the owner had just baked.

And *that* is the magic of this mostly two-lane highway. It speaks of the open road, unexplored towns, and freedom. Someday, we will drive west from Tulsa all the way to the Santa Monica pier and complete the tour. In my daydreams, I am always headed west, into the sunset.

On this day, after the Blue Whale, we continued into Tulsa. Once there, we ditched the famous route and took the expressway at the Hard Rock Cherokee Casino. There are several alignments that run through the city, but we were tired and hungry and would see them another day.

When we arrived home, we saw a group text from Lucía: "Dear all—please pray for Mexico. An earthquake hit us a few moments ago. I was at work when it happened. I can't describe the feeling. Ninety-four confirmed deaths." Lucía must have been terrified.

"Oh no no no no no," I texted back for all of us. "Please let us know, are you okay?"

We did not hear back immediately, which worried us.

We turned on the television to look for news about the quake while I prepared another dish that I had promised: fried okra, which we ate standing up while keeping tabs on developments.

We finally heard back from Lucía: "Please pray for a friend. We haven't heard from her. She was exiting university when the earthquake took place. Her name is Sofia. 119 deaths now. My family and I are safe, but my friend is still missing. It's been six hours. Flights were canceled," she continued. "The airport isn't open."

Anna texted her own words of comfort and shock.

Lucía continued, "My boss had granted me permission to come see you, and I was about to book the flights to Tulsa. But so far, one can't access or exit Mexico City due to the buildings that fell."

The Girl on the Belvedere

"I'm glad that you and your family are safe!" Anna said. "Let us know any updates. We are not getting much information here. We're watching the news but they are not saying much."

After dinner, we heard more from Mexico: "139 deaths now," Lucía texted. "At my university, forty students were injured and one is unfortunately dead. My sister is safe, thank goodness." I could not imagine Lucía's fear while waiting for news of her sister.

"Okay, good," I texted back. "That's a relief. And your friend, Sofia?"

"We don't know anything about her yet."

Anna texted, "I am so sorry! We are praying for her!"

We were all shaken by the news. Oklahoma is not immune to natural disasters; our tornadoes are well-known, and there had been a bad one in Tulsa just a few weeks before my friends arrived. However, this earthquake was massive, with hundreds dead and injured. Mexico City had been devastated, with lives lost, homes demolished, and businesses destroyed.

The next morning, I texted Lucía for more updates. "How are you? Has your friend been located?"

Lucía quickly replied, "Y'all, we found my friend. The fence at her house fell, but she is safe."

"Good news!" I said via text.

While I could not imagine the magnitude of this disaster, I could picture the devastation, panic, and confusion.

Many years before, while visiting Mexico City with my parents and brother, I had experienced a major earthquake, registering 7.5 on the Richter scale at its epicenter 300 miles away in Oaxaca.

My father and brother had just walked out of Sanborn's department store on the avenue Paseo de La Reforma, a major boulevard of Mexico City. I walked out a few seconds after them and sat down with them on the small decorative railing around a tree.

Just as I sat, the railing began pitching back and forth. "I'm breaking it," I said and stood up. The pitching did not stop. I tried to figure out this confusing situation. I was having difficulty standing.

At that moment, my mother walked out of the store and said, "I think I'm going to faint. I can't stand up."

My father said, "I know what this is. It's an earthquake." He walked us over to a large tree so that we could hold on to something and stabilize ourselves. As we clutched the trunk, I looked up and watched a lone cloud appear, then disappear, behind a skyscraper again and again.

All traffic came to a halt. People exited their cars and ran screaming through the streets. A very old woman calmly watched this scene as she held onto a stop sign near us.

Eventually, the rocking stopped, people got back in their cars, and life slowly resumed. "Only" six people were killed that day, five of them in Mexico City, but on our way back to our hotel, we noticed that almost every building displayed large cracks.

The current earthquake that Lucía had just experienced was much more devastating than that one. This one was centered 80 miles away, and killed more than 200 people in Mexico City alone and injured thousands more. I had been terrified all those years ago, and I could not imagine the fear, the panic, the dismay, and the desperation that was likely gripping Mexico. Anna, Ibrahim, and I began to plan our day, albeit with troubled minds, and it reminded me of the morning after the truck rampage in Nice, when people went about their day, forever changed.

∼

THAT DAY, we visited the Gilcrease Museum, which contains the foremost collection of Western art in the world. We saw the special exhibit, "After Removal: Rebuilding the Cherokee Nation," which told the story of the Trail of Tears and its aftermath—the story I had outlined for them at the Pawnee Bill Ranch and Museum.

"I may have a little Indian blood," I told my friends. "My family tradition holds that a Cherokee woman walked the Trail of Tears, dropped off in Springfield, Missouri, and married into my family, although I've never been able to prove it. I'm not a member of the Cherokee Nation, therefore not an Indian, but my grandmother looked Native American, as did my mother to some extent. Who knows? It's Oklahoma, and we all like to claim Native American blood, even if we don't have any. Someday, I'll research it."

I cannot see Indian artifacts and artwork without thinking of my upbringing in the dance world where I was exposed daily to the parallel cultures of Native America and Eastern Europe. Moscelyne Larkin and Roman Jasinski built the phenomenal company that is now Tulsa Ballet, carefully developing talent and adhering to the twin principles of quality and professional integrity. The senior Jasinskis' tenure was followed by that of their son, Roman L. Jasinski, who brought a world-wide repertoire to Tulsa. In recent years, the company has taken a giant leap forward, from national prominence into worldwide recognition, under Italian artistic director Marcello Angelini, who has built an empire upon the foundation left to him by the Jasinskis. Their collective history is now part of Tulsa's history, this place that is an amalgam of immigrants and native peoples.

That night, after our visit to the Gilcrease Museum, Claire and Michael invited us over to their house for dinner. They had already met Anna and Ibrahim in Quebec, but I was very sad that they would not meet Lucía, about whom they had heard so much.

Anna was awed by the beauty of Claire's home—everyone is —and walked through the house, admiring this and that. As a gift, my friends brought Claire and Michael a German tote bag and a box of candy. They always came bearing gifts, these two, and were constantly surprising me with yet another exotic food item or a freshly prepared German or Israeli dinner. Lucía would have done the same.

The next morning, Lucía sent us a video of the interior of a house in Mexico during the quake. It shook until everything inside had collapsed.

"Oh no...Is this your house?" Anna asked.

"No, a friend's," Lucía replied.

"Anyone injured?" I asked.

"No. Luckily, no one injured. My boss called me just now to ask if I was leaving today or tomorrow for the USA. Like I said, he had granted me permission to take two days off work. However, Mexico City is in chaos, and it's impossible to access or exit the city, which has collapsed buildings, or even the airport, which has damaged structures. It takes people hours just to commute from one place to the other."

"Okay, darlin'," I texted. "I understand. I'm reading all the reports, and it is just awful and tragic. It's unbelievable. I'm reading of the brave men and women of Los Topos. Bless them, and let them find survivors. We understand that Mexico is in a national crisis, a disaster of huge proportions. It makes me sad to realize you are not coming to Tulsa. We would so love to see you. You are precious to us, and we love you and miss you. Please know that I am praying for you, your family, your friends, and your country. Sending love your way."

I was indeed terribly sad that Lucía would not be joining us here in Tulsa for our mini-reunion, but the news from Mexico

City was devastating. I could tell by her comments that Lucía was shaken and grieving for all those lost and for her beautiful city. We were upset for her as well. Just like that, in the blink of an eye, lives were lost and buildings were destroyed.

THAT EVENING, we went ahead with our plan to attend a game at Oneok Field, our baseball stadium downtown. It is located in the historic Greenwood District, the site of the Tulsa Race Massacre of 1921.

A slight scuffle, or perhaps a trip of one's foot, was what triggered the massacre. A young Black man and a young White woman somehow became entangled in an elevator. Were they embracing, as one of today's leading Greenwood historians believes? Was it an attempted rape, as the young woman maintained as the elevator door opened, even though she later refused to press charges? We may never know, but when that door opened and the two were seen in close proximity, all hell broke loose.

The young man was taken into custody by the sheriff. Armed Black men gathered to prevent a lynching. Armed White men gathered to confront the Blacks. Shots were fired, and perhaps as many as ten people, Black and White, were killed. The crowd was ordered to disperse, and it did. Hours later, a group of Whites decided that not enough had been done to avenge the situation, and the assault on Greenwood began.

That massacre resulted in somewhere between fifty and three hundred of our Black citizens murdered and as many as ten thousand left homeless, their abodes and businesses burned to the ground. So many lost everything—*everything*—that day. Greenwood Avenue itself was destroyed. In its time, it had been known as "Black Wall Street," the famous street marked by incredible Black entrepreneurship. There were Black doctors, lawyers, pharmacists, grocers, barbers, pastors, teachers, and other professionals on that street. It had been a thriving, self-sufficient community.

I do not understand "the zero-sum game" as it plays out in human interactions. This is the idea that if someone else is successful, one must counteract that success, must destroy that success, in order to become successful in one's own right. That very idea can inspire hate and rage, and those emotions were what gripped and engulfed the rioters in Tulsa one hundred years ago, leading to so much death and destruction.

Innocent people were murdered where they stood. During my childhood, our elderly neighbor, a banker at the time of the massacre, once told my brother his personal story of that day, as observed through the front window of the bank where he worked. The bank's Black doorman, dressed in the formal livery of the position at that time, simply stepped out of the bank's front door to see what was happening. He was shot dead on the spot. This type of outrage was repeated all over downtown. My husband's great aunt, a young child at the time, told John of seeing a large open-bed truck going down the street, piled with Black bodies.

In the name of "safety," many Black citizens were rounded up and detained in centers such as the large municipal theatre —where I danced many years later—and the ballpark of that time. While they were being "protected," their homes and businesses were being looted, then burned.

I do not understand terror. And this was terrorism, pure and simple.

Yet there were acts of bravery, too. White employers, such as another now-deceased friend of ours, hid their Black employees upstairs in the businesses they owned, and met the mob at the door with shotguns, displaying a willingness to defend their employees to the death. The sheriff, who held the "perpetrator" in custody on the top story of the jail, disabled the elevator and deployed sharpshooters to the roof, and deputies with shotguns to the top of the stairs, to guard against the mob. No matter what aspects of the riot he mishandled—and there were many—there would not be a lynching on his watch.

Despite the fact that these events happened in my own home town, I did not hear about the massacre until 1965, when I was becoming a teenager. I was watching a live report on the Watts riot in Los Angeles, and mentioned to my parents that I couldn't believe what I was seeing.

"You know," said my father, "there was a race riot in Tulsa, too. In fact, it was the worst race riot in our country's history."

"What?" I asked, shocked and uncomprehending.

He told me the story of what had happened in Greenwood, and always cognizant of history and historical locations, drove me through Greenwood just a few days later. It was deserted and desolate, just a shell of what it must have been. It was a lesson in what can occur when mobs are allowed to rule. And mob rule is one of the ugly realities of terror.

I still have no idea how my father learned about the Tulsa Race Massacre of 1921. He was three years old at the time, and a resident of another state. The topic was quickly swept under the rug, was not taught in schools, and was never mentioned. Few Whites had ever heard of it, and even many Blacks had not.

All that has changed now, though, as we have just commemorated the massacre's one hundredth anniversary. We citizens of Tulsa yearn for peace and prosperity for *all* of our citizens. We cannot change the past, but we can continue to evolve, grow, and learn. Today, Tulsa is the home of one of the oldest and most successful celebrations of Juneteenth, the commemoration of the end of slavery. Greenwood Rising, our new museum and history center, has opened, and with that newly-turned earth we hope for a meaningful revival of our community. The Greenwood District includes many new businesses. The John Hope Franklin Reconciliation Park memorializes the massacre, and educates the public about the Black contribution to the development of the State of Oklahoma. It is connected to the new Greenwood Rising museum by the "Pathway to Hope," which features artwork honoring past Greenwood residents, and is located along busy I-244, which divided Greenwood and halted any hope for further development. I pray that the future leaders of Tulsa will now consider the impact of urban renewal on all our citizens and work to improve our larger community.

On this clear, hot, and humid Oklahoma evening, as I watched the baseball game with my friends, I thought about the massacre that had occurred exactly where I now sat. As wonderful as our new ballpark is, I think about Greenwood and its former inhabitants every time I attend a game. I can only pray that this hallowed ground will continue to develop as a place of peace, prosperity, shared pastimes, and education.

THE NEXT MORNING, we traveled Route 66 in the other direction, starting at the Cyrus Avery Centennial Plaza in downtown Tulsa. This peaceful plaza contains a bronze sculpture of the meeting of a horse-drawn wagon and an automobile, as well as the flags of the eight states that Route 66 passes through, commemorating Mr. Avery's vision of a cross-country paved road.

As we turned away from the plaza to walk back to the car, Ibrahim barely glanced at an approaching pickup truck as he prepared to step from the curb into the crosswalk.

"Wait!" I shouted, grabbing his arm.

The truck sped past without stopping; Ibrahim was shocked.

"We are terrible about crosswalks in this state," I said. "You

The Girl on the Belvedere

have to make sure a car is actually going to stop before you step into the road. Even I'm sometimes guilty of not stopping. We're not as attuned to pedestrians and bicyclists as we should be."

Once safely in the car, we headed west to the Rock Café in Stroud, famous for inspiring an animated character in the movie *Cars*. We drove through small towns boasting old motor courts and filling stations, and finally arrived at the Round Barn at Arcadia, the only round barn on Route 66, and a site listed on the National Register of Historic Places. After that, my friends then requested a quick trip into Oklahoma City since we were so close.

"Great idea," I said. I told them that there were two things we should see: the Oklahoma City National Memorial, site of the 1995 bombing, and Oklahoma City's state fair.

The National Memorial is beautiful rather than somber. There are 168 empty chairs representing those lost, with rectangular arched bronze gates at either end, one emblazoned with "9:01" and the other with "9:03," representing the time when our world collapsed. Most of those 168 souls were lost within those two minutes, either from the blast itself or the pancaking of the building.

Once we entered, I walked along the reflecting pool, leaving my friends to experience the tragic beauty of this memorial. They were very quiet, visibly moved, and needed time to process what they were seeing. I am always emotional in this sacred place, thinking of those 168 victims, the unborn children not reflected in that number, and the many, many more injured. The evening was crystalline, the burnished bronze chairs cast long shadows on the green lawn, and I was glad that Anna and Ibrahim were seeing the memorial under the best of circumstances.

I didn't think much about terrorism any longer; I left my fear behind in Europe. But seeing this beautiful site is always a good reminder of what we must guard against. Since that 1995 attack, there have been many attacks, both here and abroad. It's a terrible thing to become inured to.

From there, we drove a few blocks to the Oklahoma State Fair. I had been disappointed that Anna and Ibrahim were going to miss the Tulsa State Fair, but this would be a great substitute. I explained that state fairs were hugely popular in our part of the country. We wandered through several exhibit buildings, and they rode the Ferris Wheel. We drove home in the dark, exhausted but happy. Our "hand-squeezed lemonades" sloshed in the car's cup holders.

The next morning, we received another update from Lucía in Mexico. "We are working together as civilians to help as much as we can," she texted. "Today, my colleagues and I, with the company, managed to send three trucks for the Red Cross. My mom's business already sent two small pickup trucks to Mexico City. And my sister and I delivered some goods at our university's collection center."

"Thinking of you, Lucía," I texted, "and continuing to send you all good wishes, love, and especially peace in this difficult time." I could not imagine what Lucía and her family were going through.

We could do nothing to help Lucía. We were useless in that regard. It was frustrating and somewhat distressing.

TO TAKE our minds off of our friend's situation, we turned our attention to the long-planned visit to the Apple Store. This was the day the new products arrived, and Anna and Ibrahim were excited. Per Anna's request, we got an early start and headed to Krispy Kreme before the mall opened. The "HotLine" was on, and we were each handed a hot doughnut as soon as we stepped

The Girl on the Belvedere

into line. We ordered a whole box, and once again almost made ourselves sick. Sweet tooth sated, we drove to the mall, where security was heavy due to the product rollout. Anna bought her coveted watch, and then we walked around the mall for a bit. Ibrahim wondered if he needed new clothes for the ballet performance that we were attending that night.

"Absolutely not," I said. "The theatre is in the ballet facility, and it will be very casual. Whatever you have is fine."

We went to the theatre a little early, and I showed them where I spend quite a bit of time as the ballet's chief historian and archivist. I showed them the colorful archival costumes, the multitude of dance books, the papier-mâché masks from the ballet *Paganini*. In this room, my co-author Georgia, *une historienne extraordinaire*, spends hours compiling a massive document on the company's repertoire: every single ballet the company has ever danced, when it was performed, and who danced in it. My committee members have organized sixty years of production files, entered data into software, photographed our many artifacts, identified and organized hundreds of historic photos, and gathered posters for framing for future locations throughout the building.

A decade earlier, I had been asked to provide the "decorations" for our annual fundraiser in a ballroom downtown. When I asked the event chair if she wanted backdrops, costumes, or artifacts, she responded "All of them." My committee stepped up and helped me choose fifty-five costumes, all of which we steamed; several massive backdrops, which the stagehands hung; and scores of small artifacts for display cases. The "decorations" had become a full-on museum exhibit, complete with my commentary and costume descriptions. The fact that I could organize and produce an exhibit like this came as a complete surprise to me.

My life in the ballet has been so rich and so varied. From a dancer with Tulsa Civic Ballet, to a board member and officer with Tulsa Ballet Theatre, to the first dancer to become president of Tulsa Ballet, I have been associated with this company for forty-five of its sixty-five years.

As a small child sitting on a Belvedere that was about to be buried, I could not have imagined where this life would take me. I only knew that I loved to run, to dance, to lie on the lawn in the summer and study the stars. I could not foresee the impact that ballet and that gentle man with a funny accent, Roman Jasinski, would have on my life.

Later, seated in the theatre, artistic director Marcello Angelini stopped by to say hello. "I thought you were in Europe," he said.

"No, Europe has come to me," I replied as I introduced my friends.

THE NEXT DAY, we heard from Lucía again: "God give us some mercy. We had more earthquakes in southern Mexico, in the state of Oaxaca."

"It's too much," I replied. What more could I say? Truly it was far, far too much. It had been a terrible year for North America in general and Mexico in particular. There had been four devastating hurricanes: in Houston, in Florida, in Puerto Rico, and in Mexico. There had been the major earthquake in Mexico City just a few days earlier and now this one in Oaxaca.

I forcibly turned my attention to the present and to my houseguests. I asked them what they would like for dinner, explaining, "We are going to an afternoon football game at the University of Tulsa, but we could grill out on the patio afterward if you like. It's going to be a beautiful evening."

"Oh yes! Let's have a typical American cookout!" Anna said.

The Girl on the Belvedere

"We hear about them but we've never been to one! Can we have hamburgers?"

"Of course," I said, smiling at her enthusiasm. "Hamburgers it is."

Over dinner, we discussed the football game, the baseball game we had attended several nights earlier, the fireworks at the ballpark, and Oklahoma's crazy weather.

Anna commented, "We've been here two weeks, and I'm surprised. You're not discussing politics all the time."

"Oh, no," I said. "You've been watching *way* too much CNN International. Our life is about *us,* not the people in Washington."

We celebrated Anna's, Lucía's, and Ibrahim's birthdays, that all fall within weeks of each other, after the cookout. I texted Lucía a picture of the cake I had gotten at the bakery with their three names on it.

"Cheryl bought us a cake so that we could all celebrate together," Anna texted to Lucía. "I am so sad about all the things that happened in Mexico and that you could not come! You are here with us in our hearts."

My guests were very surprised when I served the cake with scoops of ice cream. "Birthday cake *and* ice cream?" Anna asked.

"Yes, of course," I said.

"We don't do this in Germany," she explained. "Only the cake. When I get home, my mother will make me several cakes for my birthday."

After dinner, we went inside to watch TV. I noticed a small new remote on the coffee table, but thought nothing of it. Both Anna and Ibrahim were very tech-savvy, so I assumed it belonged to one of their many devices. But soon, I noticed that Anna was staring at me. "What?" I asked, laughing.

"Notice anything new on the table?" she asked.

I looked at the tiny remote and back at her.

She nodded and said, "It's for you."

"What is it?"

"That's the remote for your new Apple TV," she said. "We bought it for you at the Apple store."

I'd heard of Apple TV, but I was clueless about how it worked. They spent the next hour showing me the ins and outs of this device and helped me set up shortcuts to my favorite programming, plus various foreign news outlets. How very thoughtful these two were!

THE NEXT DAY, we headed north to Oologah. My husband owns a horse that he keeps on a local ranch, and Anna and Ibrahim had been asking to see it. It was a typical Oklahoma summer evening, with an orange sun that promised to be spectacular as it began to set. John saddled the horse, warmed it up outside and led it into the indoor arena.

Anna went first, and it was obvious that she had ridden before. "I went to horse camp every summer as a child," she said. "I would love to start riding again."

Ibrahim was next and was a little less sure of himself. He had never been on a horse, and was grinning as he carefully dismounted.

I went last, but only stayed on for a few minutes. My legs are molded into a permanent turnout due to years of ballet, and to ride properly, one must turn the legs in from the hip, which feels uncomfortably pigeon-toed to me. I hopped off before my knees began to hurt from the awkward position. "Cheryl could have been a great rider," my sweet husband said.

"Coulda, woulda, shoulda," I replied with a smile.

After dinner with some Mexican friends, we headed home and enjoyed the rest of the birthday cake. We watched the movie

Twister. Anna and Ibrahim were riveted, knowing that we were Ground Zero for tornadoes here in Oklahoma.

I had shown them the damage from a recent EF-2 tornado that had touched down a few blocks from our house at one in the morning just a few weeks before they arrived. The structures that had not been completely blown away were now "see-throughs," with no walls and debris piled haphazardly inside.

"Did you get in your shelter that night?" Anna had asked me when I showed her and Ibrahim the damage.

"No," I said. "We rarely have to. It was August, and there were no sirens. I just assumed it was a bad windstorm, since most tornadoes occur in the spring. I've made that mistake before, but that time, our house was damaged. I should have known something was up, since the trees were whipping in circles."

During our first foray on Route 66, there had been severe storm warnings all around us. My friends had listened quietly while I tuned in to the weather warnings on the radio, trying to figure out if we were in the path of these storms. We weren't, but my friends were attentive, especially after that terrible thunderstorm in Quebec several summers ago when Ibrahim had to leave the highway multiple times.

The movie *Twister* is a perennial favorite featured heavily on TV every spring and summer, even though it's sensational in its portrayal of tornadic events. It was playing, and these two Europeans were riveted to the screen. When a cow appeared in mid-air in front of the tornado-chasing pickup truck, actress Helen Hunt said, "Cow."

"*Cow!*" the three of us shouted in unison.

The film's lead actor, Bill Paxton, is a favorite movie star in this state, especially among those who are attuned to the weather. When he died, storm chasers from Texas, Oklahoma, and Kansas honored him by lighting up the initials "BP" on a weather map using their GPS systems. He made meteorology cool.

We watched the movie's mythical happy ending and went to bed, secure in the knowledge that the next day's weather forecast was perfect for our next adventure.

22

PAWHUSKA

The next morning, we headed to Pawhuska, home of the famous "Mercantile" of *Pioneer Woman* fame. We had watched this entertaining cooking show and were agog as we stepped into this wonderland of colorful kitchen gadgets. We started with coffee and pastries on the second floor, and then walked downstairs, where Anna and Ibrahim shopped in earnest. They had just moved into a new apartment and needed to outfit their kitchen. Apparently, in Germany, one supplies one's own kitchen, including all appliances, cabinets, shelving, etc. When one vacates an apartment, the kitchen is either sold to the new inhabitants or taken along to the next home. Anna and Ibrahim had moved into an empty shell and had struck a deal with a "kitchen shop." It had taken six weeks, but their new kitchen had just been installed before they left for the States. Now, they were at the fun stage. Anna had chosen colors for the space and found several things at "The Merc" that would complement her design. She has an artistic eye, and I was quite sure that her kitchen would be warm and welcoming.

We shopped in the quaint boutiques of Pawhuska, and I encouraged Anna to buy some cowboy boots. They are always fashionable here, of course, but are also quite popular in Europe. She spied some black suede ankle boots with fringe, and from there, it took little convincing.

"You're going to be 'Too Cool for School,'" I teased.

Sure enough, several weeks later, Anna would text me a photo of herself wearing those boots in Germany, along with her new Apple watch.

WE DROVE along Grandview Avenue in Pawhuska, past the historic Osage Courthouse—we were now in Osage County, home of the Osage Nation—and continued through the gates of the Tallgrass Prairie Preserve. This is a huge preserve—the largest remaining protected remnant of tallgrass prairie in the world—and is home to a wild herd of the famous bison, also known as American buffalo. We drove for at least half an hour on the unpaved dirt road before seeing anything except the rolling Osage Hills. Then, there it was: a large herd of bison on both sides of the road, grazing peacefully.

Bison are huge animals, and I cautioned my guests to stay quiet and not get out of the car. They rolled down their windows to take some photos, and we spent perhaps thirty minutes watching these fascinating creatures.

We drove on and were still some distance from the visitor center when I saw a storm brewing to the west. "We can't chance it," I said. "We're in the middle of nowhere and can't afford to get caught in a thunderstorm, given how exposed we are." With that, I turned around and hightailed it back to Pawhuska.

As we made our way back through the rolling ancient grasslands of the Osage, I told them about the wholesale murder of the Osage Indians, the tribe that held on to their "headrights," their legal rights to the rich oil and other minerals that underpin Osage County.

I once met Dr. Elise Paschen, the award-winning poet and daughter of Osage ballerina Maria Tallchief, when she shared her poem, "Wi'-gi-e," from her book *Bestiary* (Red Hen Press, 2009) during a reading at Tulsa Ballet. It tells the story of Anna Kyle Brown, one of the Osage Indians who was murdered for her headrights. I have excerpted a portion here with permission:

> The sheriff disguised her death as whisky poisoning.
>
> Because, when he carved her body up, he saw the bullet hole in her skull.
>
> Because, when she was murdered, the *leg clutchers* bloomed.
>
> But then froze under the weight of frost.
>
> During *Xtha-cka-Zhi-ga Tse-the*, *the Killer of the Flowers Moon*.

IT WAS from this haunting poem that author David Grann took the title of his prize-winning book, *Killers of the Flower Moon: The Osage Murders and the Birth of the FBI*.

On our way home from the Osage Nation, we stopped for yet more hamburgers at the Skiatook Tastee Freez, where I introduced them to chocolate-dipped cones. We sat outside in now perfectly-clear, sunny weather, and then headed home with full stomachs, a little dazed from the day. It came as no surprise when, a month later, they texted me a photo of a German restaurant hamburger wrapped in a fake newspaper that proclaimed, "Tulsa, Oklahoma in 1891: The Birthplace of the Hamburger."

TWO DAYS BEFORE THEIR DEPARTURE, I told Anna and Ibrahim that we needed to follow the Route 66 alignments through the city itself. We started downtown, near the award-winning Bank of Oklahoma Center, designed by the famous César Pelli. This beautiful arena is a perennial "Venue of the Year" nominee and is a jewel in the crown of our architecturally significant city. After seeing the Art Deco buildings, the motor courts, the neon signs, and the filling stations, we stopped for a coffee at the newly refurbished Central Library. There is a Starbucks inside, and Anna wanted to try one of the famous pumpkin spice lattes. We followed this with a late lunch of my favorite crispy tacos at a local place. At home, Anna made delicate apple roses for our dessert, finishing our second-to-last day together on a sweet note.

The conversation at the dinner table found its way to the subject of handguns. "Do you have any?" Anna asked.

"No, we don't," I said. "And we will not. I'm opposed to them. Plus, I've seen John half-asleep at night with the remote in his hand, pointing it wildly around the room, trying to turn off the TV. If that were a gun, I would have been dead long ago, way before any intruders found us."

Everyone laughed, including my husband, my favorite source of amusement.

"Once, in the middle of the night," I said, changing the subject, "I heard a deep rumble. I stood up and listened. It was a 4.5 magnitude earthquake approaching from the west, and it shook the house as it arrived. It stopped as suddenly as it had started. It was a gift from the oil industry, a by-product of deep wastewater injection."

At the time, I had turned to John, who was soundly asleep. "We just had an earthquake," I'd said to the inert form next to me. "It's over now."

"What?" he'd said, half-asleep and unable to hear me.

"Earthquake," I said louder. "It's over."

"What?"

"Earthquake!" I said, raising my voice.

"What?"

"*Earthquake!*" I screamed.

"Oh, I feel it!" he said.

We all laughed at the story, even John.

That's my husband, who refers to the TARDIS, the spaceship on *Doctor Who*, as the "Taurus" and to the band Coldplay, whom we have seen in concert, as "Cold Plate." Yet he is also a brilliant physician, having been an American Cancer Society Fellow at Memorial Sloan-Kettering Cancer Institute in New York City.

We lingered at the dinner table until late, with Anna, Ibrahim, John, and me laughing. These two wonderful people had become such a part of our daily lives that it was hard to imagine a time when they were not with us, when they were new acquaintances, when they were strangers, when they were visitors from distant lands across the sea.

OUR LAST DAY together was a quiet one. They set up mirroring on my Apple TV and gave me a crash course on how to use it. I took them to the famous giant, the Golden Driller, and to Utica Square, our leafy, flower-bedecked shopping center.

Anna spotted Pottery Barn and wanted to go in. "In Germany, everyone says, 'Oh, it's just like Pottery Barn,' so I need to see this store," she explained. We explored every aisle, every display. Then, on an impulse, I told them that we needed to go into Williams-Sonoma.

"What is this Williams-Sonoma?" Ibrahim asked.

"It's a cooking store," I said. "It's wonderful, and you need to see it."

As we walked through the door, they both stopped suddenly, looking around, stunned. "Oh, we do not have anything like this in Germany," Anna said. I wasn't sure what she was referring to, exactly, but I could imagine. The store is large and colorful, with items for everyone's dream kitchen on display.

I smiled. "Just relax and look around," I said.

An hour later, we emerged into the evening light, and Anna said, "I love Tulsa. I could live here."

Hearing that was one of the greatest gifts of their visit.

On this last night, Ibrahim made his famous *falafel* for us. It was delicious, and he prepared some extra servings for our freezer. We finished the evening looking at their photos of Jerusalem, and they extended us an invitation to meet them there. While they lived in Germany, they promised to travel to Jerusalem whenever we chose to go, to show us the sights. I could not imagine a better way to see this ancient city and promised that we would visit as soon as we could.

The day they left, I was very sad. I asked them what they would like for lunch, and they both responded, "Chick-fil-A!"

While dining in my neighborhood version of the restaurant, we bemoaned the fact that we didn't have enough time to drive to the nearest Krispy Kreme for one last doughnut.

At the airport, we shared a pastry over coffee. Soon, their bags were checked, and it was all over except for the goodbyes. I had French class that evening and needed to leave while they were still waiting to go through security for their much-delayed flight. We hugged, they thanked me and I them, and I began to tear up. "I'm going to cry," I said. "I'm leaving."

When I reached the escalator, I turned back to give them one last wave. They were watching me and waved back. I would miss them so.

During class, I looked out the window at the beautiful Art Deco masterpiece, Boston Avenue Methodist Church, which was suddenly illuminated by the setting sun against the stormy, steely-blue sky. My mood brightened. Tulsa is such a beautiful city, and I was flooded with joy and peace, grateful that I was able to share it with these two much-loved friends. I breathed deeply and once again silently shouted my thanks to the heavens—for my excellent French professors here in Tulsa, for those immersion programs in Quebec and in Villefranche, and for these dear international friends, who keep me in touch with the world, and who keep me young.

23

GOODBYE FOR NOW

I received a photo from Anna and Ibrahim, taken on the plane. They had changed into T-shirts purchased at the airport. Anna wore a red and white shirt proclaiming "Oklahoma," while Ibrahim's was blue and gold and said "Tulsa." "Wearing Tulsa, Oklahoma all the way home!" Anna texted. "We wish you a good night, sleep tight. Thank you and John for the countless things you did for us."

"We are so happy you came—what fun we had!" I replied. "Come back soon and we'll go to Krispy Kreme first thing. *Bon voyage, mes amis!* Safe travels! Nutmeg the dog, Boris the cat, and Turtle wish you sweet dreams on your flights—*au revoir!*"

"Our hugs to them also," she said.

My home was quiet the next morning. Nutmeg looked a little lost, and I wandered about aimlessly, wondering where all the time had gone. Three weeks had seemed like such a long, good visit while we were planning it, but the days had flown by. I went upstairs to tidy the guest room and found a note from Anna, with delicate hearts hand-drawn at the bottom: "Dear Cheryl and John, thank you sooooooooo much for your hospitality, kindness, and all you did for us. Yours, Anna and Ibrahim."

I heard from Lucía, who was once again busy at work. She told me that it was really sad going into Mexico City, and that many of the smaller roads and towns were destroyed, as were areas of the city itself. But she had regained her normal sunny disposition, and was happily studying German, beginning an Excel course, and taking driving lessons.

Later, I received a text from Ibrahim: "Good morning! We are now in Amsterdam, next flight is in two hours!"

"Awesome," I replied. "Did you get a little sleep?"

"Anna, lots of sleep," he said. "I had none, but some later on. We had croissant, no sugar, missing Krispy Kreme and the donuts already."

I grinned. "Safe flight!" I texted back.

Two hours later, Anna texted me. "Frankfurt Airport now. Waiting for the train home!"

"Awesome!" I replied. "Go home and get some rest! Miss you guys!"

"We miss you, too! We're almost there!"

And an hour later, another text arrived from Anna: "Home now!"

"Wonderful!" I responded. "Hope you get some very good sleep tonight! Thank you for coming this long way to see us."

"Thank you for having us" she said. "At first, coming out of the subway here, we had no orientation at all. It was weird! Ibrahim went in the completely wrong direction. T-Town still feels like home."

"Remember that you will always have a home here."

"Thank you so much!" she said.

And with that, our minute-to-minute close connection was broken once again. They were gone.

EPILOGUE

I sit outside on the patio in the strong Oklahoma autumn sun. The chairs are empty, the wrought iron cold to the touch. The fountain still plays its watery music, the ivy still waves its shadowy patterns, the old blind cat still startles at every touch. And Nutmeg still trots up wagging her tail. The turtle that Anna discovered has not been seen since her departure.

I look around on this clear golden morning, and I feel diminished without my friends. I take a moment to reflect. What did I glean from their visit, in addition to the pure pleasure of their company?

I learned that beauty is just outside my door. I knew that in theory, of course, but it is different when you see reactions from friends from very different parts of the world.

I learned that spontaneity can be much more fun than carefully laid plans, and that there is a certain joy in an unplanned day.

And most importantly, I learned that we are always better together. All of us think differently, see beauty differently, and react differently. I was able to see my city, my state, and my country through European eyes, and as the late Roman Jasinski once told me while looking back at his long, sometimes perilous, yet always glorious life, "New country, new life, new adventure." And what an adventure my friends' visit was.

Sitting alone on the back patio, I realize that I'm much happier these days. Moments of shame and anxiety are fleeting, and I usually recognize those false voices and try to let go of guilt, of unworthiness, of negativity. I've learned to challenge my unhealthy thoughts and replace them with the positive. And I've realized that my experience is part of the larger human experience. No parents are perfect, and no children are perfect. I am not perfect, nor is anyone else on this planet. Take me or leave me, it matters not. What does matter is that I care about my life, and that the people I care for care about me also.

I think back to the first time I ever heard French, when I was four years old, in my first ballet class. I think about my truncated performing life with the ballet and decide that all is as it should be. As the very wise Roman Jasinski said to me shortly before his death, "I think that everything that happened was right. For the best. Yes." And that is true for me as well. I did not dance with a major company, perhaps, but the important thing is that *I danced*. Had I continued my ballet career, I would not have my long marriage, my children, my pets, my place at Tulsa Ballet. I would not have two college degrees, my parents' greatest gift to me. I would not speak French. I would not have my friends from around the world. And I would have missed out on the greatest adventures of my life.

I think about that day so many years ago when I sat on the Belvedere before it was buried and about being present fifty years later when it was brought back up. That car has been a constant presence in my life, a harbinger of sorts. What once was buried eventually comes to the surface, damaged but intact, ready for a makeover. Now, that the Belvedere is restored and is on its new stage at a museum, I will visit my old friend, as I am forever linked to that now-antiquated vehicle. I am and always will be the Girl on the Belvedere, that small child wondering what is to come, her whole life ahead of her.

It is a life that will include new friends—Lucía, Anna, and Ibrahim. I cannot imagine my life without them. I started life in such a restricted environment, but I am now connected to a much larger world, one that exists beyond my homeland's borders. I enjoy olive oil and *za'atar* on my morning toast. I know the taste of gingerbread from Germany and am picky about my croissants and coffee. I ask my local Mexican friends, "Is this authentic?" as I am no longer content with simple Tex-Mex. I read the *Wall Street Journal* from New York, and receive *CBC News*, *France 24*, *German News*, *Reuters*, and *Al Jazeera* news alerts on my phone. I stay in contact with my far-flung friends, and we are already making plans for our next rendezvous. Where will it be? Mexico? Jerusalem? Germany? Paris? No, I think, it will be in Quebec. Quebec, that French city with its ancient walls, that cobblestoned town containing my family's history, that magical place that started it all. I can see the four of us now, laughing in the streets, visiting over coffee, seeking out those beautiful views of the Saint Lawrence River. Quebec, Quebec, that quirky quaint city in Canada.

I can't wait.

ACKNOWLEDGMENTS

I owe a debt of gratitude to my French professors in Quebec, in Villefranche, and here in Tulsa (especially my good friend, Françoise Sullivan), all of whom have shown patience with my on-again, off-again attendance and attention.

My children, Bennett and Stephanie, are always supportive, whether I am sequestered writing, researching, or am at Tulsa Ballet going through programs, photos, or costumes. My treasured daughter-in-law Sarah is trustworthy, hardworking, fun and funny, and always ready for a new adventure.

Merci mille fois to my fabulous editor, Elizabeth Chretien, who was unwavering in her support, careful attention, and laser-like focus. She knew what I was trying to say even when I didn't, and asked all the right questions.

A special shout-out to my Beta readers, who diligently slogged through an early version of this book, and taught me so much. It is a totally different tale thanks to Marian McCarthy, Charlotte Edmundson, Linda Frazier, and Gail Algeo. My brother Larry Yadon and good friend Diane Wise encouraged me even when I was unsure of my direction.

I would be remiss if I didn't mention my coauthor of *Roman Jasinski: A Gypsy Prince from the Ballet Russe,* Georgia Snoke. Her suggestion in 2001 was, "We need to go to France to corroborate Jasinski's story!" Thus started our great adventures to Paris, Monte Carlo, London, Brighton, and New York. It was the beginning of my solo travels, and those trips gave me the courage to travel to foreign language schools and beyond.

Many thanks go to the Tulsa Historical Society and Museum, especially Executive Director Michelle Place, for use of the cover photo and unwavering support of all things Tulsa, including the raising of the buried car, the commissioning of the sculptures of the five Oklahoma Indian Ballerinas, and continued interest in the ballet.

Un grand merci to the board and staff of Tulsa Ballet, especially artistic director Marcello Angelini, who through these many years have given me so many opportunities, onstage and off, and trusted me with so much.

I am grateful to my acquaintance, poet Dr. Elise Paschen, who without hesitation gave me permission to reprint part of her poem that tells of the murder of Anna Kyle Brown, one of the many murdered Osage Indians during that tribe's Reign of Terror, foisted upon them by unscrupulous and greedy White businessmen.

My largest "thank you" goes unequivocally to my husband John, who has driven me to numerous airports, train stations, and towns, sometimes waving goodbye and sometimes joining me. I had no idea what adventures lay in store for me when I married him forty-eight years ago. I'm so glad I did.

ABOUT THE AUTHOR

Cheryl Forrest is the author of *The Girl on the Belvedere*, a "coming of age" memoir for a woman in her sixties, and the co-author of *Roman Jasinski: A Gypsy Prince from the Ballet Russe*. She is a former dancer with what is now Tulsa Ballet, and is a recipient of the Oklahoma Governor's Arts Award.

Cheryl lives in Tulsa with her husband John and pet poodle, Truffle. She enjoys French class, walking along the river with her best friend, and yoga (when she makes it to class). She is the proud mother of two, a grandmother of two, and an admirer of her lovely daughter-in-law. She serves as chief historian and archivist for Tulsa Ballet.

You may follow Cheryl's adventures and reach her at www.thegirlonthebelvedere.com.

ALSO BY CHERYL FORREST

Roman Jasinski: A Gypsy Prince from the Ballet Russe by Cheryl Forrest and Georgia Snoke

Available at Tulsa Ballet. The entire purchase price goes directly to the company. Please visit tulsaballet.org and select "store" from the menu.
Merci!